HQ 800.4. G7 HUS

D1760322

WITHDRAWN
FROM STOCK
QMUL LIBRARY

THE SINGLE HOMEMAKER AND MATERIAL CULTURE IN THE LONG EIGHTEENTH CENTURY

The Single Homemaker and Material Culture in the Long Eighteenth Century

DAVID HUSSEY AND MARGARET PONSONBY
University of Wolverhampton, UK

ASHGATE

© David Hussey and Margaret Ponsonby 2012

All rights reserved. No part of this publication may be reproduced, stored in a retrieval system or transmitted in any form or by any means, electronic, mechanical, photocopying, recording or otherwise without the prior permission of the publisher.

David Hussey and Margaret Ponsonby have asserted their right under the Copyright, Designs and Patents Act, 1988, to be identified as the authors of this work.

Published by
Ashgate Publishing Limited
Wey Court East
Union Road
Farnham
Surrey, GU9 7PT
England

Ashgate Publishing Company
Suite 420
101 Cherry Street
Burlington
VT 05401-4405
USA

www.ashgate.com

British Library Cataloguing in Publication Data
Hussey, David.
  The single homemaker and material culture in the long
  eighteenth century. – (The history of retailing and
  consumption)
  1. Living alone–History–18th century. 2. Single
  people–Social conditions–18th century. 3. Single
  people–Dwellings–History–18th century. 4. Home
  economics–History–18th century.
  I. Title II. Series III. Ponsonby, Margaret, 1952-
  643.1'08652'09033-dc23

Library of Congress Cataloging-in-Publication Data
Hussey, D. E. (David E.)
  The single homemaker and material culture in the long eighteenth century /
David Hussey and Margaret Ponsonby.
      p. cm. – (The history of retailing and consumption)
  Includes bibliographical references and index.
  ISBN 978-1-4094-1815-3 (hardcover) – ISBN 978-1-4094-1816-0 (ebook)
1. Single people–Great Britain–History–18th century. 2. Households–Great Britain–
History–18th century. 3. Consumer behavior–Great Britain–History–18th century.
  I. Ponsonby, Margaret,
  1952- II. Title.
  HQ800.4.G7H87 2012
  306.81'5–dc23
                                                                                        2011045039
ISBN 9781409418153 (hbk)
ISBN 9781409418160 (ebk)

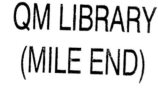

QM LIBRARY
(MILE END)

Printed and bound in Great Britain by the
MPG Books Group, UK.

Contents

The History of Retailing and Consumption
General Editor's Preface

It is increasingly recognized that retail systems and changes in the patterns of consumption play crucial roles in the development and societal structure of economies. Such recognition has led to renewed interest in the changing nature of retail distribution and the rise of consumer society from a wide range of academic disciplines. The aim of this multidisciplinary series is to provide a forum of publications that explore the history of retailing and consumption.

Gareth Shaw, University of Exeter, UK

List of Figures

List of Tables

List of Abbreviations

BCA   Birmingham City Archives, Birmingham Reference Library
HRO   Hereford Record Office, Hereford
LRO   Lichfield Record Office, Lichfield
SA   Shropshire Archives, Shrewsbury
WSRO West Sussex Record Office, Chichester
WRO   Worcester Record Office and History Centre, Worcester

Acknowledgements

In writing such a book there is always an enormous debt of gratitude to one's fellow scholars. We would particularly like to thank Nancy Cox and Malcolm Wanklyn for many fruitful discussions, insights and debates regarding the source material and for their unstintingly generous offers of access to their own research material. We are also especially grateful to John Benson for encouraging the project in the first instance and to Claire Jones for her research help and input in compiling the text. Many colleagues and friends have provided us with advice and suggestions along the way. In particular, we would like to thank Peter Borsay, Nigel Goose, Eleanor John, Leslie Martin, Steve Poole, Shirley Snow, Sylvia Watts and Lesley Whitworth. Our institution, the University of Wolverhampton, has extended important sabbatical time to us, and our colleagues have often taken up the slack in our absence. We would like to thank Karin Dannehl, Paul Henderson and Alison Toplis for their collegial support in this capacity. As always, the archivists and staff at the many record offices and repositories we have visited have been unfailingly obliging and we wish to offer our thanks to the staff at Berkeley Hospital, Birmingham Central Archives, Bristol Record Office, Coningsby Hospital, Hereford Record Office, Lichfield Record Office, Plymouth and West Devon Record Office, Shropshire Archives, Walsall Local History Centre, West Sussex Record Office, Weston Park and Worcester Record Office and History Centre, as well as the various institutions that have allowed us to reproduce pictures from their collections. Tom Gray, Emily Yates and all the staff at Ashgate have been dependably professional and encouraging. Finally, we would both like to thank our partners and families for their patience and support.

Introduction

In 1809 the retired lawyer, adventurer and former bon vivant, William Hickey, surveyed what had become of his life. Marooned in the small Buckinghamshire town of Beaconsfield, 'a country village with a very limited society' in his acerbic words, Hickey had become weary of his now mundane existence. His immediate companions – his two maiden sisters, with whom he shared a 'pretty cottage', his manservant and dog – were agreeable enough, but faded in lustre in comparison to his previous existence as a rake, habitué of the London demi-monde and latterly a successful and powerful barrister in India with a fashionable courtesan partner and a vast household. With 'comparatively absolute idleness', bad weather and indisposition tightening their grip on his already constrained situation, Hickey resolved to commit his memoirs to paper. The result was a long, occasionally peppery and always diverting concoction of half-remembered, fully embroidered and often entirely imagined scenes from a 'strange and variegated' 60 years of experience. In as much, the literary pastime of a rather isolated older man might engender limited interest beyond perhaps the racy storyline and the 'many low and indelicate anecdotes related, and many gross and filthy expressions used'. Yet the remarkable feature of Hickey's reminiscences was not its sub-Boswellian candour but that, for a man embedded in sensual pleasure, Hickey remained a lifelong singleton: his consort refused marriage but took his name for propriety's sake and after her death Hickey declined any further formal union. Pitching up finally in England, Hickey occupied a curious domestic ménage, a household of the terminally unattached – a very distillation of singleness.[1]

Singleness is the unspoken thread that runs through Hickey's writings and whilst these can be dismissed as the misty-eyed ramblings of a failed nabob, they speak profoundly of the single condition in a world in which conjugality and the marital household assumed centre stage. It is our intention in this book to address how such single men and women – bachelors, spinsters and the widowed – negotiated their domestic lives. Our position is that whilst there is much work on the condition of the singleton and, in particular, the precarious status of the single woman, there is little locating single men and women within the key arena of self-expression, the home. Where single agents intrude into the historical orthodoxy of the domestic unit of the married, they are often viewed as chaotic or individualistic consumers concerned with the hedonistic ornamentation of the self in contradistinction to the denuded and fractured materiality of their domestic life. By using a range of

---

[1]   P. Quennell (ed.), *Memoirs of William Hickey* (London: Routledge & Kegan Paul, 1975), pp. ix–x, 1–2.

dispersed and fragmentary sources and focused case studies, we argue that the unmarried homemaker represents a key variable in both the understanding of the domestic environment and the consumerist practices of homemaking too often swamped by discussion of the familial home as the normative template of cultural expression.

Some points of reference are useful here. Our main interest involves the triangulation of singleness, domesticity and material culture. As such we focus predominantly on the 'middling sort of people' – a complex, amorphous and regionally divergent social miscellany that largely, although imperfectly, cohered through shared attitudes towards status and common patterns of consumption, display and material possession. In this, we follow the work of Wrightson, Earle, French, Barry and Hunt in arguing for a categorisation based on a nuanced interpretation of status, but adopt a 'broad and pragmatic' conception of middle rank activity and aspiration.[2] This encompasses, *pace* Weatherill, a range of often dissonant and occasionally oppositional social and occupational groups, from urban trades like jobbing craftspeople, artisans and lesser shopkeepers and their rural equivalents, the substantial tenantry and husbandmen, to the relatively affluent – the minor gentry, the professions and the mercantile elite.[3] This does not mean that the research has been confined by artificial distinction: both servants with enough monetary or material resources to engage probate and the affluent, estate-holding professional have been included in the survey. Here we are especially concerned with how middling sort singletons culturally navigated the wider patterns of personal and domestic consumption or, as H.R. French has elegantly put it, charted their 'tell-tale foot-prints across the mire of the "consumer revolution"'.[4]

Although the credibility of a monolithic 'consumer revolution' located firmly in the latter half of the eighteenth century has rather taken a critical mauling in the years since this quote, we are none the less concerned with the wider practices and mechanisms of consumption.[5] In particular, we wish to chart not only the

---

[2]   For discussions of the 'middling sort', see K. Wrightson, *English Society, 1580–1680* (London: Hutchinson, 1981); H.R. French, *The Middle Sort of People in Provincial England, 1600–1750* (Oxford: Oxford University Press, 2007); H.R. French, 'The Search for the "Middle Sort of People" in England, 1600–1800', *Historical Journal*, 43/1 (2000), pp. 277–93; M.R. Hunt, *The Middling Sort: Commerce, Gender, and the Family in England, 1680–1780* (Berkeley and Los Angeles: University of California Press, 1996); the articles in J. Barry and C. Brooks (eds), *The Middling Sort of People: Culture, Society and Politics in England, 1550–1800* (Basingstoke: Macmillan, 1994); and P. Earle, *The Making of the English Middle Class: Business, Society and Family Life in London, 1660–1730* (London: Methuen, 1989), especially pp. 1–16.

[3]   L. Weatherill, *Consumer Behaviour and Material Culture in Britain, 1660–1760* (2nd edn, London: Routledge, 1996), pp. 210–11.

[4]   French, 'Search for the "Middle Sort of People"', p. 277.

[5]   For critiques of the processes, chronology and theoretical construction of consumption, see the review essays by Sara Pennell, 'Consumption and Consumerism in

ownership of goods amongst single people, an important task in itself, but also to read the simple act of material possession onto the mentalities and into the spaces that gave substance and meaning to the choreography of acquisition and use. Goods were not merely ciphers of wealth, freighting more nebulous and elusive concepts as taste, fashion or politeness, they possessed an inherent materiality: a china teacup may well have conveyed notions of respectability and cultural capital to a genteel middling sort audience, but it was also a highly decorative object, a subject of design and individual choice and, ultimately, a commodity that due to its intrinsic fragility required regular replacement.[6]

In this book, we seek to embed these approaches within the study of the material culture of the home and everyday life. We argue that home is a contested space, a cockpit wherein the cultures of consumption, arguably the most vital motive factor in the invigoration of the domestic economy, were defined and exercised. It is in these arenas that the new goods and cultural practices that came to confer important codes of behaviour were located and it is here that gendered modes of association and the spaces that came to enhance and even define them were focused. By extension, we are also interested in examining the intersections, divergences and oppositions that are inherent in the practices by which men and women understood and used domestic space. Naturally, normative social and cultural exhortation stressed the primacy of the marital home in this and, as a consequence, the position of the singlewoman was rendered especially precarious. Yet even so, both widows, who occupied a tolerable cultural association with marriage, and solitary men, were the objects of contemporary comment and debate. To understand this interplay of factors more fully, we have also chosen to extend our analysis to cover a broadly conceived period, from c.1650 to c.1850, roughly described as a long 'long eighteenth century'. We acknowledge that such a broad chronological sweep may gamble with the assumed integrity of periodisation. However, we consider the extended timeframe to be important in that it permits the continuities and commonalties that were central to the domestic strategies of single homemakers to be studied alongside the major forces of development and evolution in the material culture of the home.

In terms of sources, we have focused upon an extended survey of probate material. This is discussed in full in Chapter 2 and, whilst there has been no attempt to replicate the large-scale quantitative work undertaken elsewhere, we have ensured that the fully digitised datasets that inform our work are both

---

Early Modern England', *Historical Journal*, 42/2 (1999), pp. 549–64 and Jonathan White, 'A World of Goods? The "Consumption Turn" and Eighteenth-Century British History', *Cultural and Social History*, 3/1 (2006), pp. 93–104.

[6]   See, for example, J. Styles and A. Vickery, 'Introduction' in J. Styles and A. Vickery (eds), *Gender, Taste and Material Culture in Britain and North America, 1700–1830* (New Haven and London: Yale University Press, 2006), pp. 1–36: 21–2 and, for a wider theoretical take, the articles in Daniel Miller (ed.), *Home Possessions: Material Culture Behind Closed Doors* (Oxford: Berg, 2001).

comprehensive in coverage and, significantly, extend the chronological range of the research into the early nineteenth century. Probate and allied testamentary data form the spine to the research around which additional, more illustrative sources are arranged. For example, we have used a wide selection of other records, ranging from auctioneer schedules and court records to personal and business accounts, letters and diaries. The latter sources, a mine to the historian of material culture and the household in recent years, have comprised the standard and widely used accounts of celebrated single homemakers like William Stout and Parson James Woodforde, for example, to the private thoughts, hopes, failings and recollections of a variety of relatively obscure men and women of the middle ranks. Here the fluctuating fortunes and domestic trials of such men as the Bridgnorth printer George Gitton, the Birmingham spinster Anne Boulton and the Plymouth attorney Henry Woollcombe are used to unpick the approaches and strategies through which a household was maintained.

These works are at the core of a book organised more by theme than considerations of strict chronology. Chapter 1, 'Being Single', outlines the demographic and cultural position of single men and women across the period, arguing that, although the single estate was itself a highly common factor in the communities and economies of England and Wales, cultural attitudes tended to marginalise singleness as an aberrant other in comparison to a marital standard. Clearly, single men and women were numerous and important agents within local and regional economies: historical demographers have estimated that at least one-fifth of society remained unmarried, a figure that was swelled considerably if data for the widowed and the mass of premarital adult spinsters and bachelors are factored in.[7] In major towns, the impact of migrant and transient populations and the influence of service meant that in totality the single estate was common, even unremarkable.[8] It is also apparent that single men and women were able to construct forms of domesticity that permitted interaction with polite society. Indeed, as wider conceptions of masculinity embraced the bachelor and widower, single men were more insulated than women from accusations of impropriety. In contrast, the persistent and highly pejorative image of the 'old maid', the 'superannuated virgin' and the 'surplus woman' tended to be applied with increased vituperation to single women, and especially those who headed their own households. If anything, this position was accentuated as the nineteenth century progressed.[9]

---

[7]   See E.A. Wrigley and R.S. Schofield, *The Population History of England, 1541–1871: A Reconstruction* (London: Edward Arnold, 1981), pp. 255–65. For revisions, see D.R. Weir 'Rather Never than Late: Celibacy and Age at Marriage in English Cohort Fertility', *Journal of Family History*, 9 (1984), pp. 340–54.

[8]   A.M. Froide, *Never Married: Singlewomen in Early Modern England* (Oxford: Oxford University Press, 2007), pp. 2–3.

[9]   A.M. Froide, 'Old Maids: The Lifecycle of Single Women in Early Modern England' in L. Botelho and P. Thane (eds), *Women and Aging in British Society since 1500* (London: Pearson, 2001), pp. 89–110 and Froide, *Never Married*, pp. 154–81.

Building on this demographic contextualisation, Chapter 2, 'Singleness and Homemaking: Locating the Single Household', discusses the main sources used in the work and outlines the cultural relevance of home as a site of material possession and gendered expression. Our main sources here are probate inventories and wills. To this extent we acknowledge that testamentary materials have formed a staple means for historians to examine the cultural, social and economic basis of pre-industrial society and have engendered a raft of quantitative research.[10] None the less, concerns over the internal consistency of the probate inventory and the dramatic decline of the source from the second half of the eighteenth century has tended to limit its use in later work. Our research has centred on constructing a robust series of datasets based on the probate records of widows, spinsters and, where possible, single men with a particular focus on the administrations of peculiar courts which permit research to be extended into the nineteenth century. This has enabled us to suggest ways in which domestic space was constructed and utilised and whether that differed both in context and extent from the material culture of marital households.

Chapter 3, 'Organisation and Management of a Single Household', draws parallels between normative marital experience and the problems and opportunities faced by the single homemaker in controlling domestic space. In particular, we examine how forms of work impinged upon the single household and, in the cases of many lone women, served to shape the domestic experience. Organisation of space was central to the efficient supervision of the household and, combining probate material with diary and account book testimony, we seek to analyse the ways and means that single men and women disciplined their environment through their material possessions. Clearly, the absence of a spouse permitted some degree of latitude – a theme we return to in the following chapters – but it could also impose severe constraints upon the functionality of the household. In these instances, the homes of single people were more likely to fall into forms of material chaos wherein the norms of the culturally appropriate 'model' household, itself described and policed by conduct literature, were eroded. Here, the lone man was especially liable to let work and working materials intrude into the spaces and practices of middling sort domesticity.

This theme is further developed in Chapter 4, 'Social and Symbolic Uses of the Homes of Single People', which examines the home as a social and symbolic arena. We argue that single homemakers adopted highly flexible strategies in constructing their domestic spaces in order to counteract accusations of impropriety. For many lifelong singletons, taste as expressed through the home remained a problematic issue throughout the period. In particular, the activities of the polite household in terms of entertainment and engagement with wider society were factors that assumed a deeper importance in the lives of single men and women of the middle

---

[10] See L. Weatherill, *Consumer Behaviour and Material Culture* and M. Overton, J. Whittle, D. Dean and A. Hann, *Production and Consumption in English Households, 1600–1750* (London: Routledge, 2004).

ranks. Whereas men could quite properly engage in homosocial pursuits both within and beyond the confines of their homes, mixed company presented a range of challenges to the widower and, especially, the bachelor. This was amplified in the domestic arrangements of singlewomen and, in particular, spinsters where the strictures of decorum constrained free association. None the less, the unmarried estate could present opportunities for those with the economic wherewithal to circumvent domestic convention, and for the independent agent singleness afforded the space to pursue interests with a tenacity often denied the married. For many singlewomen, however, the persistence of male oversight and financial superintendence often made such opportunities few and far between.

In Chapter 5, 'Compromised Spaces: Lodgers, Boarders and Shared Domestic Space', we survey the opportunities for forms of domestic independence experienced by single men and women within lodging, boarding and institutional environments. Here space and privacy, the true luxuries of consumption, were constrained by the temporary and often transient nature of the accommodation. However, we argue that even in the most unpromising of situations – the bare lodging room, the almshouse cell or even the university apartment – single people were able to impose a measure of domesticity and ownership upon their often materially denuded spaces. Through the use of probate, diaries and court proceedings we emphasise how the extents and limits of 'home' were expressed and defended. Indeed, it is here that the key concern of this book – the association of goods, space and singleness – was felt most keenly.

Chapter 1
Being Single

In December 1712, Edmund Harrold, a Manchester wigmaker of declining fortunes, attended the deathbed of his second wife, Sarah. In his diary, he noted: 'My wife lay adying from 11 this day, till 9 a clock on ye 18th in ye morn. Then she dy'd in my arms … I besweech God almighty, who has taken my dear asistant from me, to asist me with grace and wisdom to live religiously and virtuously.'[1] Harrold, a man who suffered more than most from the excesses of drink and the torment – the 'madness' – of inebriation, had good cause to seek intervention. Left with a young family and a sickly newborn, Harrold was projected into the uncertain embraces of singleness. Four months later, at the demise of this child, Harrold declaimed: 'This is now 7 times that devouring death hath visited my dwelling. It has take[n] 2 dear wives and 5 sweet infants from me, and I for my part am likly to be next.'[2]

This was not to be the case: Harrold mourned the death of his daughter; but it is also clear that, like many plebeian households, 'devouring death' eased the pressure on the now abbreviated family.[3] Though shorn of his wife's support and income and now employing a housekeeper, Harrold could dispense with the wet nurse and focus on the rickety fortunes of his business. Yet, the single life did not commend itself to Harrold. Apart from the impositions upon the material integrity of his household, Harrold missed the emotional support and physical intimacy of the marital estate. After convincing himself of the moral efficacy and social necessity of remarriage, Harrold duly began courting with gusto. A potentially inappropriate and inauspicious union with the fiery Ellen Howorth briefly persuaded Harrold 'not to medle with [a] widow and children, but [remain?] a batchalor with some

---

[1]   C. Horner (ed.), *The Diary of Edmund Harrold, Wigmaker of Manchester, 1712–15* (Aldershot: Ashgate, 2008), 18–19 December 1712, p. 52. See also H. Barker, 'Soul, Purse and Family: Middling and Lower-Class Masculinity in Eighteenth-Century Manchester', *Social History*, 33/1 (2008), pp. 12–35 (pp. 18–21 for Harrold) and R. Houlbrooke, *Death, Religion and the Family in England, 1480–1750* (Oxford: Oxford University Press, 1998).

[2]   Horner (ed.), *Diary of Edmund Harrold*, 1 April 1713, p. 67.

[3]   See D. Vincent, 'Love and Death and the Nineteenth-Century Working Class', *Social History*, 5/2 (1980), pp. 223–47 and for comparable examples, D. Vincent, *Bread, Knowledge and Freedom: A Study of Nineteenth-Century Working Class Autobiography* (London: Europa, 1981), pp. 39–61 and J. Burnett, D. Vincent and D. Mayall (eds), *The Autobiography of the Working Class: An Annotated Critical Bibliography, Vol. 1, 1790–1900* (Brighton: Harvester, 1984).

money etc'. This was soon quickly forgotten and he subsequently wooed and then married the less encumbered, and suitably 'quiet and easie of temper', Ann Horrocks, in August 1713.[4]

Some 90 years later, in December 1804, the 27-year-old Plymouth attorney Henry Woollcombe looked with scorn and pity upon his solitary life and the cruel vicissitudes of love. Well connected and already embarked upon a career that would bring high public office and no little private fortune, Woollcombe confessed that his thoughts had been 'much exercised about a certain Lady' and the prospect of a long wished for marriage. In the space of just a few weeks, Woollcombe's expectations had turned to dust:

> The mail this day brought me my sentence, my hopes are gone and I am wretched for ever … How is it that I have been so deceived? Surely, surely I must indulge my fancy and divest myself of my judgement when I mix with female society. How is it possible otherwise I have been so punished, [that] I can remember such things and yet they meane nothing.[5]

Woollcombe's singleness was persistent and the space that solitude gave to private and occasionally dark reflection clawed at his sense of well-being and cultural propriety, for although Woollcombe rose through the ranks of Plymouth's social and cultural elite – becoming in succession Alderman, Mayor and Recorder and assuming a central role in the establishment of the town's principal cultural and artistic institutions, the Athenaeum and Society of Antiquaries – his unmarried status rendered him an awkward and solitary figure in company. This was markedly so in comparison to his wider family and the range of friends and acquaintances he cultivated through his professional and social life. In particular, despite the fact that Woollcombe occupied increasingly well-appointed urban residences and had access to the family's estates and country retreats in Devon, his range of polite domestic engagement, and especially mixed social intercourse, was more circumscribed than his married contemporaries'. None the less, Woollcombe pursued an idealised union and his singularly unfortunate, even gauche, attempts to realise this dream punctuated his diary with sad regularity. Thus, on Christmas Day 1818, Woollcombe, his heart captured by a visiting widow of 'irresistible' manner, reported that he attended morning service and:

> knelt at the altar near the woman whom of all others I would select for my wife. I prayed most earnestly for her welfare. I had no opportunity of speaking to her

---

[4]   See Horner (ed.), *Diary of Edmund Harrold*, 22 February–5 March 1713, pp. 61–3 for Harrold's dealings with Howorth; 22 August 1713, p. 86 for his eventual and rather low-key marriage to Horrocks.

[5]   Plymouth and West Devon Record Office, 710/391–7 Diaries of Henry Woollcombe II, 1796–1828 (hereafter: Woollcombe, *Diary*), 24 December 1804; 25 January 1805 (punctuation modernised).

& to morrow she leaves Plymouth for two months and what may happen in that time who can tell?[6]

Despite his fondly remembered past meetings and their largely imagined mutual interests, Woollcombe was not to see the object of his rather chaste and sentimental affections again. In 1827, surveying the wreckage of previous courtships and missed opportunities, Woollcombe, a man now firmly entrenched into the security of middle-age homosocial routine, had inured himself to the compensatory prospects of the single life. 'I am now settled in a comfortable, respectable house with everything about me to make me satisfied', he reported in his annual summary. 'It is true that I wished to be married & that I am disappointed, but what then – I am old enough & wise enough to see that marriage like every thing else in this world has its black side as well as his bright.'[7] This was a painful compromise, but one that clearly emphasised the importance of home as a site of material comfort and a refuge from the everyday.

Whilst an ocean of class, opportunity and advancement clearly separated the plebeian wigmaker from the affluent lawyer, the two men shared a distinct commonality. Both men were confirmed Anglicans who exhibited a wary caution towards the practices and predilections of Roman Catholics and Nonconformists alike; both were ardent bibliophiles, Harrold supplementing his living with an erratic but lucrative sideline in book dealing and Woollcombe reshaping his main house to accommodate a burgeoning collection of classics, histories, romances and legal texts;[8] both used their journals as spiritual aides-memoires to review their conduct; and both experienced periods of singleness in their adult lives. However, for Harrold singleness was merely an unfortunate interruption, a hiatus in a life that otherwise emphasised the primacy of the nuclear family and the sanctity of marital and above all generative sexual union.[9] For Woollcombe, enmeshed in the practices of male politeness, honour and sensibility, singleness was both a token of failure and a badge of otherness. Although he was insulated by the wider public cultures of masculinity – work, status and position – home, that very locus of the

---

[6]   Woollcombe, *Diary*, 24 December 1818. He met the unnamed woman, a widow, on 6 December. Despite further hopes of marriage, there is no mention of the subject again beyond 26 January.

[7]   Woollcombe, *Diary*, 31 December 1827.

[8]   Plymouth and West Devon Record Office, 2395: An account of the antiquarian and archaeological manuscripts of Henry Woollcombe, FSA, c.1839.

[9]   Ann Horrocks was Harrold's third wife; Harrold married again on her death in 1717: Horner (ed.), *Diary of Edmund Harrold*, pp. xii–xiii. For plebeian masculinity and sexual practices, see J. Tosh, 'The Old Adam and the New Man: Emerging Themes in the History of English Masculinities' in T. Hitchcock and M. Cohen (eds), *English Masculinities, 1660–1800* (London: Longman, 1999), pp. 217–38 and T. Hitchcock, 'Redefining Sex in Eighteenth-Century England' in K.M. Phillips and B. Reay (eds), *Sexualities in History: A Reader* (London: Routledge, 2002), pp. 185–202, 186–92.

family, was, as for many other single men of the period, a deeply problematic arena. And if this rang true for such an archetypal and successful bourgeois as Woollcombe – the very pillar of respectable society – how did less socially elevated men and, moreover, single women negotiate the spaces and requirements of domesticity? As recent work has confirmed, single women were far more constrained in their activities and such opportunities that singleness may have presented were policed by prescriptive codes of patriarchal decency, deference and respectability.[10] Needless to say, the legal and financial background meant that women were hardest hit and that for many marriage was the only viable solution to a life of economic makeshift or, occasionally, the comparative financial security of same-sex households – the cohabitation of widows or the 'spinster-clustering' evidenced in some early modern communities, for example.[11] Despite this, the demographic significance of unmarried single adults and the widowed remained a key factor in both the construction of the household-family, to borrow Naomi Tadmor's useful concept, and ultimately the wider economic basis of British society.[12]

Singleness and Society: The Demographic Background

The importance and centrality of the nuclear family is somewhat of a historical given. As recent work has confirmed, both contemporary comment and subsequent historical analysis have emphasised the conjugal marital household as the generative standard upon and through which all forms of household construction have been measured. The hegemony of the nuptial household has

---

[10]   See the recent work by Amy Froide: *Never Married: Singlewomen in Early Modern England* (Oxford: Oxford University Press, 2007), pp. 15–43; 'Marital Status as a Category of Difference: Singlewomen and Widows in Early Modern England' in J.M. Bennett and A.M. Froide (eds), *Singlewomen in the European Past 1250–1800* (Philadelphia: University of Pennsylvania Press, 1999), pp. 236–69; and 'Old Maids: The Lifecycle of Single Women in Early Modern England' in L. Botelho and P. Thane (eds), *Women and Aging in British Society since 1500* (London: Pearson, 2001), pp. 89–110. These points are discussed in more depth below.

[11]   For spinster-clustering as a viable survival strategy for poor singlewomen, see O. Hufton, 'Women without Men: Widows and Spinsters in Britain and France in the Eighteenth Century', *Journal of Family Studies*, 9 (1984), pp. 355–76; P. Sharpe, 'Literally Spinsters: A New Interpretation of Local Economy and Demography in Colyton in the Seventeenth and Eighteenth Centuries', *Economic History Review*, 44/1 (1991), pp. 46–65; P. Sharpe, 'Dealing with Love: The Ambiguous Independence of the Single Woman in Early Modern England', *Gender and History*, 11/2 (1999), pp 202–32; and A. Schmidt, 'Survival Strategies of Widows and their Families in Early Modern Holland, c.1580–1750', *The History of the Family*, 12/4 (2007), pp. 268–81.

[12]   N. Tadmor, *Family and Friends in Eighteenth-Century England* (Cambridge: Cambridge University Press, 2001), pp. 18–43.

thus cast a culturally normative blanket over other forms of domestic existence that proliferated in the long eighteenth century. To this extent, both contemporary descriptions of the household and subsequent historical analysis have often marginalised the arrangements of single men and women. Singleness in these conceptions was anomalous and defined, predominantly, by absence or loss. The single household was a bare cipher of the vibrant marital home, existing in a curiously transient position within wider patriarchal conceptions of male and female activity.[13] As the marital home came to occupy a culturally dominant role in patriarchal ideology as the comfortable bulwark and bastion from the muscular intrusions of the outside world, the single household thus appeared even more at odds with wider cultural practice.

A cursory examination of the domestic organisation of wider English society would seem to bear out these assumptions. Laslett's examination of 100 communities between 1574 and 1821 reveals that over 70 per cent of all households were headed by married couples. The spouses of the deceased constituted just over 18 per cent of the sample, whereas, tellingly, single men (2.1 per cent) and singlewomen (1.1 per cent) formed a wholly marginal group, barely significant in terms of the wider pattern.[14] Despite the fixity of these data, Laslett's figures are not unproblematic and certain caveats should be borne in mind. For example, the data on household headship undoubtedly favour the kind of established economic units that figured centrally in censuses and enumerations. None the less, it is clear that the marital household described the everyday, quotidian mode of existence for much of the early modern and early nineteenth century period.

Singleness was, of course, a far more common lifecycle occurrence than such simple descriptions would imply. In societies where marriage was habitually delayed to the mid or late twenties and where adult morbidity meant that many women and a few men outlived their partners, the young unmarried and the older widow (and to a lesser extent widower, as men habitually tended to remarry fairly quickly after the death of their spouse) were estates that most men and women experienced at some stage during the course of their lives.[15] Similarly, attitudes towards nominal celibacy were important in maintaining a large population of

---

[13] See A.L. Erickson, *Women and Property in Early Modern England* (London: Routledge, 1993), pp. 187–203 for a wider discussion of these themes.

[14] P. Laslett, 'Mean Household Size in England since the Sixteenth Century' in P. Laslett (ed.), *Household and Family in Past Time* (Cambridge: Cambridge University Press, 1972), pp. 145–7. See also, P. Laslett, *The World We Have Lost* (2nd edn, London: Methuen, 1971), pp. 84–112, 135–58.

[15] Erickson, *Women and Property*, pp. 153–5, 195-6; E.A. Wrigley and R.S. Schofield, *The Population History of England, 1541–1871: A Reconstruction* (London: Edward Arnold, 1981), p. 250; and R.S. Schofield, 'Did the Mothers Really Die? Three Centuries of Maternal Mortality in "The World We Have Lost"' in L. Bonfield, R.M. Smith and K. Wrightson (eds), *The World We Have Gained* (Oxford: Oxford University Press, 1986), pp. 259–60.

single men and women: Wrigley and Schofield have argued that the proportion of English men and women unmarried by the age of between 40 and 44 peaked at over a quarter (27 per cent) of the total population by the late seventeenth century, before falling off dramatically in the eighteenth and nineteenth centuries.[16] Although recent research has revised these estimates downwards, it remains that celibacy rates were notably high for much of the seventeenth century and had a direct bearing on demographic patterns of fertility throughout the period.[17]

One of the key determinants of an extended single existence was marital age. As Wrigley and Schofield have demonstrated, age at first marriage declined progressively throughout the period.[18] By the mid to late seventeenth century, men on average married at or just under 28 years of age. This fell off in the eighteenth century, with the mean age of male wedding declining to just over 26 in the 1750–99 cohort and thence to an average of 25 years and 4 months in the early nineteenth century. The pattern was mirrored in the case of women, although here the fall in marital age was perhaps even more pronounced. Women tended to get married at around the age of 26 and 9 months towards the end of the seventeenth century, although there was much local fluctuation in this trend. At Colyton, for example, in the period between 1700 and 1710, women married on average at around 30 years and 8 months.[19] A century later, the mean age of female marriage was scarcely 24, and this fell even further as the nineteenth century progressed.

Whatever the causes for this phenomenon – and Wrigley and Schofield postulate an indirect, lagged correlation with economic circumstance and the persistence and tenacity of parental control – it meant that many young adults experienced up to 10 years of single existence before marriage was considered. Of course, these global figures applied differentially and, in the case of the emergent middle class of the nineteenth century, marriage was often deferred until much later.[20] This time was subsumed in extended apprenticeship, formal education or

---

[16]   For a discussion of these trends, see Wrigley and Schofield, *Population History*, Table 7.28, p. 260.

[17]   For revised estimates, see D.R. Weir, 'Rather Never than Late: Celibacy and Age at Marriage in English Cohort Fertility', *Journal of Family History*, 9 (1984), pp. 340–54 and R.S. Schofield, 'English Marriage Patterns Revisited', *Journal of Family History*, 10 (1985), pp. 2–10. More recent research has emphasised these developments: see Froide, 'Old Maids', pp. 94–6; M. Kowalski, 'Singlewomen in Medieval and Early Modern Europe: The Demographic Perspective' in Bennett and Froide (eds), *Singlewomen in the European Past*, pp. 38–81.

[18]   Wrigley and Schofield, *Population History*, pp. 255–7, 422–4, 437–8.

[19]   P. Sharpe, 'Dealing with Love', p. 209; P. Sharpe, 'Literally Spinsters', pp. 46–9.

[20]   For deferred marriage amongst the Victorian middle class, see J. Tosh, 'Domesticity and Manliness in the Victorian Middle Class: The Family of Edward Benson' in M. Roper and J. Tosh (eds), *Manful Assertions: Masculinities in Britain since 1800* (London: Routledge, 1991), pp. 59–68 and for the later period, J. Tosh, 'Middle-Class Masculinities in the Era of the Women's Suffrage Movement, 1860–1914' in J. Tosh, *Manliness and Masculinities in Nineteenth-Century Britain* (Harlow: Pearson, 2005), pp. 103–25, 111.

service in the households of others. Indeed, younger singletons often resided and were expected to undertake unpaid work in the familial or near-natal household. Frequently, young women and on occasion men were placed in the domestic establishments of kin and occasionally family friends. Parental death, desertion or the absence of near kin characteristically alerted parochial authorities keen to minimise any potential claims for maintenance and it was highly uncommon for a younger singlewoman of marriageable age to occupy a position as an independent head of household in her own right.[21] Indeed, as Richard Wall has argued, the common experience of the urban singlewoman was as a dependant in the parental household and thereafter, if her status was appropriate, a servant, lodger or companion in the households of relatives.[22] Singlewomen were constrained by patriarchal ties of male oversight and it was not until the age of 40 – when relative longevity, imputed lack of fertility and possibly inherited or independent wealth became mitigating factors – that it became culturally acceptable for singlewomen to exist unmolested as heads of households in their own right. Whereas this position may have become somewhat ameliorated as the eighteenth century progressed, it was, none the less, expected that urban singlewomen would generally occupy situations under the direct authority of male superintendence. Through such means masculine hegemony was effectively institutionalised.

None the less, where these codes of power were subjected to stress – often under the destabilising effects of industrialisation, urbanisation and migration – male authority was quick to reassert its primacy.[23] Disraeli, for example, captures this sense of disjuncture, opprobrium and the dissolution of older forms of gendered propriety in his novel *Sybil or The Two Nations* (1845). Here Disraeli laments the growth of strange and unnatural households through the reaction of an older street trader, Mrs Carey, to two young, unmarried female mill workers setting up home together. The mill workers, Caroline and Julia, tell her: 'We keep house together; we have a very nice room in Arbour court, No. 7, high up; it's very airy. If you will take a dish of tea with us to-morrow, we expect some friends.' A shared room in the garrets of a building in a court was clearly less than salubrious and yet these young women were keen to participate in genteel forms of consumption and entertainment. Mrs Carey, however, was not impressed. Although she accepted their invitation, after they had gone on their way she commented: 'I think the

---

[21] See, for example, B. Hill, *Women, Work and Sexual Politics in Eighteenth-Century England* (London: UCL Press, 1994), pp. 233–5; Hufton, 'Women without Men', pp. 361–4; and Sharpe, 'Literally Spinsters', pp. 55–62.

[22] R. Wall, 'Woman Alone in English Society', *Annales de Demographie Historique*, 17 (1981), pp. 303–17, esp. pp. 311–12. Wall's work on Lichfield and Stoke-on-Trent make these conclusions especially apposite for the regional focus of this work. See also R. Wall, 'Leaving Home and the Process of Household Formation in Pre-Industrial England', *Continuity and Change*, 2 (1987), pp. 77–101 and Froide, *Never Married*, pp. 18–19.

[23] See also B. Hill, *Women Alone: Spinsters in England, 1660–1850* (New Haven and London: Yale University Press, 2001), pp. 43–53.

world is turned upside downwards in these parts ... this girl asks me to take a dish of tea with her and keeps house! Fathers and mothers goes for nothing ... 'Tis the children gets the wages.'[24]

If marriage was delayed the period of singleness and by implication dependency was extended throughout much of early adulthood. Similarly, the patterns of adult mortality, and especially the relatively constrained life expectancy of men in comparison to women, also translated into later age lifecycle singleness. Certainly, remarriage was an attractive proposition in many cases as later life could frequently be subsumed in poverty and straitened economic circumstance. As Sharpe has argued, the spectre of poverty at widowhood 'lurked within the psyche of both ordinary men and women to a far greater degree than is now imaginable'.[25] However, it must be remembered that widows were subject to both the partitioning of the marital estate, often receiving little more than the customary third, and, on occasion, swingeing financial penalties under the terms of their deceased husbands' wills. In such instances remarriage, if possible, would necessarily curtail hard-won financial and legal independence.[26] From Wrigley and Schofield's data, it appears that remarriage accounted for perhaps around 25– 30 per cent of all marriages by the second half of the seventeenth century, a figure that reflected recurrent mortality crises earlier in the century and one that may well have inflated the local incidence of widowhood deep into the eighteenth century. In contrast, Barbara Todd has argued that, from the position of Abingdon in the late seventeenth century at least, only 16 to 24 per cent of widows remarried – a figure perhaps reflective of the general vilification of remarrying widows Collins has located in didactic literature and conduct books. By the nineteenth century, perhaps less than 11 per cent of all marriages comprised the widowed re-entering the nuptial market.[27] Anecdotal evidence suggests that in comparison to women

---

[24]   B. Disraeli, *Sybil or The Two Nations* (Oxford: Oxford University Press, 1981 [1845]), pp. 89–90.

[25]   P. Sharpe, 'Survival Strategies and Stories: Poor Widows and Widowers in Early Industrial England' in S. Cavallo and L. Walker (eds), *Widowhood in Medieval and Early Modern Europe* (Harlow: Pearson, 1999), pp. 220–21.

[26]   Erickson, *Women and Property*, pp. 156–73 discusses settlements and limitations afforded to widows. For claims on property and possessions when marriage broke down, see J. Bailey, *Unquiet Lives: Marriage and Marriage Breakdown in England, 1660–1800* (Cambridge: Cambridge University Press, 2003), pp. 85–109.

[27]   Wrigley and Schofield, *Population History*, pp. 258–9. For remarriage, see B. Todd, 'The Remarrying Widow: a Stereotype Reconsidered' in M. Prior (ed.), *Women in English Society, 1500–1800* (London: Methuen, 1985), pp. 25–50; J. Boulton, 'London Widowhood Revisited: The Decline of Female Remarriage in the Seventeenth and Early Eighteenth Centuries', *Continuity and Change*, 5/3 (1990), pp. 323–55; B.J. Todd, 'Demographic Determinism and Female Agency: The Remarrying Widow Reconsidered ... Again', *Continuity and Change*, 9 (1994), pp. 421–50 and S. Collins, '"A Kind of Lawful Adultery": English Attitudes to the Remarriage of Widows, 1550–1800' in P.C. Jupp and G. Howarth (eds), *The Changing Face of Death: Historical Accounts of Death*

who lost their husbands, widowers tended to remarry fairly quickly – especially, as in the case of Edmund Harrold, if left with dependants. Widowers, in general, could expect less sympathetic treatment in the way of poor relief than widows.[28] On average, the 5.2 per cent of all households headed by a widower across Laslett's sample of 100 rural communities is dwarfed by the 12.9 per cent of households with a female widowed head.[29]

Even so, the economic, legal and cultural position of widows was not unfavourable. As femes soles, widows were not subject to the restrictions of coverture and thus maintained the right to contract, hold and own property in their name; conduct business; maintain apprentices and facilitate other economic concerns; administer and direct a range of financial instruments; and, by way of their increased visibility and prominence in local and urban economies, engage in forms of communal representation.[30] In short, the widow acted as an acceptable male cipher, literally 'in loco pateris' in the direction and construction of the family and as such operated with a greater degree of independence than that afforded to their married sisters – femes coverts who existed in a more constrained legal position. As such, recent work has relocated the economically robust widow to the centre of commercial life.[31] This did not mean, of course, that widows enjoyed the raft of liberties and responsibilities afforded to male heads and many found that practical economic independence was merely putative, limited by entrenched patriarchal power and subject to the supervisory gaze of both local regulation and

---

and Disposal (Basingstoke: Macmillan, 1997), pp. 34–47. For a different perspective, see A.E.C. McCants, 'The Not-So-Merry Widows of Amsterdam, 1740–1782', *Journal of Family History*, 24/4 (1999), pp. 441–67.

[28] Sharpe, 'Poor Widows and Widowers', pp. 224–5.

[29] Laslett, 'Mean Household Size', pp. 144–8. See also L. Davidoff and C. Hall, *Family Fortunes: Men and Women of the English Middle Class 1780–1850* (London: Hutchinson, 1987), pp. 324–5; Erickson, *Women and Property*, pp. 194–5.

[30] See, for example, the articles in S. Cavallo and L. Warner (eds), *Widowhood in Medieval and Early Modern Europe* (London: Longman, 1999). For discussions of coverture, see Erickson, *Women and Property*, pp. 21–31; J. Bailey, 'Favoured or Oppressed? Married Women, Property and "Coverture" in England, 1660–1800', *Continuity and Change*, 17/3 (2002), pp. 351–72; A.L. Erickson, 'Coverture and Capitalism', *History Workshop Journal*, 59 (2005), pp. 1–16 and A.L. Erickson, 'Possession – and the Other One-Tenth of the Law: Assessing Women's Ownership and Economic Roles in Early Modern England', *Women's History Review*, 16/3 (2007), pp. 369–85.

[31] See H. Barker, *The Business of Women: Female Enterprise and Urban Development in Northern England 1760–1830* (Oxford: Oxford University Press, 2006); H. Barker and K. Harvey, 'Women Entrepreneurs and Urban Expansion: Manchester, 1760–1820' in R. Sweet and P. Lane (eds), *Women and Urban Life in Eighteenth-Century England: 'On the Town'* (Aldershot: Ashgate, 2003), pp. 87–130; and D.R. Green and A. Owens, 'Gentlewomanly Capitalism? Spinster, Widows, and Wealth Holding in England and Wales, c.1800–1860', *Economic History Review*, 46 (2003), pp. 510–36.

the oversight of family and kin.[32] None the less, widow-headed households were very common and it was relatively exceptional for widows to seek maintenance or houseroom in the establishments of kin in this period unless extreme poverty or distress intervened. Even so, as Pat Thane and Sylvia Pinches have emphasised, the poor and destitute widow was not unknown.[33] Despite this work, Laslett's work on parish data has tended to stress the independence of widows: only 25 per cent of widowed women lived in the households of others, whereas the remainder either headed a household that was often maintained alongside dependents, kin, apprentices, paying lodgers and servants, or lived separately by their own means and within their own dwelling.[34]

The Never Married Singlewoman

Thus far we have examined the position of singleness as a construct of lifecycle. Young adult singletons, most of whom would progress to formal marriage, and more certainly the bereaved were intimately associated with and, for the widow and widower in particular, defined by their proximity to marriage and prescribed conjugal, heterosexual union. However, there is a need to distinguish between this group – the 'ever-married' in Amy Froide's telling phrase – and the 'never married', the proportion of society engaged in single, notionally celibate or other and often unrecorded non-marital relationships.[35] These lifelong singles – those who eschewed marriage for a variety of reasons and circumstances – were far from marginal actors in a culture dominated by the apparent authority and visibility of marriage. For a start, the never married were relatively numerous, especially in the early decades of the

[32]   See Erickson, *Women and Property*, pp. 186–7, 191–3; 200 and Anthony Fletcher's work on the changing attitudes to male domestic hegemony: *Gender, Sex and Subordination in England, 1500–1800* (New Haven and London: Yale University Press, 1995), pp. 101–25, 154–72, 204–55.

[33]   P. Thane, 'Old People and their Families in the Past' in M. Daunton (ed.), *Charity, Self-Interest and Welfare in the English Past* (London: UCL Press, 1996); S. Pinches, 'Women as Objects and Agents of Charity in Eighteenth-Century Birmingham' in Sweet and Lane (eds), *Women and Urban Life*, pp. 65–86. See also R. Connors, 'Poor Women, the Parish and the Politics of Poverty' in H. Barker and E. Chalus (eds), *Gender in Eighteenth-Century England: Roles, Representations and Responsibilities* (London: Longman, 1997) and T. Evans, *Unfortunate Objects: Lone Mothers in Eighteenth-Century London* (London: Palgrave Macmillan, 2007).

[34]   P. Laslett, *Family Life and Illicit Love in Earlier Generations* (Cambridge: Cambridge University Press, 1977), p. 198. See also B. Hill, *Eighteenth-Century Women: An Anthology* (London: Allen & Unwin, 1984) and, for the earlier period, T. Wales, 'Poverty, Poor Relief and the Life-Cycle: Some Evidence from Seventeenth-Century Norfolk' in R.M. Smith (ed.), *Land, Kinship and Life-Cycle* (Cambridge: Cambridge University Press, 1984), pp. 351–404.

[35]   Froide, *Never Married*, pp. 16–17, 33–4.

period. Although the back projection techniques used by historical demographers to reconstruct this population are subject to wide variation and regional fluctuation, it can be reasonably assumed that around 27 per cent of the population born in the mid-seventeenth century and thus reaching optimum marital age in the 1670s and 1680s remained unmarried at the terminal limit of female fertility (40–44 years of age). This pool of unmarried spinsters, attested in the contemporary attitudes of much of the virulently pro-natalist literature at the time, declined sharply as the period progressed. By the 1680s, around 16 per cent avoided marriage, dropping to 4–7 per cent in the groups born in the 1730s and 1740s. By the end of the eighteenth century, rates again began to rise, with 10–12 per cent of the quinquennial population cohorts remaining unmarried towards the mid-nineteenth century. This equates favourably to the adjusted census and enumeration data that reveal 11.7, 12.0 and 10.7 per cent of the population unmarried in the age 40–44 cohorts in 1841, 1851 and 1861. Such factors inspired concern over the 'surplus woman' problem in mid-Victorian Britain.[36] Late marriage was experienced differentially. It was widely perceived that singleness impacted most strongly among the genteel middle classes and, by the latter half of the nineteenth century, advice literature and a range of more strident medical polemic emphasised the dangers of barrenness and the celibate life.[37]

Obviously, the picture painted by such summary data is necessarily bald. It does not, for example, account for local conditions and may fail to factor in clandestine marriage, cohabitation and especially semi-formal separation. Indeed, as Ginger Frost's work suggests, cohabitation and other non-marital strategies of partnership assumed a not insubstantial place in the century after Hardwicke's Marriage Act of 1753. Such 'irregular unions', though far from commonplace, were important enough to arouse the censorious ire of Victorian commentators and legislators and were likely to have inflated the data relating to singleness.[38]

---

[36] Data from Wrigley and Schofield, *Population History*, pp. 259–65, 436–8. See also K. Levitan, 'Redundancy, the "Surplus Woman" Problem, and the British Census, 1851–1861', *Women's History Review*, 17/3 (2008), pp. 359–76.

[37] Such views are summarised in K. Gleadale, *British Women in the Nineteenth Century* (London: Palgrave Macmillan, 2001), pp. 182–5. For earlier debates, see P. Branca, *Silent Sisterhood: Middle-Class Women in the Victorian Home* (London: Croom Helm, 1975), pp. 2–5; M. Anderson, 'The Social Position of Spinsters in Mid-Victorian Britain', *Journal of Family History*, 9 (1984), pp. 377–93; J. Perkin, *Women and Marriage in Nineteenth-Century England* (London: Routledge, 1989), esp. pp. 21–20; C. Curran, 'Private Women, Public Needs: Middle-Class Widows in Victorian England', *Albion*, 25/2 (1993), pp. 217–36.

[38] G. Frost, *Living in Sin: Cohabiting as Husband and Wife in Nineteenth-Century England* (Manchester: Manchester University Press, 2008) and G. Frost, *Promises Broken: Courtship, Class and Gender in Victorian England* (Charlottesville: University of Virginia Press, 1995), esp. pp. 40–58. For a discussion of divorce, marriage breakdown and the legal position of separated couples, see R. Phillips, *Putting Asunder: A History of Divorce in Western Society* (Cambridge: Cambridge University Press, 1988), esp. pp. 71–7; L. Stone, *The Family, Sex and Marriage in England, 1500–1800* (New York: Weidenfeld & Nicolson,

Furthermore, whilst the demographic figures have established that a significant minority of the population remained unmarried throughout the period, there are some important caveats and clarifications to bear in mind. Primarily, there is little distinction between male and female components of the never married in published indices relating to the period. Wrigley and Schofield have used census material to probe gender differences in the post-1851 period, revealing that just over 11 per cent of men and 12 per cent of women surveyed remained single at the age of between 45 and 54. This cohort, born at the turn of the eighteenth century and reaching viable marriage age by the late 1820s and early 1830s, could thus reasonably be assumed as never marrying.[39] There were, of course, exceptions to this trend. Anne Nussey – sister of Henry and Ellen, friend of Charlotte Brontë and to all extents a lifelong singlewoman – was married for the first time, aged 53, to Robert Clapham in 1849.[40]

It would be dangerous and quite erroneous, however, to project the gender-specific data of the nineteenth century onto earlier periods with absolute confidence. None the less, recent work has begun to address this question. For example, Froide's examination of the Marriage Duty returns for Southampton demonstrate that within the constraints of the urban survey, whilst lone women (widows and singlewomen) headed over 27 per cent of the sample of households, in total singlewomen accounted for 34.2 per cent of the adult female population in 1694. Married women formed almost half (47.3 per cent) of those surveyed, whilst widows, arguably the most visible and legally independent of femes soles in the period, constituted only 18.5 per cent of the sample.[41] Elsewhere, households headed by a lone female were similarly prominent: almost 27 per cent of households assessed for marriage duty in Bristol were nominally headed by a woman, compared to just over 9 per cent that indicated single male headship. In Shrewsbury the imbalance towards the household headed by single women was also significant: 21.3 per cent of all households had women heads, in contrast to the 11.3 per cent

---

1977), pp. 30–32, 37–8; L. Stone, *The Road to Divorce: England, 1530–1987* (Oxford: Oxford University Press, 1995), pp. 368–82; T. Stretton, 'Marriage, Separation and the Common Law in England, 1540–1660' in H. Berry and E. Foyster (eds), *The Family in Early Modern England* (Cambridge: Cambridge University Press, 2007), pp. 18–39; D.M. Turner, *Fashioning Adultery: Gender, Sex and Civility in England 1660–1740* (Cambridge: Cambridge University Press, 2002), pp. 51–82; Bailey, *Unquiet Lives*, pp. 61–84; and E. Foyster, *Marital Violence: An English Family History, 1600–1857* (Cambridge: Cambridge University Press, 2005), esp. ch. 4, pp. 168–204.

[39]   Wrigley and Schofield, *Population History*, pp. 436–8, Table 10.4.

[40]   The marriage was short-lived: Robert died suddenly in 1855. See W. Gérin, *Charlotte Brontë: The Evolution of Genius* (Oxford: Clarendon Press, 1967), p. 396.

[41]   Froide, *Never Married*, pp. 2–3, 16–17. The data for Southampton are presented in K. Schurer, 'Variations in Household Structure in the Late Seventeenth Century: Towards a Regional Analysis', in K. Schurer and T. Arkell (eds), *Surveying the People: The Interpretation and Use of Document Sources for the Study of Population in the Later Seventeenth Century* (Oxford: Leopard's Head Press, 1992), p. 266.

headed by lone men. However, in the more dispersed settlement patterns for Kent and Wiltshire both single headship and the prevalence of the female head were less marked.[42] Singlewomen, and in particular lifelong singlewomen, clearly occupied a prominent place in societies with a large urban component. For example, inward migration and the centripetal attraction of domestic service, rather than simple endogenous growth, accounted for the dominance of the singlewoman in late seventeenth century London: over half (54.5 per cent) of all adult women in the metropolis at this time were unmarried and it is apparent that single female servants were also very significant in provincial urban economies.[43]

Froide's work on singlewomen has injected a much-needed criticality into the study of the single estate, establishing that the culturally marginal position of the urban singlewoman began to change incrementally as the eighteenth century progressed.[44] Undoubtedly, the ever-present spectre of male surveillance meant that severe restrictions were imposed upon the viability of singlewomen to exist unbridled by external oversight and regulatory activity and, for much of the period, urban authorities sought to constrain female agency wherever possible. However, a combination of age, social status, economic independence (especially in areas where proto-industry encouraged women's work), robust kin relationships and no little skill enabled some middling sort singlewomen to escape the usual fate of

---

[42]   In Kent and Wiltshire the proportions of households headed by lone women and lone men were 10.5 per cent and 9.3 per cent and 16.3 per cent and 17 per cent respectively: Schurer, 'Variations in Household Structure', pp. 253–78, especially Table 2. See also R. Wall, 'Regional and Temporal Variations in English Household Structure from 1650', in J. Hobcraft and P. Rees (eds), *Regional Demographic Development* (London: Croom Helm, 1977), pp. 89–113 and for discussions of the Kent sample, M. Overton, J. Whittle, D. Dean and A. Hann, *Production and Consumption in English Households, 1600–1750* (London: Routledge, 2004), pp. 26–7. The Bristol data are described and tabulated in full by E. Ralph and M.E. Williams (eds), *The Inhabitants of Bristol in 1696: Assessments under the 1694 Marriage Act* (Bristol: Bristol Record Society, 25, 1968). See also J. Hindson, 'The Marriage Duty Acts and the Social Topography of the Early Modern Town – Shrewsbury, 1695–8', *Local Population Studies*, 31 (1983), pp. 21–8.

[43]   For the significance of service-related female employment to urban demography and economy, see P. Laslett, 'The Institution of Service', *Local Population Studies*, 40 (1988), p. 57; P. Earle, 'The Female Labour Market in London in the Late Seventeenth and Early Eighteenth Century', *Economic History Review*, 42 (1989), pp. 328–53; D.A. Kent, 'Ubiquitous but Invisible: Female Domestic Servants in Mid-Eighteenth Century London', *History Workshop Journal*, 28/1 (1989), pp. 111–28; Schurer, 'Variations in Household Structure', pp. 270–73, 275–6; B. Hill, *Servants: English Domestics in the Eighteenth Century* (Oxford: Oxford University Press, 1996), pp. 22–43; and T. Meldrum, *Domestic Service and Gender, 1660–1750: Life and Work in the London Household* (Harlow: Pearson, 2000), pp. 128–37 and chapter 5.

[44]   See the summary of research presented in Froide, *Never Married*, pp. 15–43. There is also much useful discussion in Hill, *Women Alone*; Hill, *Women, Work and Sexual Politics*, pp. 222–3; O. Hufton, 'Women without Men', pp. 355–76.

service or quasi-incarceration in the households of natal families and near kin.[45] For example, many spinsters were able to carve out an independent existence based on an extensive network of money lending and credit.[46] Even so, only a minority of women had the advantages and wherewithal of 'capital-rich lone' women like Joyce Jeffreys.[47] Few headed their own households – perhaps as few as 15 per cent of all singlewomen in late seventeenth-century Southampton, although in towns such as Ludlow where transient or seasonal populations afforded opportunities for additional remuneration this could be higher.[48] Furthermore, it is apparent that the domestic arrangements and strategies of all but the most wealthy of the never married were limited by the vagaries of culturally acceptable female employment, something that for the middling ranks was always problematic.[49] Some widows and singlewomen were able to subsist on a combination of direct employment, service, loaning at interest and other quasi-genteel activities – education, companionship, nursing, guardianship and the like – and it has been argued that this represented an opening up of economic opportunity that was denied to married women in the eighteenth century.[50] Indeed, these opportunities may have increased, albeit

---

[45]   See, for example, the career of Hester Pinney in Sharpe, 'Dealing with Love'. See also, Sharpe, 'Literally Spinsters', pp. 45–65 and J.M. Spicksley, 'A Dynamic Model of Social Relations: Celibacy, Credit and the Identity of the "Spinster" in Seventeenth-Century England', in H.R. French and J. Barry (eds), *Identity and Agency in English Society, 1500–1800* (Basingstoke: Palgrave Macmillan, 2004), pp. 106–46.

[46]   Judith Spicksley's work on credit and the agency of the singlewoman is vital here: J.M. Spicksley, 'To Be or Not to Be Married: Single Women, Money-Lending and the Question of Choice in Late Tudor and Stuart England' in D.M. Kehler and L. Amtower (eds), *The Single Woman in Medieval and Early Modern England: Her Life and Representation* (Tempe: Arizona Center for Medieval and Renaissance Studies, 2003), pp. 65–96; J.M. Spicksley, 'Usury Legislation, Cash, and Credit: The Development of the Female Investor in the Late Tudor and Stuart Periods', *Economic History Review*, 61/2 (2008), pp. 277–301; and J.M. Spicksley, '"Fly with a Duck in thy Mouth": Single Women as Sources of Credit in Seventeenth Century England', *Social History*, 32/2 (2007), pp. 187–207.

[47]   A.L. Capern and J.M. Spicksley, 'Introduction', *Women's History Review*, 16/3 (2007), p. 293.

[48]   Froide, *Never Married*, pp. 22–3; S. Wright, '"Holding up Half the Sky": Women and their Occupations in Eighteenth-Century Ludlow', *Midland History*, 14 (1989), pp. 53–74; and S. Wright, 'Sojourners and Lodgers in a Provincial Town: The Evidence from Eighteenth-Century Ludlow', *Urban History*, 17 (1990), pp. 14–35.

[49]   For rich spinsters, see Ruth Larsen, 'For Want of a Good Fortune: Elite Single Women's Experiences in Yorkshire, 1730–1860', *Women's History Review*, 16/3 (2007), pp. 387–401.

[50]   M.R. Hunt, *The Middling Sort: Commerce, Gender, and the Family in England, 1680–1780* (Berkeley and Los Angeles: University of California Press, 1996), pp. 142–4 emphasises the relatively optimistic position of singlewomen vis-à-vis married women. There are contrary arguments presented in Hill, *Eighteenth-Century Women*, pp. 130–32 and Hill, *Women, Work and Sexual Politics*, pp. 231–2.

marginally, for professionally inclined polite spinsters, as the nineteenth century progressed.[51]

None the less, as singlewomen became more visible, attitudes towards the single estate became increasingly abusive and pejorative. Whereas singlewomen were the objects of a literature of victimhood in the seventeenth century, pitied for their lack of defining heterosexual union, by the eighteenth century the figure of the spinster had lapsed into barbed caricature. Derided for being alternately prudish yet sexually voracious, pathetically fashionable, meddling, unworldly and above all vicious, the singlewoman was transformed into the stock image of the 'old maid' and the 'superannuated virgin' – in Hufton's memorable phrase, the 'sempiternal spoilsport in the orgy of life'.[52] Dickens' representation of Miss Lucretia Tox in *Dombey and Son* (1848) aptly summarises the tone of condescension, cultural marginalisation and domestic incongruity visited upon the singlewoman. Miss Tox, we are informed:

> inhabited a dark little house that had been squeezed, at some remote period of English History, into a fashionable neighbourhood at the west end of the town, where it stood in the shade like a poor relation of the great street round the corner, coldly looked down upon by mighty mansions. It was not exactly in a court, and it was not exactly in a yard; but it was in the dullest of No-Thoroughfares, rendered anxious and haggard by distant double knocks.[53]

Such literary tropes – set pieces of the novels of the later eighteenth and nineteenth centuries – not only reveal the deep misogyny at the heart of patriarchal society but also emphasise the pervasive cultural attitude towards singleness as an identifiable and threatening other to conjugal normality. Thus, Miss Tox's dress and deportment, 'though perfectly genteel and good', was none the less characterised by 'a certain ... angularity and scantiness':

> She was accustomed to wear odd weedy little flowers in her bonnets and caps. Strange grasses were sometimes perceived in her hair; and it was observed by the curious, of all her collars, frills, tuckers, wristbands, and other gossamer articles – indeed of everything she wore which had two ends to it intended to unite – that the two ends were never on good terms, and wouldn't quite meet without a struggle. She had furry articles for winter wear, as tippets, boas, and muffs, which stood up on end in rampant manner, and were not at all sleek.

---

[51]   See Perkin, *Women and Marriage*, pp. 224–32 and G. Holloway, *Women and Work in Britain since 1840* (London: Routledge, 2005), pp. 36–40 for later examples of female employment.

[52]   Hufton, 'Women without Men', p. 354. See also Hill, *Eighteenth-Century Women*, pp. 128–9. For the earlier period, see C. Peters, 'Single Women in Early Modern England: Attitudes and Expectations', *Continuity and Change*, 12/3 (1997), pp. 325–45.

[53]   C. Dickens, *Dombey and Son* (Harmondsworth: Penguin, 1985 [1848]), p. 143.

She was much given to the carrying about of small bags with snaps to them, that went off like little pistols when they were shut up; and when fully-dressed, she wore round her neck the barrenest of lockets, representing a fishy old eye, with no approach to speculation in it. These and other appearances of a similar nature, had served to propagate the opinion, that Miss Tox was a lady of what is called a limited independence, which she turned to the best account. Possibly her mincing gait encouraged the belief, and suggested that her clipping a step of ordinary compass into two or three, originated in her habit of making the most of everything.[54]

Whilst the figure of the frustrated old maid and the crotchety spinster was viciously lampooned, the caricature masked a range of social and cultural positions and economic circumstances. For many singlewomen, the wider demands of family rendered marriage inappropriate or incompatible with a domestic situation complicated by dependants and underscored by the absence of independent wealth. Catherine Hutton, the author and daughter of William Hutton, the historian of Birmingham, is a case in point here. In 1788 the 32-year-old Hutton received an offer of marriage. This was serious enough for Hutton to consider accepting: 'The man is handsome, gentlemanly, and agreeable enough', Hutton surmised, 'but he has been an officer in the army, and a freeliver, things totally out of my sober way.' Personal predilection was largely a convenient veneer to Hutton's wider responsibilities to her mother. The pattern was repeated when in 1806 Hutton, now housekeeper to her father, received a final proposal, only for this to be rejected on the grounds of her domestic duties, wider attachments and commitments to her aged father.[55] Hutton's singleness was thus prescribed by the extension and limitations imposed upon her by the household, even though her literary proclivities – a career in all but name – also conditioned her responses.

Men, Singleness and Masculinity

It is now over 10 years ago that John Tosh posed the question: What does masculinity have to do with domesticity?[56] By locating the study of male agency and authority firmly within the contradictory ethos of the Victorian home, Tosh sought to bring together the bourgeois ideal of domesticity as a bulwark from work and the intrusions of the extramural other with an analysis of the construction

---

[54]   Dickens, *Dombey and Son*, p. 56.

[55]   C. Hutton Beale, *Reminiscences of a Gentlewoman of the Last Century: Letters of Catherine Hutton* (Birmingham: Cornish Brothers, 1891), pp. 61, 158, 213.

[56]   J. Tosh, *A Man's Place: Masculinity and the Middle-Class Home in Victorian England* (New Haven and London: Yale University Press, 1999), p. 1.

and culture of male power.[57] As Tosh emphasised, these discussions revolve around the bounds and limits of patriarchy – the jurisdiction of the husband and father within the home viewed as the wider state in microcosm – and the material expressions of domesticity that were shaped by this. In this configuration, the single male homemaker could be seen to inhabit an indeterminate space; a *pater familias* to such inferior members that might constitute his immediate household, co-resident kin, servants and the like, he was enfeebled in theory, if not perhaps in practice, by the absence of an accepted, marital relationship. Notwithstanding this compromised duality, many men through choice, circumstance, professional calling or as a simple artefact of lifecycle formed such single households. As Shepard argues, the lack of a strictly defined patriarchal role did not jeopardise their identification with the wider concerns of manhood and power.[58]

However, until comparatively recently we have known very little as to how single men organised their homes and whether the spaces occupied by them were materially different from the idealised structures of the male presence with the conjugal home. Undoubtedly, the work of both Amanda Vickery and Karen Harvey has gone some way to repositioning masculinity within the frameworks of the eighteenth-century home. Indeed, as Harvey argues, an increasing '[a]ttention to how men made homes and homes made men' in turn 'necessarily transforms our idea of "home" and "domesticity"'.[59] Through such studies there has been an increasing awareness and understanding of the wider impacts of, as R.W Connell has argued, the fault lines inherent within hegemonic 'gentry masculinity' in its various domestic guises and manifestations.[60] Thus, there is now a more nuanced approach towards the role of honour, violence and esteem in the construction of early modern male identity. Similarly, we have much more of an idea of how the intermingling codes of politeness, sensibility and respectability variously shaped

---

[57] See J. Tosh, 'What Should Historians Do with Masculinity? Reflections on Nineteenth-Century Britain', *History Workshop Journal*, 38 (1994), pp. 179–202 and, more recently, A. Shepard and K. Harvey, 'What Have Historians Done with Masculinity? Reflections on Five Centuries of British History, circa 1500–1950', *Journal of British Studies*, 44 (2005), pp. 274–80. See also J. Tosh, 'Domesticity and Manliness'; J. Tosh, 'Introduction' in J. Tosh, *Manliness and Masculinities in Nineteenth-Century Britain* (Harlow: Pearson, 2005), pp. 1–12; and M. McDonald, 'Tranquil Havens: Critiquing the Idea of Home as the Middle Class Sanctuary' in I. Bryden and J. Floyd (eds), *Domestic Space: Reading the Nineteenth-Century Interior* (Manchester: Manchester University Press, 1999), pp. 103–20.

[58] See A. Shepard, *Meanings of Manhood in Early Modern England* (Oxford: Oxford University Press, 2003), pp. 1–20.

[59] A. Vickery, *Behind Closed Doors: At Home in Georgian England* (New Haven and London: Yale University Press, 2009), pp. 49–83; K. Harvey, 'Men Making Home: Masculinity and Domesticity in Eighteenth-Century Britain', *Gender and History*, 21/3 (2009), pp. 520–40: 520–21.

[60] R.W. Connell, *Masculinities* (2nd edn, Cambridge: Polity Press, 2005), pp. 185–98, esp. pp. 191–2.

and refined masculine attitudes towards self, society and nation.[61] The location of male agency within the modes and practices of emergent consumption and, indeed, sexuality has also gone some way to explaining the distinctive motivations of men in general and single men in particular.[62] Yet where singleness has been located in these critiques of masculinity, it has predominantly been focused on distinct archetypes – the rake, the dandy, the romantic hedonist and the 'manly blackguard' and, in contradistinction, the man of sentiment and even the fop and the molly.[63] To an extent, Howard Chudacoff's American bachelor and Christopher Breward's 'hidden' and largely single Victorian quasi-*flaneur* have supplied some insights, but they are both chronologically and spatially specific studies in their own right.

---

[61]   See E.A. Foyster, *Manhood in Early Modern England: Honour, Sex and Marriage* (London and New York: Longman, 1999); Shepard, *Meanings of Manhood*; P. Carter, *Men and the Emergence of Polite Society, Britain, 1660–1800* (Harlow: Longman, 2001); W.D. Smith, *Consumption and the Making of Respectability, 1600–1800* (London: Routledge, 2002), esp. pp. 139–70, 189–222; L.E. Klein, 'Politeness for Plebes: Consumption and Social Identity in Early Eighteenth-Century England' in A. Bermingham and J. Brewer (eds), *The Consumption of Culture, 1600–1800: Image, Object, Text* (London: Routledge, 1995), pp. 362–82; P. Langford, 'The Uses of Eighteenth-Century Politeness', *Transactions of the Royal Historical Society*, 12 (2002), pp. 311–31; M. Berg, *Luxury and Pleasure in Eighteenth-Century Britain* (Oxford: Oxford University Press, 2005), pp. 199–219; and J. Tosh, 'Gentlemanly Politeness and Manly Simplicity in Victorian England' in Tosh, *Manliness and Masculinities*, pp. 83–102. See also, M. Cohen, *Fashioning Masculinity: National Identity and Language in the Eighteenth Century* (London: Routledge, 1996).

[62]   For masculinity and consumption, see Carter, *Men*, pp. 124–52; M. Finn, 'Men's Things: Masculine Possession in the Consumer Revolution', *Social History*, 25/2 (2000), pp. 133–55; D.P. Hussey, 'Guns, Horses and Stylish Waistcoats? Male Consumer Activity and Domestic Shopping in Late Eighteenth- and Nineteenth-Century England' in D.P. Hussey and M. Ponsonby (eds), *Buying for the Home: Shopping for the Domestic from the Seventeenth Century to the Present* (Aldershot: Ashgate, 2008), esp. pp. 53–4, 67–9; D. Kuchta, *The Three-Piece Suit and Modern Masculinity: England, 1550–1850* (Berkeley and Los Angeles: University of California Press, 2002), pp. 91–132; C. Breward, *The Hidden Consumer: Masculinities, Fashion and City Life, 1860–1914* (Manchester: Manchester University Press, 1999), pp. 54–99; and B. Shannon, 'Re-fashioning Men: Fashion, Masculinity and the Cultivation of the Male Consumer in Britain, 1860–1914', *Victorian Studies*, 46 (2004), pp. 597–630. For a brief survey of the intersection of male sexuality and singleness, see T. Hitchcock, *English Sexualities, 1700–1800* (London: Macmillan, 1997), pp. 24–41, 58–75.

[63]   See above and C. Campbell, 'Understanding Traditional and Modern Practices of Consumption in Eighteenth-Century England: A Character-Action Approach' in J. Brewer and R. Porter (eds), *Consumption and the World of Goods* (London: Routledge, 1993), pp. 40–57. Myers' article postulates some interesting points regarding masculine sentiment and sensibility: J.E. Myers, 'A Case of Murderous Sensibility: James Hackman, Interiority and Masculine Agency in Late Eighteenth-Century England', *Gender and History*, 20/2 (2008), pp. 312–31. For molly culture, see R. Norton, *Mother Clap's Molly House: The Gay Subculture in England, 1700–1830* (Stroud: Chalford, 2006).

With this in mind, the single man and his domestic environs still remain to be studied in depth.[64]

In this context, Froide's characterisation of the 'never married' singlewoman would appear to offer insights into the male experience. Froide isolated five factors that may have encouraged the single estate: personal sickness; the responsibility of caring for dependents or extended family; the loss or lack of financial means, especially when that was related to expected monetary provision or dowry portion; the pursuit of religious vocation; and the early death of the woman, or the untimely and devastating demise of a prospective spouse.[65] To these must be added social, sexual or personal proclivity, although here it is especially difficult to distinguish between romantic friendship, economic imperative and physical attachment in the construction of female households.[66] Certainly, cohabitation amongst single women was commonplace, but unpicking the motivation and reconstructing the households even of the more celebrated instances – the Ladies of Llangollen, Anne Damer and even Anne Lister for instance – remains a matter of debate.

Froide's determinants were emphasised when age reduced a woman's generative capability, but this did not necessarily debar late marriage: the Quaker diarist Sarah Champion, for example, was 48 and almost convinced that she 'should remain single' when she married the widower Charles Fox of Plymouth.[67] With men, greater economic independence and separation from the nurturing role culturally imposed upon women meant that the demands of familial responsibility did not weigh so heavily upon their prospects of marriage; and whilst religious inspiration and vocational calling undoubtedly inspired some men, like William Stout of Lancaster, to remain single, age was not such a barrier as that experienced by many mature women from establishing a marital household.[68] Even nominally entrenched bachelors were not insulated from the attraction of normative patterns of conjugality. The reliably dour Stout, for example, was briefly but wholeheartedly infatuated with the entirely inappropriate and capricious Bethia Green, before being politely rebuffed by

---

[64] H.P. Chudacoff, *The Age of the Bachelor: Creating an American Subculture* (Princeton: Princeton University Press, 1999); Breward, *Hidden Consumer*, esp. pp. 175–84.

[65] Froide, *Never Married*, pp. 184–94.

[66] See, for example, M.R. Hunt, 'The Sapphic Strain: English Lesbians in the Long Eighteenth Century' in Bennett and Froide (eds), *Singlewomen in the European Past*, pp. 270–96; S. Marcus, *Between Women: Friendship, Desire, and Marriage in Victorian England* (Princeton: Princeton University Press, 2007); and Hitchcock, *English Sexualities*, pp. 76–92.

[67] M. Dresser (ed.), *The Diary of Sarah Fox, née Champion, Bristol, 1745–1802* (Bristol Record Society, 55, 2003), pp. x, xvii, 123–4.

[68] J.D. Marshall (ed.), *The Autobiography of William Stout, 1665–1752* (Manchester: Manchester University Press for the Chetham Society, 1967).

a 'young [Quaker] woman of a good family, and very religiously inclined'.[69] Similarly, Parson James Woodforde was jilted as a young man, a chastening experience which, added to his natural 'shyness', seems to have promoted his later aversion to marriage; Henry Woollcombe entertained fleeting and ultimately abortive hopes of marrying on at least four occasions throughout his adult life;[70] whilst for William Hickey, singleness was a natural estate through which to pursue a lifestyle of libertinism and relatively unchecked amorous intrigue.[71] Clearly, it would be wrong to impute wider motivation from the pages of individual diaries and memoirs – at best representative of the more self-absorbed, idiosyncratic and reflective of men – but, equally, these anecdotes indicate that the pathways to singleness were varied. For example, Woollcombe increasingly consoled himself with the observation that marriage appeared to be deeply incompatible with a life divided between the twin poles of manly duty (expressed in devotion to his daily regimen of work) and the high-minded pursuit of knowledge and scholarly endeavour. 'Matrimony', he dolefully stated in 1819, 'can never admit of much time for study, and my whole way of life must be completely altered.'[72] One suspects that Woollcombe's later antiquarian and historical pursuits – activities that came to utterly consume his free time – were but an expression of such discourses born of displacement and frustration.

We started this chapter in the company of Edmund Harrold and Henry Woollcombe, and it is fitting that it closes with Woollcombe's tortuous accommodation with singleness. Yet it must be remembered that Woollcombe was, for all his failings, an eminently successful householder. Woollcombe did not exist in the kind of domestic liminality, an admixture of confusion, incompetence and ennui, in which lone men were often imagined. By the same token, he was no John Baker, erstwhile Solicitor General of the Leeward Islands who, bereft of the steadying influence of his wife, permitted his household in Horsham to fall into disorder and chaos in 1774.[73] If Baker's establishment with arguing maidservants, unruly and boisterous dung-throwing grooms and the unwholesome whiff of sexual scandal represented the perceived picture of male dystopia, of public man overwhelmed by private home as it were, Woollcombe's unremarkable and orderly household that served alternately as a centre of sociable, if largely male, recreation and company, and a scholarly retreat from the rigours of the world stands as a welcome corrective.

---

[69]   Marshall (ed.), *Stout*, pp. 140–44.

[70]   See J. Beresford (ed.), *The Diary of a Country Parson, 1758–1802: James Woodforde* (London: Oxford University Press, 1967).

[71]   Despite the irregular nature of Hickey's relationship to his mistresses and de facto wife, Charlotte Barry, Hickey clearly regarded the union as monogamous: P. Quennell (ed.), *Memoirs of William Hickey* (London: Routledge & Kegan Paul, 1975), pp. 333–49.

[72]   Woollcombe, *Diary*, 2 January 1819.

[73]   P.C. Yorke (ed.), *The Diary of John Baker, Barrister of the Middle Temple, Solicitor-General of the Leeward Islands* (London: Hutchinson, 1931), pp. 55–7, 342–4.

It is clear from the demographic picture that single men formed a significant proportion of the population, roughly equivalent to that of unmarried women. Indeed, the security of homosocial institutions like the universities or the Church offered acceptable outlets to men who through personal instance, antipathy towards marriage or same-sex attraction wished to remain formally single. Such was the virulence of officially sanctioned prosecution of openly homosexual behaviour that these solutions were undoubtedly the most practical responses to almost official homophobic denunciation.[74] Notwithstanding these forms of motivation, what remains is to position single men and women within the wider structures of domesticity and consumption. This is the subject of Chapter 2.

---

[74] See Hitchcock, *English Sexualities*, pp. 58–75; T. Hitchcock and R. Shoemaker, *Tales from the Hanging Court* (London: Hodder Arnold, 2006), pp. 14–16, 248–54; H.G. Cocks, 'Making the Sodomite Speak: Voices of the Accused in English Sodomy Trials, c.1800–98', *Gender and History*, 18/1 (2006), pp. 87–107; and H.G. Cocks, *Nameless Offences: Homosexual Desire in the Nineteenth Century* (London: I.B. Taurus, 2003).

Chapter 2

Singleness and Homemaking: Locating the Single Household

On a wintery December evening in 1788, Julius Hardy, a Birmingham button maker, sat down at his desk in his newly rented house and surveyed the circumstances which had led him to become a 'sole householder' at the age of 25. It was, he confided, 'a step I have not hastily resolved on; yet if I could have been tolerably comfortable in my later [sic] abode, I had not at present removed from thence'. As it transpired, Hardy – a pietistic Methodist of an especially, and gratingly, intransigent temperament – had spectacularly fallen out with his brother, business partner and now erstwhile landlord, Joseph. Returning home from his 'second visit to the Public', a fully libated Joseph had quarrelled with his wife and, when Hardy had boldly if unwisely intervened, terminated the ensuing discussion with violence. As a result, Hardy was struck by an iron candlestick that left 'a dreadful wound, both deep and long, on my eyebrow, almost of a semi-circular form, extending from the middle of my forehead down to the corner of my right eye'. 'With this blow', Hardy disclosed with characteristic terseness, 'I fell, and continued a short time both senseless and speechless.'[1]

Hardy bore both the physical and psychological scars of this altercation with remarkable equanimity, never mentioning the incident to his brother or wider family and continuing with the joint venture amicably. However, his 'sore accident' thrust Hardy into a life of independence. From being a mere boarder, secure in the household of kin, Hardy was transported into a de facto head of household with all the material and cultural responsibilities that entailed. Over the next two years, Hardy's struggles 'to obtain a continuance of even orderly management or good government in the little concerns of my house' provide a backdrop to his wider spiritual musings and declining business affairs.[2] As a single and really quite young man, Hardy was constrained by the contemporary

---

[1]   Diary of Julius Hardy, Button-Maker of Birmingham, Birmingham Central Library, 669002, MS 218 (hereafter Hardy, 'Diary'), 11 December 1788. See also D.P. Hussey, 'Guns, Horses and Stylish Waistcoats? Male Consumer Activity and Domestic Shopping in Late Eighteenth- and Nineteenth-Century England' in D.P. Hussey and M. Ponsonby (eds), *Buying for the Home: Shopping for the Domestic from the Seventeenth Century to the Present* (Aldershot: Ashgate, 2008), pp. 54–5, 66–7 and M. Berg, *Luxury and Pleasure in Eighteenth-Century Britain* (Oxford: Oxford University Press, 2005), pp. 199–246, esp. 232–3.

[2]   Hardy, 'Diary', 1 February, 1790.

conventions regarding the practical necessities of domestic affairs and the codes of politeness, civility and decorum that disciplined the cultural requirements of entertaining and sociability. To an extent, the dictates of Hardy's staunch religious position insulated him from any improprieties implicit in his solitary domestic arrangements. Indeed, the presence of female housekeepers and servants as well as male lodgers and a slew of button workers ripe for evangelical instruction gave the Hardy household the flavour of an ersatz 'little family'. Yet this ad hoc domestic situation remained suffused with impermanence: Hardy was acutely aware that in comparison to his abusive brother's marital home his household was markedly inferior. It was, for example, particularly unfit for receiving visiting family for long periods; and his mother's predilection for staying with Joseph, interpreted rather ungraciously by Julius as naked favouritism, was more conditioned by the material architecture of their respective households than antipathy. In this respect, Hardy held sway over a household manqué, a thrown-together ad hoc collection of semi-displaced persons, a situation exacerbated when Hardy's sole servant became pregnant by his landlord's dissolute son. It was this – a double affront to Hardy's sense of propriety and the moral rectitude of his household – that finally and after much soul-searching convinced him of the necessity of marriage to a suitably sober, if somewhat impecunious bride.[3]

Despite his clear desire to ascribe the vicissitudes of his domestic situation to providential instruction – not in itself unusual in evangelical diarists of the period – Hardy was not unlike many young single men who subsisted in makeshift accommodations until marriage or waited until an improved financial situation permitted more stable and long-term solutions.[4] Indeed, lodgings, boarding rooms, a simple room or even merely a bed in the houses of kin, acquaintances, employers or masters were part of the lifecycle of many middling sort men who, in the same vein, often 'retired' to a room in the households of family or near kin as old age and infirmity beckoned. However, what is clear here is that Hardy himself regarded the single-headed household as somewhat aberrant, a domestic other in comparison to the moral and cultural fixity of the marital home and the nuclear household.

As Hardy's behaviour tacitly implied, singlehood was problematic: normative cultural and sexual behaviour stressed the primacy of marriage and family, whilst

---

[3]   Hardy, 'Diary', 28 September–2 December; 10 December 1790. Hardy was concerned that 'greedy relations' or 'selfish byestanders' might assume that he had 'bemeaned' himself by marrying 'a person of such small pecuniary prospects': 'Diary', 10 December 1790.

[4]   See J. Tosh, 'Gentlemanly Politeness and Manly Simplicity in Victorian England', in J. Tosh, *Manliness and Masculinities in Nineteenth-Century Britain* (Harlow: Pearson, 2005), p. 90 and, for comparison, W.R. Ward, 'Mirror of the Soul: the Diary of an Early Methodist Preacher, John Bennet, 1714–1754', *English Historical Review*, 118 (2003), pp. 476–521. For an interesting examination of the concerns of male diarists, see H. Barker, 'Soul, Purse and Family: Middling and Lower-Class Masculinity in Eighteenth-Century Manchester', *Social History*, 33/1 (2008), pp. 12–35.

both prescriptive literature and religious exhortation railed against the moral perils of the single state, contrasting the godly household of marital order and familial integrity with the lassitude and immorality of wasteful singleness.[5] Yet, as the previous chapter has argued, to be single or at least unmarried in early modern and nineteenth-century England was not an atypical estate. Whereas cultural opprobrium may well have been directed at specific targets – the singlewoman, the pervasive image of the old maid or the unregulated apprentice, for example – contemporary single people organised their lives and by extension their domestic space with a great deal of complexity and thought. Far from being excluded and peripheral to the constructions of the nuclear and generative family, many single men and women of the middling sort were embedded in familial households, the establishments of kin and occasionally the domestic extensions of work.[6] Of course, single people headed households that were severally populated by near kin, relatives, non-blood lodgers and boarders, and staffed by a shifting host of paid servants and staff. However, uncovering or simply reconstituting the materiality of such households remains problematic. How, for example, did these households differ from the domestic arrangements of the marital home? In a similar fashion, how were the requirements of a polite, respectable, domestic locale negotiated by people whose status separated them from the orderly, patriarchal norm? To address these questions we have sought to focus on the domestic interior of single households using a combination of discursive sources – diaries, letters and accounts – and perhaps the stock source of quantifiable data relating to the material culture of pre-industrial England, the will and the probate inventory.

Reconstructing the Single Home: Sources, Methods, Approaches

The probate inventory has been an extensively mined source, reflecting the information it can supply on the material culture of individuals and households from the sixteenth to the eighteenth centuries.[7] By an act of 1529, executors

---

[5] The discussion on the family is too extensive for all but a brief summary here. However, see, R. Houlbrooke, *The English Family, 1450–1700* (London: Longman, 1984); K. Wrightson, ' The Family in Early Modern England: Continuity and Change' in S. Taylor, R. Connors and C. Jones (eds), *Hanoverian Britain and Empire: Essays in Memory of Philip Lawson* (Woodbridge: Boydell Press, 1998), pp. 1–22; and L. Davidoff, M. Doolittle, J. Fink and K. Holden, *The Family Story: Blood, Contract and Intimacy, 1830–1960* (London and New York: Longman, 1999).

[6] See N. Tadmor, *Family and Friends in Eighteenth-Century England* (Cambridge: Cambridge University Press, 2001), pp. 18–43.

[7] See, in particular, M. Overton, J. Whittle, D. Dean and A. Hann, *Production and Consumption in English Households, 1600–1750* (London: Routledge, 2004); C. Estabrook, *Urbane and Rustic England: Cultural Ties and Social Spheres in the Provinces, 1660–1780* (Manchester: Manchester University Press, 1998); L. Weatherill, *Consumer Behaviour and*

and administrators of estates were charged with presenting a full inventory of the 'goods, chattels, cattle and merchandises' of all persons worth in excess of £5 of movable wealth to the respective consistory court. This was to safeguard against fraud and permit the equitable division of the testator's goods, although in practice the inventory often served as a convenient schedule of appraised goods that could be used to address outstanding debt and liability that had accrued to the estate. Appraisers – often executors, kin or quite frequently skilled tradesmen with professional knowledge of the deceased's business – were responsible for valuing the goods and habitually noted the state, age and location of merchantable commodities within the dwelling place and its associated lands, business premises and outbuildings. Whilst this is not the place to rehearse the full administrative history and the subsequent scholarly application of the source, it is important to note that probate inventories provide a unique series of data that describe the types and species of goods and material possessions owned and an indication of the location, placement and potential usage of such commodities within the domestic environment.[8] With arguably over 2 million documents extant in England alone, probate inventories present a highly seductive and widely available source that when used sensitively permits a veiled access to quotidian domestic loci – the kitchens, parlours and chambers – and, more obliquely, consumption practices of the men and women of pre-industrial society who occupied these spaces. In these ways, probate has been used to supply insights into the structure, facility and organisation of the pre-industrial household of the middling sort.[9] In particular, such data have featured strongly in long-range, macro-economic, quantitative surveys of how change has impacted upon the economic motivation and material culture of households and individuals. This work has begun to piece together household economies; articulate the transformations in domestic architecture

---

Material Culture in Britain, 1660–1760 (2nd edn, London: Routledge, 1996); C. Shammas, *The Pre-Industrial Consumer in England and America* (Oxford: Oxford University Press, 1990); P. Earle, *The Making of the English Middle Class: Business, Society and Family Life in London, 1660–1730* (London: Methuen, 1989); and with particular relevance to the domestic interior, Eleanor John, 'At Home with the London Middling Sort – The Inventory Evidence for Furnishings and Room Use, 1570–1720', *Regional Furniture*, 22 (2008), pp. 27–52.

[8]   For a summary of the administrative background, interpretation and applications of probate inventories, see the articles in T. Arkell, N. Evans and N. Goose (eds), *When Death Do Us Part: Understanding and Interpreting the Probate Records of Early Modern England* (Oxford: Leopard's Head, 2000) and P. Riden (ed.), *Probate Records and the Local Community* (Gloucester: Sutton Press, 1985). In addition, see M. Spufford, 'The Limitations of the Probate Inventory' in J. Chartres and D. Hey (eds), *English Rural Society: Essays in Honour of Joan Thirsk* (Cambridge: Cambridge University Press, 1990), pp. 139–74 and also Overton et al., *Production and Consumption*, pp. 13–32 for overviews of practice.

[9]   This is also discussed in J.S. Moore, 'Probate Inventories: Problems and Products' in Riden (ed.), *Probate Records*, pp. 16–17; T. Arkell, 'Interpreting Probate Inventories' in Arkell et al. (eds), *When Death Do Us Part*, p. 72; and Overton et al., *Production and Consumption*, pp. 12–13.

and the shifting construction of domestic space; and posit suggestions regarding the acquisition and adoption of a variety of consumer goods, semi-durables and luxuries into the middling sort home. As a result, we now have an economic and cultural base line that charts the growing sophistication of the middling household throughout the later seventeenth and early eighteenth centuries whilst accounting for the functional and spatial specialisation of household activity and the gradual development of a distinctively domestic locus alongside the survival of older forms of economic practice and organisation.[10] In addition, quantitative analysis of probate material has reappraised such diverse areas as the extension of cultural practice, the construction and distribution of wealth, the significance of credit and the various strategies of inheritance.[11]

The probate inventory is not without problems and offers beguilingly plausible data for the unwary researcher. Inventories were often compiled in an irregular way; property, fixtures and certain goods were routinely omitted or alienated before the administration of the estate; chronological, geographical and social coverage is often patchy; and, as occupation was habitually noted above the marital status of the testator, unmarried male householders are not readily retrievable. None the less, the source provides a consistent series to study the material culture and development of the household over time. For the purposes of this research, we have concentrated on an indicative rather than strictly 'intensive' or 'extensive' survey of the probate and wider testamentary material of a large area of the English Midlands – in particular the counties of Shropshire, Staffordshire, Derbyshire and the parts of Warwickshire subject to the ecclesiastical jurisdiction of the diocese of Lichfield and Coventry.[12] This diocese included a large number

---

[10] For comparison, see J. de Vries, *The Industrious Revolution: Consumer Behaviour and the Household Economy, 1650 to the Present* (Cambridge: Cambridge University Press, 2008), pp. 122–88.

[11] See for example Estabrook, *Urbane and Rustic England*, esp. pp. 143–60; N.C. Cox, *The Complete Tradesman: A Study of Retailing, 1550–1820* (Aldershot: Ashgate, 2000); Berg, *Luxury and Pleasure*, pp. 222–3; J.M. Spicksley, '"Fly with a Duck in thy Mouth": Single Women as Sources of Credit in Seventeenth Century England', *Social History*, 32/2 (2007), pp. 187–207; J.M. Spicksley, 'Usury Legislation, Cash, and Credit: The Development of the Female Investor in the Late Tudor and Stuart Periods', *Economic History Review*, 61/2 (2008), pp. 277–301; and M. Berg, 'Women's Consumption and the Industrial Classes in Eighteenth-Century England', *Journal of Social History*, 30 (1996), pp. 415–34.

[12] The strengths of an 'intensive' and 'extensive' approach are discussed in Overton et al., *Production and Consumption*, pp. 8–10. For published transcriptions of probate inventories within this area, see D.G. Vaisey (ed.), *Probate Inventories of Lichfield and District, 1568–1680* (Collections for a History of Staffordshire, 4th Series, vol. 5, Staffordshire Record Office, 1969); B. Trinder and J. Cox (eds), *Yeomen and Colliers in Telford: Probate Inventories for Dawley, Lilleshall, Wellington and Wrockwardine, 1660–1750* (Chichester: Phillimore, 1980); B. Trinder and N. Cox (eds), *Miners and Mariners of the Severn Gorge: Probate Inventories for Benthall, Broseley, Little Wenlock and Madeley,*

of peculiar courts, deaneries and parochial administrations that had the right to manage their own testamentary affairs. The inventories from these peculiars – particularly Bridgnorth and parts of Ellesmere, Shrewsbury and Wolverhampton – have survived in large numbers across the period and, most importantly, continue beyond the 1730s, the point at which the extancy and quality of the source tails off dramatically in other parts of the country.[13] This cannot be overstated. Whereas the main surveys of consumption practices have been effectively hamstrung by the untimely decay of the source in terms of coverage and quality from the third decade of the eighteenth century, the survival of the probate inventory as a viable and consistently maintained record in the peculiar administrations permits a longitudinal comparison that can place the material culture of single households into a wider context. Indeed, as Erickson has argued, 'inventories become too sketchy to be of use after 1740: instead of itemising goods individually they start to summarise by room or by type of property'. Thus, the deterioration of the source effectively curtails the kind of quantitative analysis that has proved so fruitful in refocusing attention upon both cultures of consumption and the testamentary practice of widows and spinsters in the early modern period.[14]

With these concerns in mind, the core of the research has concentrated on the inventories and associated testamentary material proved at the deanery court of Bridgnorth, a small but flourishing urban settlement in Shropshire.[15] In addition,

---

1660–1764 (Chichester: Phillimore, 2000); and N. Alcock, *People at Home: Living in a Warwickshire Village, 1500–1800* (Chichester: Phillimore, 1993).

[13] The lack of inventory material for much of the latter half of the eighteenth century has informed the terminal dates of the major studies to date. Overton et al. found that between 1700 and 1749 the numbers of Kent inventories declined, whilst the intrinsic quality of the Cornish records experienced a marked decay over the same period: Overton et al., *Production and Consumption*, pp. 22–6 and 28–31. Weatherill's survey effectively terminates in 1725 as a consequence in part of the erratic survival of probate records: Weatherill, *Consumer Behaviour*, pp. 2–4.

[14] A.L. Erickson, 'Property and Widowhood in England, 1600–1840' in S. Cavallo and L. Walker (eds), *Widowhood in Medieval and Early Modern Europe* (Harlow: Pearson, 1999), p. 150.

[15] Between 1650 and 1799 there are 438 extant inventories relating to the peculiar. We would like to thank Professor Malcolm Wanklyn for arranging access to transcribed copies of the Bridgnorth material. The documents are held at Lichfield Record Office (hereafter LRO). See also M.D.G. Wanklyn, 'Urban Revival in Early Modern England: Bridgnorth and the River Trade', *Midland History*, 18 (1993), pp. 37–64; M.D.G. Wanklyn, 'The Impact of Water Transport Facilities on the Economies of English River Ports, c.1660–c.1760', *Economic History Review*, 49/1 (1996), pp. 20–34; and D.P. Hussey, *Coastal and River Trade in Pre-Industrial England: Bristol and Its Region, 1680–1730* (Exeter: Exeter University Press, 2000), pp. 58–63, 106–9, 113–17, 128–31 for a discussion of the economic development of Bridgnorth and the trade of the River Severn in this period. We are also grateful to Dr Nancy Cox for access to the inventories digitised by the Dictionary Project and the transcriptions of Ellesmere peculiar. See N.C. Cox and K. Dannehl (eds), 'The

a random sample of the surviving probate records of the Lichfield Consistory Court has been added. These records include a further body of inventories made to furnish information in testamentary disputes that not only survive in significant numbers into the early nineteenth century but also are extensive and detailed. To this extent, both the Bridgnorth series and the longer Consistory Court records provide a sense of commonality and fixity across the majority of the period. Probate material, abundant from the seventeenth century, thus continues in such forms until well into the later eighteenth century and, rather more sporadically, into the early nineteenth century: in terms of probate, the terminal date for the research is thus extended to 1838. To the Bridgnorth and wider Lichfield material we have also added a number of probate records from the dioceses of Hereford, Worcester and Chichester. This is by no means a comprehensive survey and it has not been our intention to replicate the work of, for example, Weatherill, Shammas and Overton et al. in seeking to provide longitudinal surveys of consumption practice. However, it provides us with a manageable, digitised resource that can begin to tease out the patterns of material possession and how this both defined and was defined by homemaking across the period.

In essence, our research focuses on identifying the homes of singlewomen: widows and spinsters who, as femes soles, were liable to engage probate and were routinely described through status titles in the records.[16] However, this was not the case for men where the primacy of occupational designation obscured their marital situation.[17] In a smattering of instances, men were described solely as bachelors and their records have been duly captured. The reason for this designation is unknown, although it appears to have been due to a number of interrelated testamentary factors: the comparative youth of the testator; intestacy or the reported presence of nuncupative instructions that required legal formalisation; or questions concerning the often disputed administration of the estate. For example, the administration of Richard Saxton of Derby in 1743 described the testator as a bachelor. His movable wealth amounted to over £62 and, unusually for male testators at this date, his clothing and personal effects were described in full.[18] Beyond his fairly well-stocked house and modish apparel, little is known of Saxton. Yet Saxton is markedly unusual: in the regular series of probate it is

---

Dictionary of Traded Goods', British History Online, http://www.british-history.ac.uk/source.aspx?pubid=739 (accessed 10 July 2010).

[16] See L. Weatherill, 'A Possession of One's Own: Women and Consumer Behaviour in England, 1660–1740', *Journal of British Studies*, 25 (1986), pp. 131–56. See also A.L. Erickson, *Women and Property in Early Modern England* (London: Routledge, 1993), pp. 187–203 and S. Staves, *Married Women's Separate Property in England, 1660–1833* (Cambridge, MA: Harvard University Press, 1990), pp. 131–61.

[17] See M. Pelling, 'Finding Widowers: Men without Women in English Towns before 1700' in S. Cavallo and L. Walker (eds), *Widowhood in Medieval and Early Modern Europe* (Harlow: Pearson, 1999), pp. 37–54.

[18] LRO, Richard Saxton (Saxon), bachelor, Derby, 1743.

practically impossible without detailed prosopographical information to separate
the widowed and unmarried from the bulk of administrations described only by
occupational descriptors or status labels. We have isolated a small sector of known
widowers and bachelors from the Bridgnorth sample where local taxation and
parochial records provide corroborative information. However, even with such
painstaking work, this can only capture a fraction of single male households. The
vast majority of men who died without spouse are thus likely to be overlooked.[19]

Positioning the Single Home: Domestic Goods and Gender in Context

Many historians of material culture have attempted to chart the growing
sophistication of the (marital) household and the extension of domestic practices
through the impact and ownership of a range of goods and consumer durables. In
this way, Lorna Weatherill sought to locate change in the ownership of a set of
'key' diagnostic goods in a wide sample of probate inventories as a representative
index of consumer behaviour in late seventeenth- and early eighteenth-century
England.[20] These goods encompassed nominally 'traditional' household items
like tables, cooking pots, pewter and table linen, the basic equipage of a modest
domestic establishment, through to identifiably 'new' goods such as knives and
forks, china and utensils for hot drinks, commodities that indicated novel forms of
cultural practice, especially in polite forms of eating and the taking of refreshment,
and the fashion for certain transoceanic groceries. Other goods – pewter dishes
and pewter plates, earthenware and saucepans, for example – provide insights
into the domestic relationship with food as the main determinant of household
activity and expenditure. By extension, mapping these goods onto the domestic
arena can indicate the growing centrality of the home as a locus of consumer
activity. In a similar fashion, the possession of books, clocks and pictures suggests
communication, engagement with the wider world and cultural sophistication,
whilst looking glasses, pier glasses and window curtains emphasised attitudes
towards the presentation of the self and the desire for comfort and privacy.

---

[19]   We would like to thank Malcolm Wanklyn for access to transcriptions of the
Bridgnorth parish registers and local taxation records. This kind of analysis is particularly
relevant where communities can be reconstructed with some degree of confidence: see D.
Dean and M. Overton, 'Wealth, Indebtedness, Consumption and the Lifecycle in Early
Modern England', paper presented to the 14th International Economic History Congress,
available at http://www.helsinki.fi/iehc2006/papers3/Overton122.pdf (accessed 6 June
2010).
[20]   Weatherill, *Consumer Behaviour*, pp. 203–7. See also C. Shammas, 'The Domestic
Environment in Early Modern England and America', *Journal of Social History*, 14 (1980),
pp. 1–24; Shammas, *Pre-Industrial Consumer*, Appendix 1; and C. Shammas, 'Changes in
English and Anglo-American Consumption from 1550 to 1800' in J. Brewer and R. Porter
(eds), *Consumption and the World of Goods* (London: Routledge, 1993), pp. 177–205.

Cross-tabulating these goods – middling rank 'decencies' that enhanced and occasionally rationalised the rough edges of everyday existence – with the key variables of time, space, occupation, location within the household and gender has suggested a number of provocative avenues of research.[21] A central, although perhaps least surprising, factor was proximity to or communication with a major urban centre, especially London. Here the diffusion of metropolitan taste was articulated through the ownership of expressive (and expensive) goods like china or decorative goods like pictures that transmitted a high degree of cultural capital. None the less, however much towns acted as conduits of culture, they were not singular '"islands" of active consumption surrounded by "traditional" values in the countryside'; consumer goods, petty trifles, durables and decorative items were to be found in the inventories of rural testators, albeit with less frequency.[22] Similarly, the various species of goods were consumed (or rather owned) at subtly different rates throughout the country, and these indices of possession were matched by comparable gradations according to occupation and less explicitly status.

These findings have posited some central assertions that are fundamental to this research. In particular, Weatherill emphasised that social position mapped imperfectly upon the dynamics of individual and household consumption: in terms of diagnostic expressive and decorative goods, china and utensils for hot drinks in the main, socially subordinate groups like the major mercantile and dealing trades outstripped superordinate gentry consumers.[23] To this extent middling sort consumers have been positioned as the truly dynamic element in the gearing of consumption and the primary motive force behind explanations of what is a highly contested 'consumer revolution'. In addition, by using an interpretation of Erving Goffman's dramaturgical conceit linking the symbolic interaction of the self with the ownership of select goods, Weatherill postulated that domestic space could be

---

[21] Weatherill sought to distinguish these goods from 'luxuries' with the imputation of waste and excess and 'necessities', items required for the everyday functioning of household economies. The terms are elusive and chronologically and culturally imprecise. See Weatherill, *Consumer Behaviour*, pp. 14–16 and for a more sophisticated discussion of luxury, M. Berg and E. Eger, 'The Rise and Fall of the Luxury Debates' in M. Berg and E. Eger (eds), *Luxury in the Eighteenth Century: Debates, Desires and Delectable Goods* (Basingstoke: Palgrave Macmillan, 2003), pp. 7–21 and Berg, *Luxury and Pleasure*, pp. 21–45.

[22] L. Weatherill, 'The Meaning of Consumer Behaviour in Late Seventeenth- and Early Eighteenth-Century England' in J. Brewer and R. Porter (eds), *Consumption and the World of Goods* (London: Routledge, 1993), p. 209. In comparing Bristol with its immediately bucolic environs, Estabrook has argued that a distinctive urban culture of possession can be evidenced in eighteenth-century England: *Urbane and Rustic England*, pp. 128–56. For critiques, see J. Stobart, A. Hann and V. Morgan, *Spaces of Consumption: Leisure and Shopping in the English Town, c.1680–1830* (London: Routledge, 2007), esp. pp. 9–13.

[23] There are, however, problems in such a simplistic hierarchic encapsulation of English society, primarily as nominal 'gentry' often migrated to 'merchants' and 'major dealers' in simple status designations: see Weatherill, *Consumer Behaviour*, pp. 184–5.

usefully read as describing 'frontstage' social and cultural activity wherein public elements of display and the performance of taste were permitted and 'backstage' arenas where less visible, functional and production-based conduct took place.[24]

This oppositional diarchy is perhaps rather too rudimentary to explain the ambiguous and highly nuanced cultural performance of consumers, but it does suggest useful ways of viewing the domestic interior through the lens of cultural meaning rather than as simply a two-dimensional pattern of ownership at the point of what was essentially a post-mortem survey. Perhaps more significantly, Weatherill argued that, whilst no definitive 'feminine material subculture' could be actively imputed from probate evidence alone,[25] women testatrixes may have owned 'different things because their tastes were allowed a free hand in the absence of a male head of household'.[26] These tastes may have been expressed in the ownership of more decorative and expressive pieces, like china wares, or goods in which women's domestic activity – looking glasses or window curtains for example – has been traditionally, if rather paternalistically located. By implication, this denigrates women's consumption to the peripheral, the ornamental and the banal, whilst valorising male activity and male possession, trade tools, commercial stock and the like as productive and substantive. Even so, these tentative postulations offer tantalising ways of analysing probate data: women may well have owned subtly different things, but those things and indeed the domestic environment in which they were housed and displayed were also shaped and conditioned by the pressures and occasionally the opportunities of singleness.

Following Weatherill's work, Table 2.1 presents the frequency of a range of goods as owned by spinster and widow testatrixes over the course of the period. This segments the data into 25-year blocs, with the exception of the nineteenth century for which the extant records do not permit a significant sample along such temporal lines. Appended are three cumulative indices of ownership derived from Weatherill's data that relate to the total experience of women testatrixes, the regional, North-West Midlands sample and total inventoried possession between

---

[24] E. Goffman, *The Presentation of the Self in Everyday Life* (Woodstock, NY: Overlook Press, 1959). For the use of inventory data in describing rooms and their functions, see U. Priestley and P.J. Corfield, 'Rooms and Room Use in Norwich Housing, 1580–1730', *Post-Medieval Archaeology*, 16 (1982), pp. 93–123; E. John, 'At Home with the London Middling Sort: The Inventory Evidence for Furnishings and Room Use, 1570–1720', *Regional Furniture*, 22 (2008), pp. 27–32; and Overton et al., *Production and Consumption*, pp. 121–36.

[25] Weatherill, 'A Possession of One's Own', pp. 131–3. See also critiques of this stance by Amanda Vickery: 'Women and the World of Goods: A Lancashire Consumer and her Possessions, 1751–81' in J. Brewer and R. Porter (eds), *Consumption and the World of Goods* (London: Routledge, 1993), pp. 274–304, esp. pp. 274–8; A. Vickery, *The Gentleman's Daughter: Women's Lives in Georgian England* (New Haven and London: Yale University Press, 1998), pp. 160–64.

[26] Weatherill, 'Meaning of Consumer Behaviour', p. 211.

Table 2.1   Ownership frequency of goods: widows and spinsters, 1650–1850

Date	Tables	Cooking pots	Saucepans	Pewter	Pewter dishes	Plates	Earthen-ware	Books	Clocks	Pictures	Looking glasses	Table linen	Window curtains	Knives and forks	China	Utensils for hot drinks	Silver
	%	%	%	%	%	%	%	%	%	%	%	%	%	%	%	%	%
1650–74 n = 68	59	68	0	75	74	19	7	13	0	3	12	60	1	0	0	0	25
1675–99 n = 69	65	61	4	78	46	25	14	30	7	7	35	65	7	1	3	0	43
1700–24 n = 55	65	67	7	75	47	38	22	27	15	15	40	58	18	7	4	5	31
1725–49 n = 60	73	68	25	85	75	58	23	13	22	25	35	58	17	8	5	15	15
1750–74 n =54	83	63	35	78	61	56	48	9	44	37	50	41	26	17	15	48	20
1775–99 n=26	92	62	15	62	35	31	54	38	46	31	62	46	27	38	31	46	38
1800–50 n =20	95	75	60	20	0	20	90	50	65	45	90	55	70	65	65	90	35
Women 1675–1725 n = 217	77	66	12	89	47	22	33	18	13	12	36	46	17	4	4	2	37
N/W Midlands n =390	87	62	13	94	42	21	17	15	7	4	14	28	3	1	0	1	8
Total 1675–1725 n=2,902	89	70	11	93	48	27	37	19	19	13	33	42	13	4	4	4	23

Note: The final three rows are derived from L. Weatherill, *Consumer Behaviour and Material Culture in Britain, 1660–1760* (2nd edn, London: Routledge, 1996), pp. 168, 44, 26 respectively.

1675 and 1725. The table is only an indication of the ownership of key 'diagnostic' goods and collapsed within the data are a number of variables. The most prominent of these is the nature of the regional sample. As Weatherill discovered, the 'North-West Midlands' – an area dominated by the mixed pastoral and arable economies of north Shropshire and Staffordshire – was particularly sluggish in acquiring the kinds of consumer durables evidenced in the national sample. Her data indicated that 'lower proportions of all goods were recorded ... new goods were almost unknown, decorative ones were very unusual, and clocks were rare'.[27] Although our sample has a much more significant urban component than this, and should thus be expected to demonstrate a greater affinity with such goods, it is also clear that the Shropshire and Staffordshire components that constitute the bulk of our survey have impacted upon overall levels of possession.

Secondly, there are a number of materially limited singlewomen captured within the sample. These women, often subsisting on the income from property leases, debts and bonds at interest and other financial devices, were essentially *rentiers* and in comparison to the main householders and substantial testators of the sample had relatively denuded estates, certainly in terms of the extent and description of such household goods that were listed. In addition, the Midlands sample contains the inventories of singlewomen in service who, as in the case of *rentier* widows, had a sparse scattering of goods – often little more than a bed of sorts, some linen and perhaps some rudimentary and portable storage, a box, chest or occasionally a set of drawers. These women had just enough in wearing apparel, sundry goods and, in particular, ready money and money at interest to warrant probate. The presence of these factors has tended to depress the overall picture of ownership. This was likely to have been felt with more certainty from c.1725 when the main Bridgnorth series becomes increasingly concerned with the monetary portions of nuncupative and intestate estates to the exclusion of detailed descriptions of material goods. It is thus wholly probable that the increased levels of ownership reported in the mid- to late eighteenth century are themselves underestimates of a more thoroughgoing trend.

It is also clear that practices of record were occasionally erratic and the sample is not free from the widespread tendency of eighteenth-century appraisers to summarise species of good into convenient categories or such generic phrases as 'goods unseen' or 'other necessaries', practices that tended to increase in the later period. In these instances, absence of goods should not always be interpreted as primarily negative evidence: as Overton et al. have intimated, if non-possession is correlated with wealth and other contingencies – size of the household, other goods and location, for example – it can reveal important lacunae in the data.[28] As certain goods became widespread even everyday decencies, their inclusion in testamentary records was subject to a more subtle decline. Commodities like table linen, brass kettles and cooking pots, and even pewter – expensive and noteworthy

---

[27] Weatherill, *Consumer Behaviour*, pp. 57–8 and Tables 3.1–3.3.
[28] See Overton et al., *Production and Consumption*, pp. 16–18 for important omissions.

items at the beginning of the period – were the kinds of goods a polite middling sort household and its appraisers would find so commonplace and so quotidian a century later to either comparatively devalue, omit or simply lump together into amorphous assemblages of household accoutrements. It is thus highly likely that goods such as table linen, an absolute requirement of any household with pretensions of basic respectability, were often subsumed into general chamber or parlour descriptions. Clear underreporting should not however be automatically conflated with non-possession.

With regard to the data, there are some anomalies and deviations from the national picture emphasised by Weatherill and subsequently Overton et al.'s survey of Kent and Cornwall. Firstly tables and pewter are underrepresented in the Midlands sample, whereas specific pewter tableware – dishes and plates – was somewhat more in evidence. Similarly, Midlands appraisers appear to have been more willing to record table linen, especially tablecloths and other napery ware, than the national sample. Certainly, both pewter and linen were the sorts of generic goods that were often reduced in the kind of expedient shorthand employed by hard-pressed appraisers, often appearing unspecified in descriptions of kitchen contents and household and personal linen. Elsewhere, the findings are broadly consonant with the wider results. There are more books – often simply a Bible – and rather fewer instances of households possessing earthenware, a factor that may reflect the geography of the sample.

It is, however, from c.1725 that most change is apparent in the inventories of widows and spinsters. In all the major categories of 'new' goods, significant increase in the level of ownership is reported. Thus, saucepans – practically absent from the seventeenth- and early eighteenth-century tranches of data – were found in one in four of households by 1725–49. Apart from the last quarter of the eighteenth century, where the proportionately higher numbers of intestate record described above appear to have impacted on the record, the trend, indicative of new methods of cookery, continued. By the nineteenth century, most households would be expected to own such items. Similarly, there is a steady rise in the ownership of earthenware and looking glasses. From the mid-eighteenth century, female headed households were likely to own at least one looking glass, and frequently more, at death. None the less, it is in the possession of clocks, window curtains, table cutlery, china and utensils for hot drinks that most development is apparent. These goods were either wholly missing from the households across the first 75 years of the sample or were present in fairly insignificant numbers. All of these goods were undoubtedly commonplace in the rather constrained numerical sample of records for the nineteenth century, but it is equally clear that the ownership was widespread in the homes of fairly modest households from c.1750 onwards. For example, in 1768 Elizabeth Jeffries, widow of Bridgnorth, left barely £19 of household goods and yet whilst her movables contained the basic requirements of independent living – a range of pewter and pewter tableware, tin, iron and brass cooking equipment, tables, beds, a selection of earthenware, napery and linen wares – she also possessed a wide range of new and decorative goods. Thus, there was a selection of earthenware in the kitchen and her two parlours housed two looking glasses, seven pictures, some small silver goods, china ware and glasses.[29] In these cases, the significance of Bridgnorth in the wider sample cannot be overemphasised. As a river port, Bridgnorth gave access to the wider commercial and cultural opportunities afforded by trade and, in particular, the large back-cargoes emanating from the transoceanic entrepôt of Bristol.[30]

The main factor captured in the data is not merely the greater penetration of such items through the social hierarchy, but the increased diversity, specialisation and quality of the goods owned. Middling sort widows like Jeffries enjoyed a range of commodities that were almost wholly restricted to wealthy and culturally literate consumers barely 40 years before. To an extent this proceeded from production efficiencies that brought a raft of commodities into the spending capabilities of the ordinary consumer. However, changes in fashion and the material culture of the home were also reflected in the indices of consumption.[31] Thus, the period from c.1750 saw the adoption of such commodities as carpets, upholstered furniture, cotton furnishings, small mahogany and rosewood items, mahogany furniture, and drinking glasses. Ownership of these goods was graded by status, access to the market and availability. For example, the homes of the clearly wealthy were characterised by substantial items of high-quality furniture – bedsteads, dining tables and sideboards in mahogany or walnut – and often suites of furniture and matching textiles in damask, chintz and moreen. These items involved a major investment in the material culture of the home, but also indicated a heightened conception of domestic space and an increasingly sophisticated awareness of household goods as objects of desire.[32] Such trends are clear from auctions of house contents that always stressed the best that a house had to offer. In 1815, Fairfax Moresby Esq. was selling up his house and contents in Lichfield.[33] The auctioneer boasted that his goods were mostly London made and they included large quantities of mahogany cabinetry and a drawing room 'suit of Elegant Furniture, as window Curtains, Sofa, and Chairs of rich striped Satin; the Curtains lined and fringed, Drapery Valance, rich white and gold Cornices'. This was a fashionable and elegant assemblage for a provincial town and could not be

---

[29]   LRO, Elizabeth Jeffries, widow, Bridgnorth, 1768, £19 4d.

[30]   Bridgnorth was an important trading node on the River Severn, and was more likely than other landlocked Shropshire and Staffordshire towns to have direct experience of the kinds of traded commodities shipped upriver from Bristol: Hussey, *Coastal and River Trade*, pp. 90–91, 171–3.

[31]   The following summary of ownership is based on research in Margaret Ponsonby, 'The Consumption of Furniture and Furnishings for the Home in the West Midlands using Local Suppliers, 1760–1860', unpublished PhD thesis, University of Wolverhampton, 2001.

[32]   See, for example, C. Steedman, 'What a Rag Rug Means' in I. Bryden and J. Floyd (eds), *Domestic Space: Reading the Nineteenth-Century Interior* (Manchester: Manchester University Press, 1999), pp. 26–30.

[33]   *Aris's Birmingham Gazette*, 13 March 1815.

matched in more middling sort homes. However, in the High Street in Bridgnorth in 1810 the widow Mrs Whitehead had a comfortable home. Her combined parlour/dining room had carpet on the floor, a mahogany table and chairs with hair seats and brass nails, and a pier glass with a gilt frame.[34] More practical than lavish, Mrs Whitehead's home demonstrates the spread of smart furnishings and a knowledge of fashion to provincial homemakers. Like Whitehead, the polite middling sort and middle-class home of the later eighteenth and early nineteenth century emphasised solidity and durability above extravagance. Thus furniture in vernacular materials – oak, ash and deal – was often mixed with statement pieces in walnut or mahogany;[35] suites of furniture were rare and where matching items were evidenced, they were constructed in cheaper materials, for example horse hair rather than leather or even a good-quality textile.

In addition, as the period progressed, many of the goods that denoted or enhanced levels of personal consumption and comfort in the seventeenth century were themselves subject to obsolescence and substitution. By the latter half of the eighteenth century, commodities such as pewter, especially in the form of tableware, buffets, delft ware, vernacular table forms and benches, and wooden trenchers were decidedly unfashionable for polite display or use and where they were present at all, were relegated to the service areas of genteel households. Indeed, the retention of these outmoded, often rough-hewn commodities reflected negatively on the taste and economic wherewithal of individual testators and can thus be used as a practical discriminator of the wider cultural association of the household. Product obsolescence and the spiral of replacement was most evidenced in the homes of higher ranking testators, whereas for many people of the lower middling sorts – and certainly those squeezed by economic necessity (poor widows and spinsters living off annuities, for instance) – these goods remained key to their everyday lives and featured prominently in both their inventoried wealth and in the main rooms of their homes. Despite these factors, the levelling off of pewter consumption as demonstrated in Table 2.1 is indicative of a process of substitution. Whereas pewter continued to be used for many everyday household implements and was retained in many middle ranking households due to its high unit value, portability and durability, it had been effectively replaced as respectable tableware by forms of earthenware – white ware, delft ware and from the 1760s decorative English earthenware. By the early nineteenth century even porcelain was relatively prevalent in the homes of the middle ranks. As ceramic goods were themselves subject to wear and breakage, obsolescence and the necessity of replacement, and thereby the potential acquisition of more fashionable designs, became important factors in household management.[36]

---

[34] Shropshire Archives 6001/4/4645–4647, Auction notice 7 February 1810.

[35] See Vickery: 'Women and the World of Goods', pp. 280–81.

[36] S. Richards, *Eighteenth-Century Ceramics: Products for a Civilised Society* (Manchester: Manchester University Press, 1999), pp. 89–126.

Gender and Ownership: The Domestic Interior

The trends in ownership posit some broad conclusions regarding the velocity of change over the period. However, whilst ownership trends are undoubtedly important in providing an overview of the materiality of consumption, individual items need to be contextualised within the domestic setting. The 'bare facts of possession' can only advance research in a rather reductive and largely linear trajectory: they give us a frozen snapshot of the home post-mortem, but tell us little about the motivation and impetus of live consumers or the provenance and ultimately use of the commodities described. To this extent, an indication of the potentially different attitudes towards household space and the wider apprehension of domestic goods can be gained by comparing the marital household with the estates of widows. In particular, when the deaths of the erstwhile husband and wife occurred within a relatively short time, an especially sharp light is thrown on the construction of the household. For example, on his death in 1671 Simon Beauchamp, gentleman of Bridgnorth, left inventoried wealth of over £1,300, consisting mainly of trade goods – cloth and assorted grocery wares in the cellar, shop and warehouse (£600) – and debts and ready money (£594 4s).[37] Some five years later Beauchamp's widow, Anne, left a much reduced estate of under £450, the bulk of which (£250) was tied up in due debts.[38] Clearly, the intervening years had seen the drastic scaling back of the business consonant with the reduced requirements of widowhood. Thus, whilst Anne retained the rump of the shop trade – a not inconsiderable £96 12s remained in merchantable commodities – a proportionately higher percentage of her wealth was located in household goods. Furthermore, whilst some key goods were missing – highly masculine items such as swords, pistols, fowling pieces and a halberd – other items and indeed other spaces entirely absent from Simon Beauchamp's inventory are listed. In particular, Anne Beauchamp possessed a strange collection of 'one sett of yellow Curtains of serge, one little truncke, two boxes [and] two rundletts' in a closet. This could be explained by the acquisition of goods in the hiatus between the two inventories or, more plausibly, that, despite the law of coverture, Anne retained goods that were identifiably and inalienably hers within marriage. These goods and the feminine private space in which they were housed were thus wholly omitted from Simon's inventory.[39] Their prominence in 1677 suggests a subtly altered view of domestic space, and one that reflected the influence of gender and singleness on how the home was both physically constructed and mentally imagined.

----

[37]   LRO, Simon Beauchamp, gentleman, Bridgnorth, 1671, £1,338 5s.

[38]   LRO, Anne Beauchamp, widow, Bridgnorth, 1677. The inventory listed goods and debts worth £457 16s (erroneously £491 17s 2d).

[39]   For the use of closet space as feminine sanctuary, see K. Lipsedge, '"Enter into Thy Closet": Women, Closet Culture, and the Eighteenth-Century English Novel' in J. Styles and A. Vickery (eds), *Gender, Taste and Material Culture in Britain and North America, 1700–1830* (New Haven: Yale University Press, 2006), pp. 107–22.

Whilst Beauchamp's inventory represented a widow in retreat – both in terms of economic and cultural space – that of Priscilla Pugh, a widow and upholsterer from Shrewsbury, indicated that other strategies were captured in the probate record. Pugh's husband had died in 1706 leaving a considerable movable estate of over £346, most of which (£294 1s) was committed to trade stock and book debts.[40] When Priscilla's inventory was proved in 1724, the balance between commercial and domestic concerns remained relatively intact: her estate was valued at just under £338, of which almost £270 was tied up in shop goods and debts.[41] Clearly, Priscilla had maintained the business as a going concern, probably with the assistance of apprentices and kin. This much echoes what has been written on the independent widow and her ability to carve out an economic niche within patriarchal forms of governance and surveillance.[42] However, it is the construction of the domestic environment that is instructive. From the rather summarily compiled inventory of Edward Pugh, wherein household goods were described generically and the domestic spaces entirely omitted, it can be roughly surmised that the Pugh household was traditionally furnished. By 1724, in keeping with the rising tide of polite consumption, the widow possessed not only an extensive range of the basic commodities – joined furniture, cooking equipment, pewter tableware and table linen – but also many goods designed to enhance comfort and reflect the respectability of the owner. Thus, Priscilla owned upholstered furniture, window curtains, saucepans, a chocolate pot, two coffee pots, two tea kettles, china, white ware, carpets and a large cache of silver and plate. Moreover, there were designated spaces in which such goods were genteelly presented. Pugh's parlour, for example, contained a looking glass, 12 chairs, a round table, one Dutch table, a corner cupboard, two stands and two tea tables.

A further case also throws light on these gendered forms of possession. In 1728, in the small Derbyshire village of Tideswell, Thomas Creswell died.[43] Described as a yeoman in his will and an ironmonger in the inventory, Thomas left a large dwelling house, a 'new building' clearly designed for residential and commercial purposes, a well-stocked shop and an inventoried estate that boasted

---

[40]   LRO, Edward Pugh, upholsterer, Shrewsbury, 1706. The estate was valued by James Davis and Thomas Burley at £346 19s 4d, consisting mostly of textiles (£144 1s) and book debts (£150).

[41]   LRO, Priscilla Pugh, widow, Shrewsbury, 1724. Thomas Davis and Thomas Burley appraised the estate at £337 18s 4d. Shop goods, predominantly rugs and stuff, amounted to £169 19s and debts 'dubious & payable' came to £100.

[42]   H. Barker, *The Business of Women: Female Enterprise and Urban Development in Northern England, 1760–1830* (Oxford: Oxford University Press, 2006), pp. 141–51, 157–64.

[43]   In 1782, the German pastor Carl Philip Moritz described Tideswell as consisting of two rows of stone houses with a couple of inns. C.P. Moritz, *Journeys of a German in England in 1782*, translated and edited by Reginald Nettel (London: Jonathan Cape, 1965), pp. 156–7.

over £633 in movables, bonds, securities and other credits. However, book debts, trade arrears and funeral expenses loaded the estate with over £662 of debt.[44] By his will, Creswell bequeathed the required third part of his real estate and copyhold lands to his wife Anne 'during her natural life in full of her dower', the residue being dispersed to their four minor children. Anne also received her due third of the goods and chattels, albeit limited to her remaining unmarried, and retained the governance of the retained lands as joint executrix of the estate. Thus far, Thomas's settlement resembled the kind of testamentary limitations to provision imposed by a minority of men of some substance and wealth concerned with preserving the integrity of their patrimony.[45]

In as much, Anne's situation was fairly unremarkable. However, in 1735 Anne died and the discrepancies between the two Creswell administrations reveal factors that cannot be explained solely by simple liquidation of assets or the acquisition of goods in the intervening seven-year period. Thus, whilst the main core of the ironmongery business appeared to have been leased out – the inventory speaks of 'John Cromwell's shop' in the new building – it is clear that Anne still traded on her own account and that the business, in a more abbreviated fashion, remained a viable concern.[46] It is with the decorative and expressive goods – the key diagnostic commodities isolated by Weatherill as indicative of enhanced consumer habits – that the two inventories differ.[47] In particular, Anne's inventory listed a range of additional domestic niceties – including a 'tea table, 3 hand boards, a set of blue and white china, 6 coffee pots, 5 plates, slop bason, milk jugg, [and] 2 sugar dishes' – that were entirely absent from the marital home. Similarly, as with the Beauchamp estate, the guns and other weaponry that were prominent in Thomas Creswell's inventory were conspicuously missing in the widow's inventory. Whilst it is tempting to read into the guns and china ware distinctive and almost oppositionally discrete forms of household consumption along gendered lines, these reported divergences in possession could, of course, simply reflect the nature of the source: omissions, abridgements and descriptive consolidations are common artefacts of probate inventories and it is entirely possible that such goods were located elsewhere in the household in 1728, or simply included in such blanket phrases as 'all husslements seen & unseen'.[48] Similarly, such items could well have been excluded from the goods legally accruing to the husband under the law of coverture by way of formal, pre-marital contract, or, more likely, informal

---

[44]   LRO, Thomas Creswell, ironmonger, 1728.

[45]   Sexual jealousy as well as purely dynastic considerations may also underpin some of the restrictions imposed on widows: Erickson, *Women and Property*, pp. 166–9.

[46]   See P. Earle, *Making of the English Middle Class*, pp. 159–68 and M.R. Hunt, *The Middling Sort: Commerce, Gender, and the Family in England, 1680–1780* (Berkeley and Los Angeles: University of California Press, 1996), pp. 125–33 for similar instances.

[47]   Weatherill, *Consumer Behaviour*, pp. 28–31, 166–9, 172, 179, 187–9.

[48]   This form of words is appended to Thomas Creswell's inventory.

agreement.[49] Certainly, Anne was previously married – as, it appears, was Thomas – and thus was likely to have brought goods beyond her acknowledged personal 'paraphernalia' into the Creswell household.[50]

The differences between the marital and widow-headed establishment may well have been expressed in terms of detail rather than structure. In the 1735 document, major items of furniture like the clock and case had perhaps understandably depreciated, and there is a much smaller range of iron wares and general shop goods in line with a partial liquidation of stock as a result of the partition of the estate. However, it is the relationship to goods and not the goods per se that is important here. Anne's will clearly indicates the wider affective significance of commodities. Indeed, whereas Thomas Creswell was mostly concerned with the dynastic conveyance of land and property, his wife apportioned domestic items with precision and care. Thus, Sarah Oldfield, the Creswells' eldest daughter, bequeathed the standard shilling by her father in probable recognition of her earlier marriage settlement, was given interest on £100 by her mother.[51] Anne's daughter by her previous marriage, Alice Hill, was to receive 'the drawers in my room, the looking glass & green two-arm'd chair, & her silver spoon, & her gold ring', whereas her son, John Creswell, was bequeathed 'my large silver tankard, a gold ring & all his father's clothes and plate buttons & his watch'. Other key goods – her rings, clothes, Bible, table linen, silver plate, brass and copper goods, delft ware, books, the '36 best plates & hard mettle dishes' and 'my tea table with all the furniture thereunto belonging to it' – all resonant of personal use and charged with both display and affective meaning were distributed amongst the children. In Anne's will singleness and gender combined to charge the household and its wider material constructions with key significance.

The examples suggest patterns of subtly different forms of gendered ownership. It is perhaps not sufficient to build a thesis of persistent female acquisitiveness, but there are suggestions, nuances even, where the widow and spinster-headed household may have been expressed through the possession and location of certain goods. In this context, it is important to emphasise the increasing sophistication and specificity of room use.[52] The closet has already been identified as an 'architectural

---

[49] Erickson outlines a number of cases where such informal agreements separated household goods: Erickson, *Women and Property*, pp. 144–7.

[50] Erickson, *Women and Property*, pp. 174–86.

[51] The amount was to be devised to Thomas Creswell, an elder and now independent son from a previous marriage, on the event of Sarah Oldfield's death.

[52] For an overview of room use and interiors, albeit for a metropolitan location, see P. Guillery, *The Small House in Eighteenth-Century London: A Social and Architectural History* (New Haven and London: Yale University Press, 2004), especially chapters 1–3. A more socially elevated taste is described by H. Grieg and G. Riello, 'Eighteenth-Century Interiors – Redesigning the Georgian: Introduction', *Journal of Design History*, 20/4 (2007), pp. 273–89, whilst Hamlett's recent work provides important qualifications as to the gendering and segregation of space in the later nineteenth-century household: J. Hamlett,

place' of female refuge and privacy away from the interventions and disruptions of mixed company;[53] Mary Penn, a widow of Broseley, tellingly possessed a 'Writeing Closet' with a 'desk and a few pictures' in 1740, for example.[54] Elsewhere, wider changes in the domestic interior reflected both the growth of discrete areas of gendered practice and competence within the structure of an increasingly idealised setting. For example, throughout the period, the parlour developed as the locus of public display and polite entertainment and the main physical space wherein issues of taste and distinction were subtly displayed. It was also the room most suitable for the women of the house to sit when they had leisure. Largely as a consequence of these factors, the parlour or latterly drawing room tended to house respectable decorative goods; and such items as carpets, rugs, painted floor cloths, window curtains, ceramics, looking glasses and pictures steadily appeared from the early eighteenth century.[55] By the 1780s wealthier homes had invested in modish wallpaper and upholstered seating.[56]

The emergence of the parlour from a room of multifunctional omnicompetence to a refined space for the reception and entertaining of polite company is revealed across the Midlands sample. For example, in 1674 Joan Easthope, a widow of Bridgnorth, left an estate of over £56 and a moderately well-equipped house of at least seven rooms. Her ground floor accommodation consisted of a kitchen, a general purpose hall and a parlour. This contained a bed, bedstead and assorted furniture, a coverlet, one 'old stript coveringe', a table, frame and a joined form, a livery cupboard and an old chair.[57] If Easthope entertained any sort of company in her parlour, and there is reason to suppose that the hall with its grate may have sufficed for this, it was amongst the accoutrements of general storage and sleeping.

By 1722, however – when Jane Maddox, widow of Bridgnorth, died in possession of a well-appointed house and an inventoried estate of over £314 – the parlour could be a much more cultured space. Maddox left eight chairs, two tables, a clock and case, six caster dishes and a chimney piece valued at £5 6s in her parlour.[58] Similarly, the inventory of Catherine Brown, proved at Bridgnorth in 1774, reveals a parlour that was also clearly a discrete space, removed from the

Material Relations: Domestic Interiors and Middle-Class Families in England, 1850–1910 (Manchester: Manchester University Press, 2010).

53   Lipsedge, 'Enter into Thy Closet', p. 119.

54   See Trinder and Cox (eds), *Miners and Mariners*, pp. 212–13.

55   S. Sarin, 'The Floorcloth and other Floor Coverings in the London Domestic Interior 1700–1800', *Journal of Design History*, 18/2 (2005) pp. 133–46.

56   See A. Vickery, '"Neat and Not Too Showey": Words and Wallpaper in Regency England' in J. Styles and A. Vickery (eds), *Gender, Taste and Material Culture in Britain and North America, 1700–1830* (New Haven and London: Yale University Press, 2006), pp. 201–22.

57   LRO, Joan Easthope, widow, Bridgnorth, 1674.

58   LRO, Jane Maddox, widow, Bridgnorth, 1722. The inventory valued goods at £314 11s, of which £210 was tied up in money, plate, wearing apparel and book debts.

sleeping chambers and the more functional kitchen and brew house. Brown had an oval table, a square table, five chairs and one picture worth in total barely 9s located in her parlour.[59] Brown also owned a coffee pot and copper tea kettle amongst her meagre possessions: her goods were appraised at less than £18. Brown's near contemporary, Elizabeth Jeffries, had two corner cupboards, two tables, two looking glasses, a chimney piece and seven old pictures in her parlour when her inventory was appraised in 1768. Like Brown, Jefferies was not wealthy – her movable wealth amounted to just over £19 – but she also possessed earthenware and the utensils and equipage to make hot drinks.[60]

The implication of change is none the less somewhat illusory: older practices clearly survived into the later period. Thus Mary Veal's parlour contained an old feather bed, bolster and old bedstead along with a poor collection of hurden sheets and napery ware, presumably housed in the old chest that was also listed when her estate was proved in 1740.[61] As the administration reveals, Veal was clearly an old widow, and her goods, such as they were, reflected her reduced circumstances. Such experiences, together with the numerous examples wherein rooms are simply not named, caution us against adopting too rigid or linear an interpretation of development.

It was also from the later seventeenth century that a room set aside for dining became desirable for many middling sort homemakers. Samuel Pepys, for instance, had a dining room in his modish London house in the 1660s.[62] As with the development of the parlour and in the increasing recognition of private space in the form of clearly designated chambers, the practice of using a dining space in an ad hoc or largely miscellaneous capacity gradually gave way to a functionally separate room with a defined purpose. Thus, the all-purpose buffet or corner cupboard that was often housed in a parlour was replaced by a sideboard and cellaret in a dining room. Specialism of function was also accompanied by gender demarcation, most obviously in the distinctive use of the dining room as a male space for largely, although not exclusively, postprandial homosocial activity. In these ways, the use of gender-specific furnishings alongside a general proliferation of domestic objects became much more pronounced, especially in the nineteenth century.[63] To this extent, the crowded parlour and separate dining

---

[59] LRO, Catherine Brown, widow, Bridgnorth, 1774.

[60] LRO, Elizabeth Jeffries, widow, Bridgnorth, 1768. The movables were valued at £19 4d.

[61] LRO, Mary Veal, widow, Bridgnorth, 1740. The estate was valued at £18 11s 4d, of which two old tenements at lease accounted for £10.

[62] D.N. Durant, *Living in the Past: An Insider's Social History of Historic Houses* (London: Aurum Press, 1988), p. 34. For the adoption of dining rooms as part of the state rooms in grander houses, see G. Jackson-Stops and J. Pipkin, *The English Country House: A Grand Tour* (London: Phoenix Illustrated and National Trust, 1993).

[63] For the introduction of gender-specific furniture to wealthy households, see C. Edwards, *Turning Houses into Homes: A History of the Retailing and Consumption*

room – the domestic norm of bourgeois high Victorian sensibility of the 1860s – had its roots in the developments of the eighteenth century. None the less, it must be remembered that these processes were incremental and keeping a room for the sole purposes of dining continued to be unusual in provincial middling sort homes in the eighteenth century. Even where the practice was adopted the room was more usually deemed an eating room or dining parlour.

Undoubtedly, the evolution of the home as a distinct space to work and the emergence of the idea of domestic ideology are closely linked to many of the changes outlined here. Much has been written about these developments, particularly whether the monolithic imposition of the concept of separate gendered spheres of operation and influence is appropriate or not. It is clear, however, that in the cluttered, permissive spaces of the late eighteenth- and early nineteenth-century home maintaining hermetically sealed distinctions between the public and the private – a pervasive feminine interiority and a masculine other dominated by work, interaction and commercial discourse – was something of a practical, if not theoretical, impossibility.[64] None the less, the way that the home was conceived in advice literature, novels and personal diaries emphasised its centrality as an emotional space, an asylum from the world and a bulwark against the invasion of work.[65] As the concept of the household as primarily a functional, economic

---

of Domestic Furnishings (Aldershot: Ashgate, 2005), p. 99. The spread of gender differentiation in design is described by A. Forty, *Objects of Desire: Design and Society 1750–1980* (London: Thames & Hudson, 1987), pp. 63–6 and the gendering of rooms is outlined by J. Kinchin, 'Interiors: Nineteenth-Century Essays on the "Masculine" and "Feminine" Room' in P. Kirkham (ed.), *The Gendered Object* (Manchester: Manchester University Press, 1996), pp. 12–29. For dining rooms as a male space, see M. Hutchinson, *Number 57: The History of a House* (London: Headline, 2003) and Hamlett, *Material Relations*.

[64]   The clearest statement of the development of separate spheres can be found in L. Davidoff and C. Hall, *Family Fortunes: Men and Women of the English Middle Class, 1780–1850* (London: Hutchinson, 1987). See also R.B. Shoemaker, *Gender in English Society, 1650–1850: The Emergence of Separate Spheres?* (London: Longman, 1998), esp. pp. 16–35 and 113–21. For critiques of this position, see A. Vickery 'From Golden Age to Separate Spheres: A Review of the Categories and Chronology of English Women's History', *Historical Journal*, 36/2 (1993), pp. 383–414; Vickery, *The Gentleman's Daughter*, pp. 196–7, 232–3; and L.E. Klein, 'Gender and the Public/Private Distinction in the Eighteenth Century: Some Questions about Evidence and Analytic Procedure', *Eighteenth-Century Studies*, 29/1 (1995), pp. 97–109.

[65]   For advice literature, see Davidoff and Hall, *Family Fortunes*, p. 182; Tadmor, *Family and Friends*, pp. 53–62 and V. Jones, 'The Seductions of Conduct: Pleasure and Conduct Literature' in R. Porter and M.M. Mulvey (eds), *Pleasure in the Eighteenth Century* (London: Macmillan, 1996), pp. 108–32. Thad Logan's work on the 'cult of domesticity' as a distinct development in nineteenth century is also significant here: T. Logan, *The Victorian Parlour* (London: Cambridge University Press, 2001), p. 25.

and productive unit receded,[66] a link between the nature of domestic furnishings and the psychological investment in the home was established. Upholstered furniture, an abundance of textiles and a greater proliferation of objects thus gave the impression of physical comfort, and simultaneously policed and nurtured the companionate marriage and the integrity of the generative family unit.[67]

In these contexts, marriage was thought desirable for both sexes and the inability to marry, or choosing not to marry, was seen as, at best, unfortunate or, at worst, an aberration worthy of ridicule. The single homemaker was thus not merely assailed by the practical and economic aspects of homemaking. The lack of a spouse to undertake specifically gendered work made the home imbalanced in both contemporary eyes and in the pages of prescriptive literature. Moreover, the absence of an appropriate host or hostess for the entertaining of mixed company could undermine the construction of the home as a site of secure, polite interaction. Underpinning these considerations was a persistent, almost ubiquitous implication that single households and even those populated with near kin, servants and other companions were in some ways emotionally and morally deficient. Given the rigidity of these assumptions, how could single people create a home that was viewed by society as respectable when such homes lacked the essential ingredients of a nuclear family? Organising these spaces thus offered distinct challenges to single householders: it is to this that we now turn.

---

[66] See Edwards, *Turning Houses into Homes*, pp. 5–7 and Overton et al., *Production and Consumption*, pp. 33–64.

[67] L. Stone, *The Family, Sex and Marriage in England, 1500–1800* (London: Weidenfeld & Nicolson, 1977), pp. 217–53 and revisions in A. Fletcher, *Gender, Sex and Subordination in England, 1500–1800* (New Haven and London: Yale University Press, 1995), pp. 154–72 and Tadmor, *Family and Friends*, pp. 18–43.

Chapter 3

Organisation and Management of a Single Household

In 1817, Anne Boulton declared herself 'anxious to get settled in some home of my own'.[1] Despite being 49 years of age and well provided for by her father's will she had great difficulty in accomplishing this wish. A desire for independence and a sufficient income were not always enough to overcome the practical problems and social mores of setting up and subsequently managing a home independently. Anne's childhood friend James Watt junior, the son of the maker of steam engines and partner of Matthew Boulton, experienced a somewhat different trajectory of being a householder. In 1798, aged 29, he was able to lease a cottage at the Soho Foundry site and begin his independent homemaking.[2]

The differences in the homemaking experience of Anne and James highlight the gender differences of setting up an independent household. But more than that, they also show that even when the circumstances were propitious single people could be reluctant to branch out on their own. In the case of Anne and James, they both had independent incomes sufficient enough to cover the expenses of renting a house and employing servants to maintain it. They also were wealthy enough to decorate and furnish their homes in some style; and yet the experience was not wholly welcomed and, in Anne's case in particular, it was fraught with problems. If this was so when circumstances were to modern eyes ideal, then for many of the single people examined later in this chapter the problems of independent homemaking were far worse. Anne Boulton and James Watt junior therefore offer us a useful template for judging some of the challenges faced by single people when organising and managing their homes. Single people needed to ensure that their households ran smoothly despite lacking a spouse. Increasingly, their domestic interiors needed to be protected from being sullied by income-generating activities and they needed to combat any imbalance in their domestic arrangements produced by gendered practices.

James Watt junior was forced to embrace an independent lifestyle at an early age since he was sent to Europe to complete his education. When he returned to England, he lived at home with his father, stepmother and younger siblings and would have

---

[1]   Shena Mason, *The Hardware Man's Daughter: Matthew Boulton and his 'Dear Girl'* (Chichester: Phillimore, 2005), p. 156.

[2]   Mason, *Hardware Man's Daughter*, pp. 123–59 deals with Watt's various homes. For an overview of James Watt junior and his circle, see Jenny Uglow, *The Lunar Men* (London: Faber & Faber, 2003).

continued there indefinitely. However, he found his stepmother's faultfinding intolerable and so felt compelled to move to a separate dwelling. Although rather humble, the cottage on the foundry site was quite large enough for his first foray into homemaking. There seems to have been two bedchambers, plus one for a servant. Downstairs was a kitchen and a parlour. He had very little in the way of crockery, with just six plates listed for his immediate needs. However, he soon outgrew the cottage and wanted something better and so after only a year he began renting The Rookery, a small house in Handsworth, then on the outskirts of Birmingham. His stock of crockery, silver and linen was more numerous and far more ambitious, for example, he recorded lists of best and common ceramics. He also went from having one servant to three, including a housekeeper and a manservant. No list of furniture survives for this house but he left some items behind at the foundry cottage for the use of Mr Murdoch, the engineer at Boulton and Watt. These items included a bed, dressing table, looking glass, washstand and curtains in one of the bedrooms and in the parlour six chairs, a table, a carpet and window curtains.[3] This suggests that these items were in some way makeshift and that he wanted something better at The Rookery. James purchased some things from friends for his new home but also commissioned new items, including a wash-hand stand from Seddon's for £9, Seddon being an important London cabinetmaker. Unspecified items were ordered from Mr Smallwood, an established firm of cabinetmakers in Birmingham at the time, and his bill came to £134 9s.

In 1808, Watt moved again, this time to a house owned by Matthew Boulton called Thornhill and bordering the estate of Boulton's own home at Soho. Thornhill was an attractive house with prominent bays on both sides of the building making large reception rooms, namely a drawing room and dining room. From a smaller room Watt created a library. The house also had extensive grounds that he took a keen interest in and spent a great deal of money laying out and planting trees. Again, no listing of the contents during Watt's residency survives, but from tradesmen's bills and drawings of built-in bookshelves it is clear that his ideas for this home were more ambitious than at The Rookery. The prestigious cabinetmaker George Bullock did the more important rooms. This work included two bedrooms, the staircase, the housekeeper's room, the drawing room and the library and the bill came to £157 5s 8d. Smallwood was employed again but this time merely to paper and paint servants' rooms in the attic, for which he charged £25 9s 3d.

Watt would perhaps have been content to stay at Thornhill – certainly the money and effort he lavished on the house suggests this. With 4 acres of grounds, his interest in gardens could be satisfied and the property was large enough to house his extensive collection of books and fossils, and a large stock of wines.[4] However, he moved again in 1818 to make way for Anne Boulton to take up

---

[3]   Birmingham Central Archives (BCA), Watt Papers, MS 3219/6/35, James Watt 'Household Memorandum', p. 9. This notebook contains details of Watt's first three attempts at independent homemaking.

[4]   BCA, Watt Papers, MS 3219/6/1/521, 2 August 1817.

residence. Watt's fourth and final home was the early seventeenth-century Aston Hall. His father in a letter to his land agent commented on this move, telling him that James 'is to have a lease of Aston hall for 10 years where he will be magnificently and conveniently lodged. He is also to have a 3 acre walled garden, a flower garden, two large fishponds and a part of the park, all within about 2 miles of the manufactory.'[5] Watt lived here until his death in 1848.

Each property rented by James Watt junior was larger and more ambitiously furnished than the last. Whilst Watt provided himself with comfortable, attractive and fashionable homes, he also took a great interest in the gardens; and in his last house he developed a somewhat individual antiquarian taste, perhaps inspired by the age and grandeur of Aston Hall. Such homemaking and control of a household would not have been possible except in his own homes. When he moved into the humble cottage Watt probably assumed that he would eventually marry, and the cottage was merely a kind of pre-marital apprenticeship at homemaking. His increasingly ambitious house furnishing perhaps reflected his confirmed bachelor status.

There are some interesting parallels but also some differences in the homemaking of James Watt and Anne Boulton demonstrating perhaps gendered preferences but also responses to the practical considerations of homemaking for unmarried women. Anne and James had been friends since childhood and had come close to marrying at one stage.[6] Like James, Anne only moved out of her family's home, at the age of 50, due to a personality clash, this time with her brother's new wife. Anne had kept house for her father at Soho House after her mother died in 1783 and then did the same for her brother. When he married, she tried to make the best of things, although she had to give way as mistress of the house to a woman almost 30 years her junior and with whom she did not get on.

However, while James was free to rent a cottage on the Soho Foundry site this option was not open to Anne. When desperate to move she mentioned the possibility of renting the cottage, to Annie Watt, James's stepmother, who thought it highly unsuitable and urged Anne to think again. Apart from the dirt and noise of the foundry, presumably it would also have been in close proximity to the mainly male workforce. Anne looked at various properties but none seemed suitable for various reasons and she grew ever more frantic to move out of her old home. Despite having a good income from money settled on her by her father, establishing her own home was a problem and a lonely business for Anne Boulton.[7]

Setting up home without a spouse meant many decisions had to be made and some friendly advice was sometimes welcome. James Watt senior, for example, wrote to his son in 1808 giving advice about where to go in London for wallpaper, carpets and furniture.[8] A friend of James gave Anne advice on which shops to

---

[5]   BCA, Watt Papers, extracts from the correspondence of JW and JWJ 1798–1819.

[6]   See Mason, *Hardware Man's Daughter*, pp. 139–48.

[7]   Anne Boulton had over £1,000 a year from interest and an annuity. Mason, *Hardware Man's Daughter*, p. 132.

[8]   BCA, Watt Papers, MS 3219/6/1/305, 22 February 1808.

Figure 3.1   Anne Boulton used the architect and furniture designer Richard Bridgens to produce plans for changing her home, Thornhill, to her requirements. *Source*: Reproduced with the permission of Birmingham Libraries and Archives.

use in London, from some of which she later made purchases – although none apparently from the retailers of second-hand/antique goods that were listed.[9] All the illustrations of her interior stay within the Classical style.

Anne and James both used the firm of Smallwood for furnishings and decorating work. They both demanded a higher standard for substantial items. Anne bought goods from Thomas Hensman in New Street, Birmingham, probably the town's leading cabinetmaker at this time,[10] as well as from Gillows in London. Anne also followed James's lead in patronising Richard Bridgens, who handled the making of window curtains and produced a number of designs for decorating and furnishing the drawing room at Thornhill, as well as some suggestions for attractive sunshades or a veranda for this south-facing room (see Figure 3.1)[11] The numerous drawings produced by Bridgens and decorating firms such as Rickman and Hutchinson during the first few years of Anne Boulton's time at Thornhill, testify to her enthusiasm for homemaking but also her need for visual representations of furniture and decorative features before making a decision about what work to commission.

The homemaking of James Watt and Anne Boulton shows that, even in the best of circumstances, when a single person had economic independence and the freedom to establish their own household this was often undertaken with some reluctance. An independent lifestyle presented both with practical problems but Anne experienced the added restrictions imposed on women. However, they both were able to indulge an interest in homemaking with some freedom of choice and lifestyle since in both cases they had sufficient income to be independent. Gender differences are in evidence but also their life experiences were different and these influenced their homemaking. James had led an independent life since he was a child and was sent away to school. He spent extensive periods abroad throughout his life, whereas Anne never travelled outside Britain and had been protected by her family. These life experiences were also dictated by social expectations of the role of men and women generally at the time of their homemaking. Anne would have suffered censure if she had taken an inappropriate property, and family and friends as well as the wider community would have closely monitored how she lived. The cottage at Soho was off-limits to a lady of gentility, whereas it was an acceptable base for a man of that class.

Sharing the Burden: Single People Sharing a Home

The cultural impropriety that might have adhered to Anne Boulton's independent household was in part mitigated by her high standing in local society as the daughter and sister of important men, added to which Anne shared her home at

---

[9]   BCA, MBP MS 3782/14/83/19, n.d.
[10]   BCA, MBP MS 3782/14/21/1/27, 1820.
[11]   Signed R. Bridgens Jan. 1820: BCA, MBP MS 3782/13/142/22/21.

least some of the time with a female friend such as Ann Keen, who was less well provided for than herself.[12] Juggling economy and propriety made independent living difficult if not impossible for many single people of the middle ranks. The financial burden perhaps increased in the nineteenth century as the requirements for establishing and maintaining a home became more demanding as the century progressed. Many middle-class young people put off marriage until their late twenties – until the prospective husband was established in his chosen career.[13] A stop-gap solution for a singleton not ready or able to marry but who desired or needed an independent home life was to become a lodger in someone else's household, sometimes that of a relative. However, if a longer-term arrangement was needed, especially for single people who thought they might never marry, then an alternative was to share a home with another single person. There were times when two people were better than one for taking care of the practical side of running a home, for the sake of economy and for the companionship usually associated with marriage.[14]

The economic aspect of the single life is highlighted in advice literature, for example *The Home Book* in 1829 gives tables for household expenses for families of different size and status (see Table 3.1).[15] Two tables dealt with independent women. Both households consisted of two women living together rather than a single woman as the head of a household. The first table included two female and one male servant and the expenses were £216 18s 6d for a year. The second table was for a household with just one female servant and the expenses were £112 18s 6d. In the 1820s, £150 was usually taken as the minimum income a year to sustain a middle-class household so *The Home Book*, aimed at a middle-class audience, was encompassing single women who were barely able to sustain a genteel lifestyle.[16]

---

[12]   Mason, *Hardware Man's Daughter*.

[13]   The problem of how much income was necessary was much debated at the time. See John M. Robson, *Marriage or Celibacy? The Daily Telegraph on a Victorian Dilemma* (Toronto and London: University of Toronto Press, 1995). See also Patricia Branca, *Silent Sisterhood: Middle-Class Women in the Victorian Home* (London: Croom Helm, 1975), p. 4.

[14]   For discussion on companionship in marriage, see L. Stone, *The Family, Sex and Marriage in England, 1500–1800* (London: Weidenfeld & Nicolson, 1977), pp. 217–53 and Naomi Tadmor, *Family and Friends in Eighteenth-Century England* (Cambridge: Cambridge University Press, 2001), pp. 21–4.

[15]   A Lady, *The Home Book: or Young Housekeeper's Assistant* (London: Smith, Elder & Co., 1829), pp. 169–70. Nineteenth-century advice literature often gave such tables of household expenses. Single ladies, but never men, are often dealt with. However, by the mid century some tables dealt with single people who were in lodgings rather than householders. See J.H. Walsh, *A Manual of Domestic Economy* (London: Routledge, 1857), p. 606. Lodgings are dealt with in Chapter 5.

[16]   John Burnett, *A Social History of Housing 1815–1970* (Newton Abbot: David & Charles, 1978), p. 96.

Table 3.1   Household expenses for two ladies and a maidservant (1829)[17]

	Weekly			Quarterly			Yearly		
	£	s	d	£	s	d	£	s	d
14 lbs Meat, at 9½ d	0	11	1	7	4	1	28	16	4
13 lbs Bread & 3 lbs Flour	0	3	0	1	19	0	7	16	0
2 lbs Butter, at 14d	0	2	4	1	10	0	6	0	0
Vegetables	0	0	7	0	7	7	1	10	4
Milk	0	0	10½	0	11	4 ½	2	5	6
Beer	0	1	0	0	13	0	2	12	0
Washing put out	0	3	6	2	5	6	9	2	0
½ lb Soap for home	0	0	4	0	4	4	0	17	4
5½ ounces Tea, at 9d	0	4	1½	2	13	7½	10	14	6
1½ lb Sugar, at 11d	0	1	4½	0	17	10½	3	11	6
½ lb moist Ditto	0	0	4	0	4	4	0	17	4
1 lb Cheese	0	0	6	0	6	6	1	6	0
Spices, &	0	0	3	0	3	3	0	13	0
Rice, Groats, and Currants	0	0	3	0	3	3	0	13	0
Black Lead, &c	0	0	2	0	2	2	0	8	8
4 Gallons Oil, at 8s	0	0	0	1	12	0	6	8	0
Servants' Wages	0	0	0	3	3	0	12	12	0
6 chaldrons Coal	0	0	0	0	0	0	16	4	0
Wood	0	0	0	0	0	0	1	0	0
£ 1	9	8½	24	0	10½	112	18	6

The shared household was certainly a more economical solution[18] but perhaps too the book suggests that co-residence was a more acceptable solution for unmarried women's living arrangements. By including single women as head of households, *The Home Book* at least suggests that this was a normal situation that occurred often enough to be acknowledged.

None of the tables in *The Home Book* gave figures for a single male-headed household or for two men living together. One obvious reason for this was that since men were the chief providers of income in the middle-class home an unmarried man or a widower setting up a home would be less affected than a woman in a similar position, and therefore the tables of expenses for a family home could be

[17]   Lady, *The Home Book*, p. 170. The main extra expense in the table for two women with two female servants and a footman was in servants' wages, which amounted to £46 4s per year. A further £26 was required for the footman to board elsewhere, which would have avoided paying servant tax for him. This household could make a small saving by doing the washing at home.

[18]   Davidoff and Hall suggest female relatives lived together to 'pool resources'. L. Davidoff and C. Hall, *Family Fortunes: Men and Women of the English Middle Class 1780–1850* (London: Routledge, 1987), p. 315.

used by men. However, it might also be the case that *The Home Book* avoided the single male-headed household since it lacked respectability, although age and status must have played important roles in determining how society both locally and at large regarded individual household arrangements.[19]

In the examples of inventories consulted, many single people were found to be sharing a home. The combinations found were widowed men with an adult unmarried daughter still living with them; two sisters sharing a home; or a brother and sister living together. The census[20] shows the make-up of households with numerous examples of extended family and additional people living alongside the head of household. Using the 1851 census for three locations, a simple estimate of single heads of household and how many lived with relatives can be made.[21] The results showed rather predictable patterns of behaviour. In the centre of Worcester, using 150 households, approximately 12 per cent had an unmarried head.[22] These consisted of five bachelors, four widowers, six widows and three spinsters. Of these, two bachelors, three widows and one spinster had other adult family members living with them. In the village of Strensham, in Worcestershire, out of the 93 households that made up the village approximately 10 per cent had an unmarried person listed as head: these were five bachelors, one widower, two widows and one spinster.[23] Three of the bachelors and one widow had other family members living with them. So, for example, John Evans – aged 27, an unmarried farmer of 67 acres – had his widowed uncle and aunt living with him at the time of the census in 1851. His aunt, Elizabeth Grove, was his housekeeper; and his uncle, David Evans, worked as an agricultural labourer. Another unmarried farmer, aged 48, had his unmarried brother and sister, aged 42 and 50, living with him and no doubt helping him to farm his 158 acres.

An even more noticeable concentration of singletons was found in a few respectable streets of Shrewsbury, where among just 46 households there lived three widowers, three bachelors, seven widows and seven spinsters who were recorded as heads of household.[24] Of these 20 households, two widowers, one bachelor, four widows and four spinsters shared their homes with other members of their family. For example, Sarah Bayley a retired governess aged 71, was listed as the head of household and her 63-year-old widowed sister, Mary Brown, lived with her and was described as 'dependent on her sister'. Rebecca and Mary

---

[19]   For an example described in 1766 in the *Gentleman's Magazine* of two women sharing a home, with one disguised as a man, see Bridget Hill, *Eighteenth-Century Women: An Anthology* (London: Allen & Unwin, 1984), p. 128.

[20]   The 1851 census was the first to record the relationship of everyone to the head of household.

[21]   The occupants of almshouses and lodging houses were not included in these figures. For a discussion on these living arrangements, see Chapter 5.

[22]   1851 census, St Helen's parish, Worcester.

[23]   1851 census, Strensham parish, Worcestershire.

[24]   1851 census, St Chad's parish, Shrewsbury.

Millar, aged 64 and 49, were two unmarried sisters living together and both were described as 'gentlewomen living on interest'. Similarly, Dianna and Katherine Wood were sisters aged 34 and 31; both were unmarried and 'gentlewomen' and their only listed live-in servant was a girl of 13, which to some extent suggests rather meagre living arrangements. In the same parish was an example of a brother and sister keeping house together – John Richards, the head of household, was a 78-year-old widower who was described as the 'hostler at [the] Lion Hotel' and his sister, a spinster of 50, was his housekeeper.

These instances of single-headed households identified in the 1851 census reveal a trend already established in the eighteenth century: that single people living on unearned income were more likely to set up independent households and tended to congregate in urban areas that displayed certain characteristics.[25] Towns like Shrewsbury, Ludlow and Chichester had many facilities on offer.[26] County and cathedral towns developed a social, cultural and commercial presence that attracted gentry residents, especially for the winter season; and middling sort residents, including unmarried women living on annuities, came to live economically while still being able to enjoy the benefits of town life.

Perhaps unmarried professional males were particularly likely to live in this kind of extended family household. Unmarried women in such households often never married since they were genteel and educated but relatively impoverished and therefore lacked suitable suitors. Using the 1851 census, numerous examples emerge in different kinds of location. For example in the village of Strensham there were two professional households at the schoolhouse and rectory. Thomas Cotton – a bachelor aged 31, described as the schoolmaster – occupied the schoolhouse and his sister, Mary Cotton, a spinster aged 20, lived with him and was listed as a governess. At the rectory the widowed clergyman aged 70 lived with his spinster daughters, aged 37 and 32, and his spinster sister aged 71, plus two unmarried female servants. Similarly, in Worcester the Berkeley's Hospital almshouses were looked after by the chaplain, Edwyn Bultner, an unmarried man of 53, and Jane, his 45-year-old unmarried sister. Their only live-in servant was recorded as a spinster of 49.

---

[25]   Mark Girouard, *The English Town* (New Haven and London: Yale University Press, 1990). See also Peter Clark (ed.), *The Transformation of English Towns, 1600–1800* (London: Hutchinson, 1984); Peter Borsay (ed.), *The Eighteenth-Century Town, 1688–1820* (London: Longman, 1990); Peter Clark and R.A. Houston, 'Culture and Leisure, 1700–1840' in P. Clark (ed.), *The Cambridge Urban History of Britain: Volume 2, 1540–1840* (Cambridge: Cambridge University Press, 2000), pp. 575–614.

[26]   Ludlow had lost its importance in the seventeenth century after the demise of the Council of the Marches but it continued to have a 'season' and to exert an influence in the surrounding area. See Susan Wright, 'Holding up Half the Sky': Women and their Occupations in Eighteenth-Century Ludlow', *Midland History*, 14 (1989), pp. 53–74 for comments on the high percentage of female-headed households and the continuation of a season.

St Chad's parish in Shrewsbury included a number of respectable streets inhabited by middle-class people either practising a profession or retired from one. For example Thomas Bayley, a bachelor of 61 and schoolmaster of an endowed school, had living with him his two nieces, Sarah and Ann, who did his housekeeping. They were both unmarried and aged 24 and 26. Another example of a professional bachelor in Shrewsbury who relied on his extended family was Henry Wace. In the 1861 census the family was living in College Hill, a central and smart address in the town which suited the legal profession followed by the male Waces. At that time the family consisted of the widowed father, Richard Wace (aged 82), his son Henry (aged 46 and unmarried) and his younger son George (aged 41), together with his wife Elizabeth and their young son and daughter. From this family home the Wace men ran their legal practice and were prominent in local affairs.[27]

The professional men who headed these households gained reliable housekeepers from within their own families. They were also men who were in a position sometimes to help unmarried female relatives who in some cases would never marry and therefore not have a husband to support them financially. Co-residence offered both the head of household with an income and the relative dependent on them financial and emotional advantages. Household work, management of servants and entertaining in the home could be shared between a brother and sister or uncle and nieces instead of between husband and wife. To what extent the suspect nature of a bachelor's residence was mitigated by living with female relatives rather than relying solely on servants is difficult to ascertain. Although some single women benefited from more independence by being the mistress of a father's or brother's house rather than marrying,[28] inevitably stresses and strains resulted from many of these living arrangements and women, while providing the managerial and physical tasks demanded of an efficient housekeeper, lost out on the status and respect due to a wife. This was the case of Anne Boulton, who had kept house for her father for many years and continued, after his death, to manage Soho House for her brother until his late marriage made her feel superfluous. There are many examples of famous men, lifelong bachelors or men who married late in life, benefiting from having a sister to do their housekeeping for them. One such example was the artist Joshua Reynolds, who never married and who Ian McIntyre suggests was 'a bit of a cold fish'.[29] His younger sister, Fanny, a poet and artist, kept house for him for nearly 25 years. They seem to have fallen out and despite the many years that Fanny had managed his home, Reynolds simply replaced her with one of his nieces. Fanny was forced to move

---

[27] *Directory of Shropshire* (Manchester: Slater, 1844), *Directory of Shropshire* (London: Bagshaw, 1851) and *Directory of Shropshire and Staffordshire* (London: Post Office, 1870) all give the address as College Hill, the same address as the residence in the 1861 census.

[28] Leonore Davidoff, *The Best Circles* (London: Croom Helm, 1973), p. 50.

[29] Ian McIntyre, *Joshua Reynolds: The Life and Times of the First President of the Royal Academy* (London: Penguin, 2004), p. 86.

into lodgings. Samuel Johnson, who addressed Fanny as his 'Dearest Dear', and his friend, Mrs Thrale, thought Reynolds had treated her badly.[30]

The complex inter-relationship of the single householder, extended kin and the use of domestic space is well illustrated through the various domiciliary arrangements of the Quaker merchant William Stout of Lancaster. In 1691, Stout decided to 'keep house' in a rather crudely subdivided building adjacent to his ironmongery shop. Stout had leased the back portion of 'John Hodgson's great house', comprising the 'great parlor, seller under it and three bedrooms above' with a brewhouse shared between the families of two other tenants. In order to bring some direction to this five-roomed dominion, Stout engaged his sister, Elin, who had hitherto aided Stout's fledgling business on market days and now 'freely offred to come and be my house keeper'.[31] Elin's 'ill state of health ... [and] the care and exercises that always attended a married life, and the hazard of happiness in it' had effectively condemned her to a life of singlehood and de facto extended familial servitude.[32]

Ostensibly, the relationship between William and Elin was economically and materially unequal; for example, there is no evidence of any formal financial arrangement offered by William or his brothers, Josias and Leonard, for whom Elin also periodically kept house. Elin appears to have existed on irregular pocket money, occasional handouts and the remnants of the portion conferred on her at the death of her father.[33] Indeed, whilst such forms of service emphasise the extent and pervasiveness of patriarchal norms in structuring households – Stout's mother also kept house for Josias intermittently until ousted by a combination of infirmity and, belatedly, a new wife – this did not reflect in a wholly pejorative fashion on Elin's status.[34] Far from being regarded solely as a domestic drudge, Elin, the only other professed Quaker in the wider family, acted as the bona fide governess of Stout's domestic affairs, organising the shop, disciplining apprentices as well as maintaining cordial relations with neighbours – a factor perhaps lost on the stoically terse and direct Stout. This was not therefore, to paraphrase Bridget Hill's assertion, merely a 'suitable occupation' for the unattached and by extension inferior female family members, although the Stout family clearly benefited

---

[30]   McIntyre, *Joshua Reynolds*, pp. 88 and 328–9. See also the example of William Pitt and his sister in Amy Froide, *Never Married: Singlewomen in Early Modern England* (Oxford: Oxford University Press, 2005), pp. 61–4.

[31]   J.D. Marshall (ed.), *The Autobiography of William Stout of Lancaster, 1665–1752* (Manchester: Manchester University Press for the Chetham Society, 1967), pp. 102–3.

[32]   Marshall, *Stout*, p. 87.

[33]   Elin briefly kept house for Josias and Leonard Stout between 1698 and 1699: Marshall, *Stout*, pp. 120–3, 127. Elin received £80 from her father and further annuities from her mother: Marshall, *Stout*, pp. 72–3, 103.

[34]   Froide argues that debility and the care of relatives and kin were consistent factors in the lives and experiences of many singlewomen: Froide, *Never Married*, pp. 160–69, 184–94.

from what was in practice unwaged labour.[35] In a curiously emotive passage in an otherwise largely dispassionate account, Stout reveals how this relationship, nominally couched in the language of service and deference, translated into something far more affective. In 1702, Stout, recalling a transient brush with the possibility of marriage, recounted:

> I consented living with my sister Elin, who was as carful and dilligent to serve me as much or more than if I had been her own sone. And I was tender to her, who was very infirme of body and subject to many infirmities. I kept her a good maid servant, and we had always two of my brother Leonard's children with us; tooke them at two years old, and kept them till they were six years old and capable to goe to Boulton Schoole. And my sister was as carfull to nurs and corect them as if they had been her own children.[36]

This fondly imagined family cobbled together by necessity in Stout's newly bought and much extended house was in direct contrast to the more frosty and utilitarian approach to domestic arrangements after the death of Elin in 1724. Stout took on each of his four nieces in turn to provide domestic support, although perhaps because of their youth, inappropriate romantic attachments or more likely their persistent disregard for Stout's well-meaning but hectoring advice, these relationships were increasingly fraught and unsatisfactory.[37] Finally, in 1742, after a period of boarding out, Stout settled his household affairs on 'Mary Hall, daughter of my neece'. Hall's previous training in the Stout household in what appears to be an unregulated period of informal domestic tutelage had equipped her in the 'knowledge of my way of living':[38] plain and frugal if a little sanctimonious. Despite the evident kin alignment this last arrangement was defined wholly by service and Hall was clearly expected to perform the bulk of the menial household tasks.

Stout regarded the household as principally an extension of work, moral probity and good governance and viewed kin through the same critical prism, frequently upbraiding them for frivolity, high living and lack of 'substance'. Indeed, such was his aversion to the niceties of polite company that he removed himself from the social spaces of his nephew's house whilst boarding with him, shunning the 'costly household goods and ... entertainments' and maintaining the 'street rooms' above his old shop as austere and solitary living quarters. He would only take his 'victuals in the house', there 'being no way easy' with his profligate nephew's 'way of living,

---

[35]   B. Hill, *Servants: English Domestics in the Eighteenth Century* (Oxford: Oxford University Press, 1996), pp. 120–21 and 127. See Froide, *Never Married*, p. 184 for a more critical discussion of Elin Stout and service.

[36]   Marshall, *Stout*, p. 142.

[37]   Marshall, *Stout*, pp. 192, 200–201, 203–5, 215–16.

[38]   Marshall, *Stout*, pp. 232–3.

or his conduct abroad; he being soe outward and expencive'.[39] Yet whilst this ethos reflected the particularly ascetic precepts of Stout's own comprehension of his faith, kin were often important social extensions to the single household. For example, between 1779 and 1803, the Reverend James Woodforde, parson of Weston Longeville, Norfolk, presided over an extended mixed household that consisted of up to five servants and his niece Nancy.[40] Although Nancy clearly had some responsibility in organising the domestic routines of the parsonage and the daily direction of the female staff, and indeed was given an annual allowance of £10, her role fell somewhat short of the kind of housekeeping omnicompetence afforded to Elin Stout.[41] In this Woodforde was keen to exercise a measure of control, minutely detailing the bulk purchases of everyday domestic items like foodstuffs and fish, as well as accounting for the household's needs in cloth and his own more idiosyncratic and personal acquisitions.[42] For example, in 1783 Woodforde bought over 27 yards of quite expensive 'stuffs for Gowns &c' – traditionally the province of the woman of the house – from a travelling salesman, congratulating himself that he 'gave both my Maids a Gown apiece of it and of the same Colour, something of the Pea Green'. Having liveried his servants, Woodforde then 'gave Nancy also, to make a Skirt for her of a light blue 6yds',[43] an action that neatly positioned his niece in terms of her social position and economic dependence in the household.

However, as a well-connected man of some local importance, the provision of hospitality and a fair degree of domestic largesse were key to Woodforde's existence. Thus, whilst Nancy may well have been shorn of the range of domestic responsibilities required of and demanded by a wife or housekeeper, her presence in the Woodforde household permitted the kind of genteel association that may have proved uncomfortable or unacceptably impolite in a wholly masculine configuration. For example, Woodforde regularly entertained friends, relations and members of the nearby squirearchy and furthermore expected reciprocal generosity and gift exchange. In these instances, the parsonage was transformed into a centre

---

[39]   Marshall, *Stout*, p. 216–18.

[40]   See J. Beresford (ed.), *Woodforde: Passages from the Five Volumes of the Diary of a Country Parson, 1758–1802: The Reverend James Woodforde* (6th edn, London: Oxford University Press, 1967 [1935]), p. 293 (10 January 1787).

[41]   For Nancy's annual wage, see Beresford, *Woodforde*, p. 293 (16 January 1787).

[42]   For Woodforde's purchases, see Beresford, *Woodforde*, pp. 130–31 (16 January, 26 March, 29 March, 17 April 1777); 203–4 (5 June 1783); 293 (16 January 1787); 353 (3 June 1789); 388–9 (7–8 December 1790); 424 (23 October 1792) and M. Finn, 'Men's Things: Masculine Possession in the Consumer Revolution', *Social History*, 25/2 (2000), pp. 138–42.

[43]   Beresford, *Woodforde*, p. 202 (6 May 1783). For female purchases for the household, see C. Walsh, 'Shopping at First Hand? Mistresses, Servants and Shopping for the Household in Early-Modern England' in David Hussey and Margaret Ponsonby (eds), *Buying for the Home: Shopping for the Domestic from the Seventeenth Century to the Present* (Aldershot: Ashgate, 2008), pp. 13–27.

of refined leisure, high living and, as befitted the age, diversionary forms of gambling, in which Nancy Woodforde acted entirely as the hostess.[44] Indeed, the acquisition of a suitably quiescent female relative for both companionship and to insulate bachelors and widowers from accusations of putative sexual impropriety was a major concern for many male householders in this period.[45] Through such means, Nancy Woodforde thus acted as a cultural emollient to her uncle's wider social pretensions and the conduit through which Woodforde, as a bachelor, was able to operate within the wider cultural mores of his circle.

A similarly permissive if more curious *ménage* was that created by Elizabeth Purefoy, widowed in 1704 at the comparatively young age of 32, and her infant son Henry, then aged 7, who remained subsequently unmarried. The Purefoys occupied Shalstone Manor in Buckinghamshire and lived out a distinctly gentrified existence enabled in part by their respectively single status which afforded Elizabeth, who maintained a matriarchal control over Shalstone even after her son's majority, much latitude in the material construction of the household. Both widow and son were thus active in improving Shalstone. For example, in 1735 Elizabeth ordered quilting for 'one of the new-fashioned low-beds without a cornice' from Anthony Baxter, a London-based tradesman, and also acquired a number of second-hand goods from London dealers and more proximate house sales, including inkstands, soap dishes, a 'Buroy with glasse doors', an 'India Tea board' and 13 stools for the servants' hall.[46] Henry Purefoy also engaged with Baxter in 1738 to obtain material – preferring white Indian damask to fashionable 'best chintz' – for the window curtains and valences of Shalstone's two parlours.[47]

The niceties of choosing parlour curtains was not in the astronomer William Herschel's mind when he sent for his young sister Caroline to keep house for him after he had established himself in Bath as a musician and music teacher in 1772. Although he saved Caroline from the ill-treatment of her mother, he expected hard work and total commitment from her. When she first arrived in England they rose at 6 am and Caroline's day consisted of 'household accounts, shopping, laundry, three-hourly singing lessons, instruction in English and arithmetic, music copying, formal practice on the harpsichord kept in the front

---

[44]   See, for example, the visit of the Custances on 9 November 1786: Beresford, *Woodforde*, p. 287.

[45]   Davidoff and Hall, *Family Fortunes*, p. 391; Hill, *Servants*, pp. 115–27, especially pp. 118–19. Nancy was often Woodforde's de facto 'partner' when receiving married company like the Custances and Beauchamps: see Beresford, *Woodforde*, p. 380 (15 July 1790).

[46]   G. Eland (ed.), *Purefoy Letters 1735–1753* (London: Sidgwick & Jackson, 1931), pp. 97, 110. For the use of second-hand goods, see Clive Edwards and Margaret Ponsonby, 'Desirable Commodity or Practical Necessity?: The Sale and Consumption of Second-Hand Furniture' in Hussey and Ponsonby, *Buying for the Home*, pp. 117–38.

[47]   Eland, *Purefoy Letters 1735–1753*, p.104, 4 June 1738; p. 105, 16 July, 1738, 6 August 1738.

room, and reading aloud from English novels.' She did some astronomy in her spare time.[48]

William prospered as an astronomer; the highlight of his career was the discovery of a new planet, to be named later as Uranus. They moved to a larger house near Windsor so that he could be the King's Personal Astronomer, with a salary of £200 a year. Caroline had a separate apartment, made in rooms over the stables for her occasional use, consisting of a bedroom and writing room – plus a flat roof from which she could make her own observations. Caroline specialised in discovering comets, for which she was rewarded with a salary of £50 a year from George III, a very unusual development for a female scientist. She commented that this was 'the first money I ever in all my life thought myself to be at liberty to spend to my own liking.'[49] Despite her importance in William's household she felt that she 'could only look upon myself as an individual who was neither Mistress of her brother's house, nor of her Time, and for that reason neither could, nor would, ever' invite anyone to her home. She was essential to William's work, keeping notes that he dictated while studying the stars through the powerful telescopes of his own design and manufacture. However, at the age of 53 William married a rich widow and Caroline was demoted from being his housekeeper to living permanently in the few rooms over the stables. In her diary Caroline recorded her brother's wedding day, not as a forthcoming happy event but as 'the time I was to give up the place of a Housekeeper which was the 8th of May 1788.' After this entry the rest of the page remained blank, for she ended the account of her life then and did not resume keeping a diary until 1840.[50]

Despite the cooling of relations between her and her brother Caroline became close to William's son; and in this she mirrored Dorothy Wordsworth, who also lost her position in her brother's household when he married late in life but later became her nephew's housekeeper.[51] Both of these relationships in their different ways were intense, based on shared interests, although it has been noted that the latter took on a somewhat unhealthy complexion when Wordsworth eventually married.[52]

The Reverend Henry Nussey illustrates the need for a housekeeper in the form of a wife, or failing that, a sister. He is remembered as the man whose offer

---

[48]   Richard Holmes, *The Age of Wonder: How the Romantic Generation Discovered the Beauty and Terror of Science* (New York: Pantheon Books, 2008), p. 82.

[49]   Holmes, *Age of Wonder*, p. 179.

[50]   Michael Hoskin (ed.), *Caroline Herschel's Autobiographies* (Cambridge: Science History Publications, 2003), p. 95. Caroline eventually moved into lodgings and later in her life she returned to live in Germany.

[51]   Holmes, *Age of Wonder*, p. 203.

[52]   Ashton and Davies describe Dorothy's feelings for her brother as 'morbid and extravagant'. Helen Ashton and Katherine Davies, *I Had a Sister* (London: Lovat Dickson Limited, 1937), p. 108.

of marriage Charlotte Brontë turned down.[53] His desperate search for a wife is suggested in his diary where he recorded proposing, unsuccessfully, to a young woman; and just weeks later he tried again, with his sister Ellen's best friend. He suggested, rather unromantically, that Charlotte would help him take on pupils, and perhaps he was hoping for financial as well as practical help. Either way, Charlotte declined, preferring to wait for someone with more to offer.

Henry Nussey took up his position of curate in rural Sussex in 1838. The day he arrived he recorded in his journal: 'And where am I now? In the Rectory of the Parish of Earnley nr Chichester in a very low & flat neighbourhood near the sea.'[54] His dismay at finding himself in such an unpromising place was also conveyed on his first Sunday in the parish when he went to church with some trepidation but found in the 'most rustic & primitive looking Church, a very good & attentive congregation. Their responses and singing were delightful.' That said, the village had little to offer someone with an Oxford education, who had lived in York and who was from an old established land-owning family with literary leanings. Fortunately he got on well with his 'kind Rector', Mr Browne, and found that he could visit and take tea with a few families nearby, including Mr Osborne and his extended family with whom he spent Christmas day and enjoyed the evening with the family playing sacred music. He was also able to dine occasionally with clergy families in Chichester, which was 6 miles away. He recorded calling on the bishop a number of times but never found him at home.

The limitations offered by his life in Sussex left Henry feeling lonely and perhaps a little depressed. In addition, he experienced some domestic problems. His housekeeper suited him 'very well in her capacity but was rather of too lively & gay turn of mind'. She and her husband moved away and he engaged another couple, who he described as 'well disposed and simple-hearted creatures of the name of Bridle'. He thought they were not as proficient as his first servants but hoped things would work out with them assisting him 'in [the] temporal [and] I may be made useful to them in Spiritual' matters. Within a few months he was busy proposing marriage, but to no avail. Fortunately, he had numerous sisters to help him. They seem to have taken it in turns to come to keep house for him over the six or seven years of his residence in Sussex. At the time of the census in 1841 it was the turn of his eldest sister, Ann. The census recorded their ages as 25 and 40, although in reality Henry was 29 and Ann was 46. Their household also included three young men aged 13–14 so Henry's plan of taking in pupils had been put into practice, but with a sister's help rather than a wife's. There was also a live-in servant girl, suggesting that with sisters to keep his house he did not need a housekeeper and her husband. His sisters helped Henry make money and saved him money, as well as making his life more pleasant and his home run more smoothly. He did eventually succeed in finding a wife after he moved

[53]   Christine Alexander and Margaret Smith, *The Oxford Companion to the Brontës* (Oxford University Press, 2003), p. 352.

[54]   British Library, Egerton Mss. 3268A, Henry Nussey journal.

to Derbyshire to become the vicar of Hathersage. Miss Emily Presscott came with 'a handsome fortune' so surely now Henry was set up in life; with his career established, the money to fund a substantial house with genteel furnishings and finally with a wife by his side he could enjoy all the advantages of mixing in good society. He could even look forward to children and therefore founding his own dynastic line. However, finding a suitable marriage partner did not always secure a happy and profitable future. Henry and Emily did not get on and the marriage was not a success. Within a few years they took the drastic step of separating and Henry Nussey died in France, his marriage and career in tatters.[55]

Marriage was not necessarily the route to a happy home life; sometimes a brother and sister cohabiting achieved a more successful companionate relationship. The circumstances surrounding Charles and Mary Lamb setting up home together were tragic. Both of them had inherited mental instability from their father's family and in Mary this manifested itself in fits of manic depression throughout her life, becoming more frequent and lasting longer over time. Like so many unmarried daughters, she was expected to remain at home to care for her parents, a burden that became intolerable for her. Her father was 70 and senile and her mother was paralysed, added to which she and Mary had never been close; but now Mary had to share a bed with her mother and tend to her every need. Her father's sister, Aunt Hetty, who was old and feeble physically and mentally, also lived in their cramped lodgings. Into this appalling situation came a further difficulty when Mary's elder brother, John, had an accident badly injuring his leg and came home to convalesce. Mary was also trying to earn a living as a dressmaker at this time. On 22 September 1796 something happened to push Mary over the edge, and she killed her mother with a knife and injured her father. She was put into a private asylum as a temporary measure but a public institution, probably the dreadful Bethlem Hospital, would have been her fate if Charles had not pledged to care for her for the rest of his life. Mary was 34 and Charles 24 when they set up home together, an arrangement that lasted 35 years.[56]

In between fits of depression Mary was calm and happy, and the brother and sister seem to have had a contented life together. They lived in various rooms, particularly in the Inner Temple, the area where they had grown up. Mary was a good housekeeper and they managed to live reasonably well on the £90 a year that Charles received at East India House, supplemented with the money they gained from their joint literary efforts such as *Lamb's Tales from Shakespeare* and *Poetry for Children*. When they moved into 4 Middle Temple Lane they had two rooms on the third floor and five attic rooms above. They hung Hogarth prints in narrow black frames on the walls and made one of the attic rooms into a study

---

[55]   Winifred Gérin, *Charlotte Brontë: The Evolution of Genius* (Oxford: Clarendon Press, 1967), p. 129. For comments on separation, see J. Bailey, *Unquiet Lives: Marriage and Marriage Breakdown in England, 1660–1800* (Cambridge: Cambridge University Press, 2003), pp. 198–204.

[56]   Ashton and Davies, *I Had a Sister*, pp. 17–79.

for Charles. Mary made up a fire in the grate and carried up a table and one chair for him, but Charles found the bare room uncongenial and said he could not write 'in that dull unfurnished prison'. Mary improved the room with bits of carpeting on the floor and a few prints on the white-washed walls. The brother and sister then proceeded to cover the walls with pictures cut from books. The result, Mary wrote to a friend, was that 'the poor despised garret is now called the print room and is become our most favourite sitting room'.[57] Charles and Mary Lamb were extremely fond of each other and sympathetic to each other's moods resulting from the mental problems that they shared. Despite the worsening of Mary's condition Charles remained devoted to her and referred to their relationship as a 'double singleness'.[58] The Lambs appear to have been individually shattered entities and co-dependent on each other. Their household was a substitute marriage of sorts, or as normative a relationship permitted within the confines of psychic (and material) dysfunction.

In many instances a sister stood in for a wife for her unmarried or widowed brother. However, as James Gee remarked after his wife had died in 1806 and his widowed sister Mary came to keep house for him, he would have preferred to remarry as although she 'pleases me in every thing that lies in her power, yet a sister is not like a wife'.[59] James paid Mary just £3 a year in wages but since she had no home when she went to live with him perhaps she was content with her new role. As a needy widow Mary had few opportunities at her disposal, and in such cases poverty and the meagre provisions of the poor law awaited the destitute.

Coping Alone: Women Farming Without a Spouse

Of all occupations, farming was a way of life that dictated what needed to be done at every moment of the day. Of the many tasks involved, many required hard physical labour. The experience of running a farm would have been influenced by the availability of other family members to contribute labour; the financial resources available to pay for extra labour; and the location of the farm and its specialisation.[60] The probate inventories of farmers from the sample provide examples of single people engaged in this way of life, although many were no doubt struggling to survive without a spouse. In particular, women who inherited a farm were severely disadvantaged in the male world of ploughing, sowing, harvesting and dealing with the livestock. However, traditionally it was women who looked after the farmhouse, the dairy, the chickens and the vegetable garden.

---

[57]   Ashton and Davies, *I Had a Sister*, p. 62.

[58]   Ashton and Davies, *I Had a Sister*, p. 57.

[59]   'The Life and Times of James Gee of Walsall 1746–1827' Transcription, Walsall Local History Centre, 920GEE, pp. 70–75.

[60]   Joan Thirsk (ed.), *The Agrarian History of England and Wales, vol. 5 1640–1750* (Cambridge: Cambridge University Press, 1984).

A single woman who needed to employ male labourers to help her run a farm would have been in the difficult position of employing men and watching over their work to ensure her farm was successful.

The inventories of widows and spinsters consulted here include a number of women engaged in farming. At least 20 women were running farms at the time of their decease, either as unmarried singlewomen or continuing the farm after the death of a spouse. One example of an extensive operation was the farm of Martha Davis in Byford, beside the River Wye in Herefordshire.[61] The total value of the farm was an impressive £488 9s 6d. Clothing and household goods amounted to the relatively low sum of £33 19s 6d. The majority of her wealth was tied up in animals, valued at £229 6s – which included the unusually large number of 12 oxen valued at £70. This area of Herefordshire was good arable land, if rather heavy soil, and the oxen would have been used primarily to work her 92 acres used to grow wheat and barley, although she could have earned additional money from renting them to other local farms. Davis also had a dairy herd of 30 cows, as well as sheep, pigs and horses, making the most of the lush pastureland beside the river.[62] Various crops, a wagon and a quantity of horse bridles made up the remainder of the inventory. Davis had family, including adult sons, to help her and it would seem she headed a large and successful farming operation.

Continuing a farm as a widow – especially if it had been successful and if the widow could rely on family help – was less difficult than as an unmarried woman running a farm independently. Most singlewomen involved in farming in the sample headed modest smallholdings. For example, Jane Foster ran a farm in Hampton near Ellesmere, Shropshire, until her death in 1688.[63] The value of her farm stock, household goods and wearing apparel totalled £29 9s 8d. The most valuable items in her inventory were her four cows, valued at £6. The farm had other livestock in the form of three yearling calves and an unspecified number of sheep and pigs, valued at £1 12s. Geese and poultry made a further contribution to food provision and additional income. Small quantities of corn, hay, manure and cheese testify to the nature of her enterprise. In the same village some 70 years later, another spinster, Elizabeth Owen,[64] was running a modest smallholding at the time of her death in 1764. Although farming on a small scale, the sheer diversity of her activities was captured in her inventory with references to cheeses, turves [for fuel], corn, muck, straw, hay, hemp, potatoes, a spinning wheel, a kneading trough and two cows.

An independent but hard and frugal existence is suggested by the inventory and administration of Elizabeth Whitehouse. She died in 1801, having rented a

---

[61]   Hereford Record Office (HRO), Martha Davis, widow, Byford, 1731: inventory and will, in which she leaves the farm to her eldest son.

[62]   Joan Thirsk, 'The South-West Midlands: Warwickshire, Worcestershire, Gloucestershire, and Herefordshire' in Thirsk, *Agrarian History*.

[63]   Lichfield Record Office (LRO), Jane Foster, spinster, Hampton, 1688.

[64]   LRO, Elizabeth Owen, spinster, Hampton, 1764.

farm in West Bromwich from a Mr Walker of Birmingham.[65] After her death he took possession of two pigs and a quantity of potatoes and sold them for £2 8s to cover rent owing to him. In administration documents her executor was anxious that he should not be charged for these missing items. The rest of the inventory listed her goods that had been sold by an auctioneer on the premises. Wheat and barley were sold for £12 2s. The only other farm stock listed was some wheat straw sold for £1 2s 6d and some manure worth 7s. Her clothes were valued at just 10s. Other items listed sold for a few shillings each – the most valuable assets were a clock and case for £1 11s 6d and the beds with mattress, pillows and blankets that sold for £1 1s and £2 19s 4d. In addition to her two pigs, Whitehouse had presumably had a cow at some point – evidenced by a milking pail, butter tub and milk pan being listed. The presence of barrels and 18 glass bottles suggest she had brewed her own beer.[66]

The parish of West Bromwich, in the seventeenth and eighteenth centuries, had been noted for poor farmers who were squatters on the land and who had combined keeping some livestock with industrial activities. By the later eighteenth century, the economy of the area had progressed to being mainly industrial.[67] No indication of any additional forms of employment is in evidence in Whitehouse's inventory, but she did have a lodger to supplement her income. Despite the paucity of goods and their low value for the beginning of the nineteenth century, Whitehouse had numerous decorative goods. These included looking glasses, pictures, books and a bookshelf, a desk, earthenware, curtains, pewter and brass items, plus sufficient furniture to live comfortably in her farmhouse – although no upholstered seating was listed, which would have been expected in better-off middling homes by this period. Although her farming activities may have been curtailed due to illness and old age, the low value of her wearing apparel suggests a meagre existence.

Not all spinsters running farms were just getting by. One exception to this was Ann Fox, who had an extensive farm and house in Cleobury Mortimer, Shropshire,[68] and was sufficiently well off to be able to leave bequests to local charities. Fox named three servants in her will, Nancy, Sally and John Dallance, although their roles were not included. Bridget Hill[69] and Carolyn Steedman have

---

[65]   LRO, Elizabeth Whitehouse, spinster, West Bromwich, 1801.

[66]   It has been estimated that in 1700 about half of all beer was brewed privately in England and that about one-fifth continued to be as late as the mid-nineteenth century, although the brewing industry was well organised by this time. Richard Wilson, 'The British Brewing Industry Since 1750' in Lesley Richmond and Alison Turton (eds), *The Brewing Industry: A Guide to Historical Records* (Manchester and New York: Manchester University Press, 1990), p. 1.

[67]   David Hey, 'The North-West Midlands: Derbyshire, Staffordshire, Cheshire, and Shropshire' in Thirsk, *Agrarian History*, pp. 145 and 148.

[68]   Shropshire Archives (SA), 6000/15309 Auctioneer catalogue for Ann Fox, spinster, Cleobury Mortimer, 1813.

[69]   On the fluidity of servant labels see Hill, *Servants*, pp. 22–33.

both illustrated that there was no clear distinction between the indoor and outdoor work for servants on a farm, particularly for a maidservant 'who was likely to clean the house, cook the dinner, plant beans in the kitchen garden and milk a cow as part of a day's work'.[70] Additional outdoor help could also be employed, especially on a seasonal basis.

The farming concern of the spinster Jane Irland provides a similar picture to Martha Davis in that she died just six years earlier, in 1725, and her farm in Bury, Sussex, was valued at a similar amount, £421. However, the details of the inventory suggest a rather different operation. Unlike Martha's somewhat poorly furnished home, much of Irland's wealth resided in an array of household goods that amounted to about £120. In addition, she had a bond valued at £50 from which she would have earned interest.[71] The farmhouse was similar to many homes in the early modern period in that the greatest value was derived from the beds and bedding, with the contents of several bedchambers being valued at more than £15 each. These were quite high valuations for a middling household and suggest some good-quality goods, although, unfortunately, individual items were not valued to verify this point. No parlour was listed, although there was a parlour chamber. The farm stock came to about £250 and included wheat, barley, beans and 'tears' [tares], a kind of vetch grown for animal feed and to improve the soil and an indication that at least some of her farmland was enclosed. Livestock included horses, 108 sheep, 47 lambs, pigs and 14 'beasts'. Bury, being situated on the chalky soil of the South Downs, provided a more rugged terrain than the lush pastures of the Wye valley in Herefordshire, and included common land for grazing sheep. Irland's mixture of livestock, arable and legumes corresponded to what was usual for the area.[72] While many aspects of this farm suggest a progressive and successful enterprise, a number of peculiarities exist. The number of lambs is low compared to the number of sheep. A 'milk room' was included but no cows, only 'beasts', were listed – and this is usually the description given to beef cattle. In addition, eight tons of 'old hay' was listed, although the inventory was made in June and normally the stock of hay would have been used over the winter months. Old age or illness in the final year or months of Irland's life may have brought about changes and retrenchments to her farming practices.

The relatively high number of female farmers encountered in the sample for the Midlands region might be to some extent explained by the importance of dairying in Shropshire, Cheshire and Wales, which also accounts for cheesemaking

---

[70]   Carolyn Steedman, 'The Servant's Labour: The Business of Life, England, 1760–1820', *Social History* 29/1 (2004), pp. 1–29, p. 11.

[71]   West Sussex Record Office (WSRO), Jane Irland, spinster, Bury, 1725. On the value of land and movables and inheritance, see Amy Louise Erickson, *Women and Property in Early Modern England* (London: Routledge, 1993), pp. 64–5.

[72]   Brian M. Short, 'The South-East: Kent, Surrey, and Sussex', in Thirsk, *Agrarian History*, p. 274.

equipment featuring prominently in the inventory sample.[73] Pastureland could support a viable farm with less acreage than arable, and therefore male farmers were perhaps more likely to leave wills that divided farms between their offspring, including daughters.[74] In the example of Jane Ireland in Sussex the nature of her inheritance is not known. Perhaps she was the only child; and, other than aristocrats who strongly favoured leaving their wealth and titles to a male heir, many men preferred lineal female kin to inherit rather than collateral male heirs.[75]

By-Employment without a Spouse

Diversity and self-sufficiency of household production were routine in the early modern period. This included combining food production and a wide variety of other activities that produced goods to sell. The combination of arable farming, which did not require year-round activities, with metalworking trades such as nailmaking was common in the West Midlands. By-employment of this kind was a method of offsetting downturns in trade and poor harvests. Jan de Vries has argued that an industrious revolution took place as a spur to industrial production as people chose to work harder and increase their wage-earning capacity to enable them to purchase market-supplied goods and services rather than supplying their own needs.[76] However, Overton et al. map the continuity of by-employment and suggest that in the eighteenth century it continued as an entrepreneurial activity rather than as risk aversion. For example, they suggest that retailers, victuallers and innholders combined their enterprises with brewing and farming.[77] Such a mixture of activities is illustrated by the sale of the contents of the hotel in Darlaston, Staffordshire, the property of Mr Dorsett in 1815. The large quantity of domestic goods befitting a hotel setting was supplemented by brewing equipment, shop fixtures, grocery and drapery goods, two milking cows, wheat, straw, manure and farming implements.[78]

For whatever reason it was practised, many of the inventories in the sample suggest some form of by-employment. During the early modern period, the division

---

[73]   Gloucestershire and Somerset were also important areas for dairy production; and as London's population increased, nearby counties such as Hertfordshire became important producers to supply the needs of the capital.

[74]   Erickson, *Women and Property*, pp. 40–41.

[75]   Erickson, *Women and Property*, p. 63.

[76]   Jan de Vries, 'Between Purchasing Power and the World of Goods: Understanding the Household Economy in Early Modern Europe' in John Brewer and Roy Porter (eds), *Consumption and the World of Goods* (London: Routledge, 1993).

[77]   M. Overton, J. Whittle, D. Dean and A. Hann, *Production and Consumption in English Households, 1600–1750* (London and New York: Routledge, 2004), pp. 65 and 71.

[78]   *Aris's Birmingham Gazette* 9 January 1815, Auction notice for the hotel, Darlaston belonging to Mr Dorsett, marital status unknown.

between work and home was more blurred than subsequently. The home was the site of production of goods to be consumed and used by the family as well as the centre for the consumption of items produced elsewhere. The balance between the two varied according to the area of the country, the status of the households and whether they were based in rural or urban communities. Rural areas were slowest to relinquish by-employment activities since market-produced goods were less likely to be available and agricultural land offered many possibilities for augmenting food production. Small towns, however, could still present a rural aspect well into the nineteenth century and therefore it was acceptable to have a few chickens or even pigs for the household's use. For example, Margaret Rhodes lived in Bridgnorth in a well-equipped and nicely furnished house, but the final item in her inventory was '4 Pigs £5 10s' and in her kitchen was listed a 'bacon cratch' for hanging the meat to cure, a situation that was replicated in many homes over this period.[79]

The most interesting aspect of the production/consumption equation is how it related to gender. Many of these activities were female related, although roles and responsibilities were not rigidly adhered to.[80] Overton et al. stress the importance of the family unit for household production such as spinning, dairying, brewing and preserving foodstuffs to take place. Households where there was a husband and wife were at an advantage over those headed by women.[81] It should be noted that Overton et al.'s reason for this conclusion was because most of the inventories for women that they sampled described 'part households', that is where the woman was a lodger or living with family. Their research also found that status influenced whether these additional household activities could be carried out. Brewing and baking required the most specialist equipment and were therefore mainly reserved for the households of the gentry. Most yeoman farmers participated in dairying, brewing and baking and some of the less affluent husbandmen had involvement in spinning, dairying and preserving foodstuffs.[82]

A few households in the sample had evidence of spinning or other textile production. This was mostly in the form of spinning wheels, but a knitting frame and a worsted winder were also listed. Only one inventory for a man, Thomas Lovatt, listed a spinning wheel and, presumably, his unmarried sister Jane who lived with him used this.[83] Most of these items connected with textile production occurred in rural homes and some were in farmhouses where dairying and brewing were also being carried out. For example Ann Simpson, a widow with a farm, had

---

[79] LRO, Margaret Rhodes, widow, Bridgnorth, 1759.

[80] Amanda Flather, *Gender and Space in Early Modern England* (London: The Royal Historical Society, The Boydell Press, 2007), p. 77.

[81] For their discussion of household and gendered by-employment, see Overton et al., *Production and Consumption*, chapter 4, pp. 65–86. De Vries also suggests that the family unit was essential for by-employment: de Vries, 'Between Purchasing Power', p. 118.

[82] Overton et al., *Production and Consumption*, p. 80.

[83] LRO, Thomas Lovatt, bachelor or widower, Claverley, 1786.

80 gallons of ale listed at the time of her death in 1750.[84] A few of these items were in the homes of poor women for whom textile-related production might have been the main source of income. Sarah Weaver, for example, a widow who died in Shrewsbury in 1691, seems to have had an extensive business as a stocking maker with over £100 in stock in her shop and therefore combined retail and production on premises that overlapped with her living accommodation.[85]

In Shropshire, where cheesemaking was undertaken on a large scale, rooms were often set aside for storing cheeses while they matured. These cheese rooms were chambers on the first floor or a garret and had latticework over the windows, to allow free movement of air, rather than glass windowpanes.[86] Latticework partitions between rooms were sometimes used to increase ventilation. Cheese rooms were often listed as such in inventories and even had the name written over the doorframe, thereby stressing the use of the room so that window tax was not paid. The rooms were fitted with movable shelves for the cheeses to mature. The use of lattice to ventilate the rooms meant that cheese rooms could not conveniently be used as bedchambers. Mary Smith, a farmer in Draycott in the Clay, Staffordshire, had 70 cheeses in her cheese room when she died in 1759.[87] Smith's farming was on a relatively small scale, with six cows. Cheese chambers were also found in the homes of gentlemen farmers such as Edward Baldwyn (d. 1700) and Robert Gage (d. 1723).[88] Both men were substantial arable and pastoral farmers in Worcestershire. They also had apple orchards for cider and, in the case of Robert Gage, hops for brewing.

Many gentlemen farmers who employed labour were engaged in brewing as a profitable sideline as well as for household consumption.[89] Their homes and farming concerns were extensive enough for them to have 'Maids' and 'Manservant' rooms listed in their houses and these servants would to some extent have doubled as outdoor help with their farming concerns. Similarly, Dame Mary Wintour, a gentlewoman living in Huddington in Worcestershire in a 22-room house, engaged in mixed farming with livestock – which must have included sheep to justify a 'Wool Chamber' – and large-scale brewing since among her service rooms £60 of hops were listed in the 'Hop Chamber'. When Wintour died in 1697, she had been a widow for 49 years and had successfully continued to oversee the estates that

---

[84]   LRO, Ann Simpson, widow, Broseley, 1750.

[85]   LRO, Sarah Weaver, widow, Shrewsbury, 1691.

[86]   Cheese rooms were probably only listed in inventories when cheeses were present so it is not possible to say with any accuracy what percentage of homes had them using this source. For pictorial examples see Linda Hall, *Period House Fixtures and Fittings 1300–1900* (Newbury: Countryside Books, 2005), pp. 204–5.

[87]   LRO, Mary Smith, spinster, Draycott in the Clay, 1759.

[88]   WRO, Edward Baldwyn, bachelor or widower, Longdon in Treddington, 1700; Robert Gage, widower, Woodend in Wichenford, 1723.

[89]   Wilson, 'British Brewing', p. 1.

she had inherited.[90] Mary Smith's farm, by contrast, was valued at just £60 9s and her nephew had removed goods during her funeral to make sure of his inheritance.

As many goods and services became more readily available, the need for some degree of self-sufficiency within middling households decreased. The last dated inventory with cheesemaking items was that of Ann Fox in 1814; and the last with a spinning wheel was in 1799 when Sarah Harvey and her mother inherited the farm when her father died.[91] After the mid-eighteenth century, such activities were increasingly performed outside the home by specialist commercial enterprises and only rural households might be expected to continue them. Even so, the presence in many homes of work-related rooms throughout the period reminds us of the important role of housework/household management within the home. Such rooms went far beyond a kitchen and perhaps a scullery that were usual in more recent times, and instead encompassed a wide range of specialist rooms for particular activities and storage. Terms found in the sample included dairy, cheese room/chamber, bakehouse, laundry, wash house, pantry, buttery, larder, brewhouse (used for brewing beer but also for laundering clothes, this being a common term in the Midlands region of England), hop chamber, cellar, small beer cellar and garret. Even small houses had several of these ancillary rooms and larger houses and rural farmhouses had these and many others, such as coach houses, stables and saddle rooms.

As the material culture of the home evolved during the later eighteenth and early nineteenth centuries, so people's relationship with the interior of their home changed. The expectations of what a home should consist of and the role that it should play in their lives also changed. The home was filled with more items of furniture, which were made in increasingly elaborate styles with costly materials. In addition, the use of more textiles such as carpets and elaborate window curtains meant that caring for the home had become more onerous. The scene in *Cranford* where the new carpet has to be protected from the sun and newspaper paths put down when visitors call is a humorous but telling comment on the need to protect the investment in material goods in the home.[92] The women of the household were increasingly expected to stay at home rather than go out to work. However, far from being a leisured alternative the nineteenth-century home required a good manager to take care of the huge investment in its material culture and to oversee the work of servants in caring for it.[93] For the lower middle-class home much of

---

[90]   Malcolm Wanklyn (ed.), *Inventories of Worcestershire Landed Gentry 1537–1786*, Worcestershire Historical Society New Series, vol. 16 (Worcester: Worcestershire Historical Society, 1998), inventory of Dame Mary Wintour, widow, Huddington, 1697.

[91]   SA, 6000/15309 Auctioneer catalogue for Ann Fox, spinster; LRO, Sarah Harvey, spinster, Calton, 1799.

[92]   Elizabeth Gaskell, *Cranford* (Harmondsworth: Penguin, 1976 [1851]), pp. 52–3.

[93]   Barbara Caddick, 'The Material Culture of the Household: Consumption and Domestic Economy in the Eighteenth and Early Nineteenth Centuries', unpublished PhD thesis, University of Wolverhampton (2010).

the work still devolved to the women of the household. In addition, the greater elaboration of entertaining in the home required a hostess rather than simply a housewife who could prepare a basic meal and serve it in a simple manner.[94]

Working from Home: Demarcations and Overlaps

A blurring of the domestic and public world of work was prevalent throughout the period due to income-generating activities and living accommodation being combined at the same premises.[95] Farming was and still is the prime example but throughout our period many people engaged in trades and retailing that combined their business and domestic lives. A common solution was for the trade or shop to be based at the front of the premises, with the family's living accommodation being at the back of the building and on upper floors.[96] For much of the period, the shop part of the house was not purpose-built but merely the front room. James Gee's experience was a common one. He lamented in his diary: 'I can not now call my house my own by reason of people coming in at all hours for something or other ... My parlour, which was a pretty one, is now turned into a shop and, in consequence, when I have a fancy to read ... I hide myself up stairs.'[97]

The idea that there was a division between work and home, or at least that this was a desirable situation, was established by the early nineteenth century. The development of proto-capitalist industrial methods had begun much earlier, certainly by the seventeenth century,[98] and with it came the idea that the wives of wealthier businessmen should not take a practical hand in running the business. Such ideals were not always possible to carry out. While the trend during the eighteenth century and more particularly in the nineteenth century was for the separation of the home from work as the home became solely related to the private sphere,[99] this separation was far from complete. This was particularly so in small-scale enterprises, and especially in small provincial towns and rural areas where work and work-based practice necessarily intruded into the domestic environment.

How much the overlap between home and work particularly affected single people is complex. Many historians have suggested that the possibilities for women to run their own business decreased from the later seventeenth century onwards, although the openings for single women were possibly less constricted

---

[94]   Entertaining in the home by single people is dealt with in Chapter 4.

[95]   Overton et al., *Production and Consumption*, p. 33.

[96]   Nancy Cox, *The Complete Tradesman: A Study of Retailing 1550–1820* (Aldershot: Ashgate, 2000).

[97]   Gee's wife ran the shop when his income fell due to a decline in trade. 'The Life and Times of James Gee of Walsall 1746–1827' Transcription, Walsall Local History Centre, 920GEE.

[98]   Overton et al., *Production and Consumption*, p. 4.

[99]   Davidoff and Hall, *Family Fortunes*.

in comparison to the position of married women.[100] While this is undoubtedly true, some women did continue their late husband's or father's trade, albeit in a smaller way, selling second-hand furniture for example instead of trading as cabinetmakers or upholsterers where more trade skills acquired during a long apprenticeship were required. Alternatively, the business might be continued by a widow with the help of apprentices and bringing her sons or other kin into the trade. The possibilities for running a petty trading enterprise, selling groceries for example, increased during the period and therefore offered women the possibility of working from home without compromising their good name. Many women survived by doing poorly paid work, such as sewing, or took in washing at their homes. Some women also seem to have survived through a *rentier* existence and, in urban areas, through money-lending activities.[101] Single women engaged in trades and enterprises that could be conducted from their homes and which would have encroached on their home lives in a variety of ways. Single men were also affected by the same trend to separate work from the home but one of the points to be considered here was whether work affected domestic arrangements more or less in the homes of single men than women. To what extent were clear divisions maintained? Were men who depended on servants to maintain their homes more likely to allow work-related activities and objects to encroach on their domestic surroundings than single women?

It was assumed throughout the period that it was women's responsibility to organise the home and make sure that it ran smoothly. This responsibility is nicely captured by Mrs Eliza Warren in her advice book of 1868: 'Wives! If you would retain your husband's love with a deeper affection than when in its youthful freshness, cultivate every winning charm of mind and manner – every grace of proper attire, but let your household management be such as shall ensure comfort, pleasure, and recreation.'[102]

When work-related matters overlapped with the domestic arrangements good organisation became even more imperative for the sake of both home life and financial well-being.

The homes of professional men were automatically free of the dirt and disorder of manufacturing work that so many tradespeople lived alongside in the long eighteenth century; however professional people were among the last to separate their homes from their work.[103] As with many of the professional classes, physically (and indeed psychologically) distinct spaces for work and domestic practice were either slow to evolve or were resisted by the nature of the vocation. Physicians and solicitors gave up a room in the house as a consulting room, and schoolmasters and clergymen often had scholars boarding in their homes, as we have seen in the

---

[100]   Froide, *Never Married*.
[101]   See Wright, 'Holding up Half the Sky', pp. 62–3.
[102]   Quoted in Robson, *Marriage or Celibacy*, p. 79.
[103]   Davidoff and Hall, *Family Fortunes*, pp. 364–69.

case of Henry Nussey. His house had one room for his three scholar/boarders; they shared a bed but each had a chamber pot for their own use.[104]

For single men – and, more conjecturally, women – the demands of work were likely to be amplified. In the absence of a normative home and family unit upon which the cult of domesticity could be culturally fastened, many single men found that work habitually intruded into the apparent sanctity of the home. For example, in July 1818 Henry Woollcombe described his daily and Sunday regimen in the following way:

Friday 31st July

Rise at six – prayers. Office till eight – breakfast – library – office at nine till eleven – church committee till one – office till ½ past two – school till four – dinner – read Childe Harold till six – office till eight – tea – Mr Grim came in – walked with him to the Lyceum till 9 – Read & wrote till ten – prayers – bed at ½ past ten

Sunday 2nd Aug

Rise at 7 – prayers – breakfast – read Child Harold – church ½ past ten till past one – walked on Hoe – Read – church three till ½ past four – dinner – Read Monthly Review – much entertained – tea – Jago [partner in Woollcombe's legal business] came in – walked in my garden – read till ten – prayers – bed[105]

Woollcombe was a man who frequently bemoaned the tedium and drudgery of work as mere 'duty'. He admitted, some five years later, to be 'engrossed in [a] business which I do not love [and] neglect a thousand things which I desire to do'.[106] Indeed, his true attachment to literary endeavour and self-improvement is clear in the extract. Yet Woollcombe remained fixated by work, undertaking hours in his formal office and interspersing light reading and his various other administrative and charity responsibilities with legal business conducted in the library at home. Similarly, as a High Anglican, Woollcombe attempted to observe the Sabbath as best he could in recreation and pious reflection, although his reading matter was of a dubiously uplifting and improving quality in this extract. None the less, discussion with his business partner occupied much of his evening, and it was not unknown in periods of financial crisis or pressing commitments for Woollcombe to devote much of the day to work-related activity.

In smaller retail, manufacturing and commercial enterprises many wives continued to be a vital part of the day-to-day running of the concern, as well as the

---

[104]   WSRO, Add. Mss. 2245, Henry and William Peat notebook.

[105]   Plymouth and West Devon Record Office, 710/391–397 Diaries of Henry Woollcombe II, 1796–1828 (hereafter: Woollcombe, *Diary*), 31 July and 2 August 1818.

[106]   Woollcombe, *Diary*, 1 May 1824.

wives of professionals such as solicitors and teachers where the division between work and home was necessarily blurred. This situation affected married couples as well as singletons, but certain aspects particularly applied to them. Single men were more likely to miss the organising skills of a wife and, as in the example of Woollcombe, feel less need to stop work and make distinct their leisure time. Single women were more likely to take on income-generating work that could be accomplished within the domestic domain if they were without a husband's wages to support them. The homemaking of single people was always to some extent compromised since the team of major breadwinner and supporting home manager and additional source of income – namely a husband and wife – was disrupted, despite attempts to ameliorate this through shared households.

The fusion of the domestic and the commercial is readily apparent in the enumeration of goods in an inventory, even if the resulting compromises are implied rather than explicitly stated. In rural areas in particular, divorcing work and home was not a practical arrangement and inventories of rural householders often reveal overlaps between the different aspects of the inhabitants' lives. Farming was the most difficult work to keep separate from the home since it is a way of life rather than a job. Rural homes were also more likely to continue with some degree of self-sufficiency in food production as well as providing household necessities such as candles and soap. Many of the examples looked at in this research were located in rural rather than urban locations. This factor has the tendency to stress old-fashioned habits and ways of life. Examining the relationship between the home and the place of work, the solutions resorted to and the presence of work-related items in the domestic areas of the home all reveal gendered attitudes to homemaking as well as possible compromises due to the makeup or deficiencies of the households of singletons.

All the farmhouses in the sample with a bachelor living alone included work-related items in the domestic areas of the house. These included a saddle, a bridle and butchering equipment. However, despite some overlaps several farmhouses did establish a clearly defined parlour space without a bed or work equipment present when the inventory was made. An attempt to demarcate work and the domestic space was achieved in the farmhouse of Thomas Thomas, whose home was looked after by a woman whom he described in his will as 'Ann Beddard who now lives with me'.[107] Ann was probably responsible for the best parlour only containing an oak table, corner cupboard, five ash chairs, a japanned tea board and six cups and saucers – and therefore all that was necessary for a parlour and nothing else. For much of the eighteenth century such furnishings and the lack of work- or sleep-related articles defined the nature of a parlour and demonstrated that it was not a multifunctional room. However, by 1796, when Thomas died, such a pared-down parlour would have seemed rather spartan to fashion-conscious middling sort people, especially those living in towns. The parlour displaying the most awareness of fashionable consumption amongst the rural farming examples

---

[107]   LRO, Thomas Thomas, bachelor or widower, Bobbington, 1796.

was in the home of the much wealthier Ann Fox (d. 1814).[108] Along with a table and chairs was a mahogany card table, a pier glass, tea and coffee china and even a floor carpet. This was a substantial home with appropriate uses of the rooms in the house, but it stopped short of any extravagance. It was therefore suited to the rural township of Cleobury Mortimer as well as to Ann's life as a religious spinster.

Work-related items were unlikely to be in evidence at the home of butchers since the trade entailed little investment in tools, and animals were not kept for long on the premises but rather in a field near the outskirts of town, as in the example of Francis Law, a widower who died in 1761.[109] No tools connected with his trade were mentioned in the contents of his home. However, at the end of the inventory were listed items at a farm at Severn Hall outside the town of Bridgnorth where Law resided. At the farm were cows, sheep and a couple of horses, along with hay and some farm tools. A town butcher, such as Law, operated differently from a farmer who also slaughtered some of his animals at the farm. Farm outbuildings often included a 'slaughter house', although it was usually situated some distance from the farmhouse. James Mullock's farm in Shropshire was an instance of this arrangement;[110] and tools connected with this work at a farm would have been closer to home than in the case of Francis Law and therefore more likely to spill over into the domestic rooms such as the farmhouse kitchen, which often doubled as a functional part of the farm. However, Mullock allowed these items to penetrate further into his domestic terrain and stored several butcher's pads in the house, one in a bedchamber and the other in the lobby on the upper floor. The nature of such items made them highly inappropriate for the domestic situation.

The intrusion of working life into the domestic space of the home threatened its domesticity both in the way that the home functioned and in the way that it was perceived by the inhabitants of the house and by visitors. One of William Herschel's music pupils described Herschel's lodgings in Bath, where he gave lessons, as having both music- and astronomy-related items littering the rooms in some profusion. The rooms were 'heaped up with globes, maps, telescopes, reflectors etc under which his piano hid, and the violoncello, like a discarded favourite, skulked away in a corner'.[111] As the music gave way completely to astronomy, Herschel applied himself to producing telescopes that took over ever more space. His sister Caroline, who had come from Germany to keep house for him, was dismayed by the way that their home was being transformed: 'To my sorrow I saw almost every room turned into a workshop. A Cabinet-maker making a Tube and stands of all descriptions in a handsome drawing room! Alex [another brother] putting up a huge turning machine … in a bedroom.' The telescopes had metal mirrors that were first made in moulds of horse dung and were then hand ground to produce

---

[108]   SA, 6000/15309 Auctioneer catalogue for Ann Fox, spinster.

[109]   LRO, Francis Law, widower, Bridgnorth, 1761.

[110]   SA, 6000/12167 Auctioneer's notebook, James Mullock, bachelor, Whitchurch, 1804.

[111]   Holmes, *Age of Wonder*, p. 89.

Caroline Herschel.

Figure 3.2   Caroline and William Herschel are depicted in an attractive parlour in this c.1890 lithograph. In reality, their workshop was less domestic and their gender roles were less well defined.
Source: Wellcome Trust, London.

the correct surface. This was precise and exhausting work. The polishing of the mirrors had to be done continuously since even a slight break meant that the metal hardened and the mirrors would then mist over and be useless. William, assisted by his sister Caroline, did this work in an unheated, stone-floored basement in rough clothes amidst the smell of chemicals and horse dung.[112] While this was the reality of their ground-breaking work, described by Caroline in her journals, the pair were celebrated 100 years later in a coloured lithograph that depicted them in a sedate parlour, nicely dressed, and while William works Caroline offers him a cup of tea (see Figure 3.2).[113]

This sanitised view of the late eighteenth-century reality of the Herschels' home was required for nineteenth-century middle-class consumption when not only had domesticity been given a bourgeois gloss of perfection but also gender roles were more clearly defined, in part to underpin the production of masculinity.[114] To nineteenth-century eyes, Caroline's apparent failure to maintain an appropriate home setting threatened her femininity and, crucially, her active participation in physical work threatened William's masculinity. The home that needed to accommodate their work had all the hallmarks of a workshop, but for the late Victorians this celebrated brother and sister had to be shown with their domesticity intact.

Early modern manufacturing and retailing was usually situated alongside housing. The move towards having specific areas of towns for industrial and commercial enterprises, although beginning earlier, was still evolving in the nineteenth century. Despite the growing desire for separating the home from the dirt and disorder of the work environment a great many people in the long eighteenth century continued to live and work on the same premises. Working long hours, the employment of all family members and the need to keep commercial interests secure from burglars and casual housebreakers all made this a convenient arrangement. Many of the small-scale businesses run by women would have made them more likely to live 'over the shop' and perhaps single men were less likely to move to the smarter areas of town or the newly emerging suburbs if they had no wife to aid the establishment of a genteel home. This may have been the case with Jonah Bissell, a successful metal wares manufacturer in Birmingham. His substantial business was worth £965 when it was auctioned over three days in1842.[115] However, he continued to live alongside his business in the centre of Birmingham and used a sitting room that was next to his kitchen and storeroom and looked out over a yard at the rear of the property. This allowed

---

[112]   Holmes, *Age of Wonder*, pp. 86.

[113]   Wellcome Library, London, V0002731. Coloured lithograph of Sir William Herschel and Caroline Herschel, c.1890.

[114]   John Tosh, *A Man's Place: Masculinity and the Middle-Class Home in Victorian England* (New Haven and London: Yale University Press, 1999).

[115]   Bissell also had funds amounting to £950 at his death. BCA Family Papers: will and auction pamphlet for J. Bissell, MS319/1–14.

him to keep an eye on the workers in his extensive premises, which included a large warehouse with 141 lots listed by the auctioneer, an inner warehouse, lower warehouse and yards.

Although men were more likely to be affected by the problems associated with 'messy' trades, in the West Midlands region of England many women worked in branches of the metalworking industry. Although no documents came to light relating to the nail- and chainmaking activities associated with the Black Country a number of women, all widows, were engaged in arduous and dirty trades. One of the earliest inventories consulted was for the widow Wheggrom in Broadwater, Sussex, who seems to have had a saddlery workshop making or selling such items as 'britch bands', 'belligirts', 'bellituggs', halters and horse locks.[116]

Katherine Daintry was operating as an ironmonger with a shop or workshop in Newcastle under Lyme, Staffordshire, at the time of her death in 1694.[117] The shop contents of iron, steel, iron wares, rosin, clogs and patens, a long list of worked iron goods, locks and kitchen equipment, tools, tin ware and brass gives an indication of the diversity of her stock. Part of her premises was another shop that she leased to a Mrs Allen, perhaps thereby removing further living accommodation. Daintry's household goods were basic and although she was able to keep her kitchen, houseplace and bedchambers as separate spaces, there was no parlour and the extent of her comfortable seating was two chairs with woven seats. None the less such a bare and comfortless interior was not unusual for the period. More surprising is the lack of a parlour 100 years later in the home of Jane Browne. She was continuing her husband's trade as a plumber and glazier in the High Street of Bridgnorth when she died in 1797.[118] Her husband had been a churchwarden and the couple had five surviving children, one of whom, Walter, continued with the business after Jane's death. This was a prominent business and the premises were extensive, with a glazing [work]shop, a plumbing [work]shop, and the 'Front Shop' with a shop window and scales that seem to be have been for retail. Although the rooms were numbered rather than named, there were seven with beds, followed by a kitchen or houseplace. A separate parlour is not indicated by the listing and was perhaps sacrificed to make way for bedrooms and workspace.

A rather small business concern in filemaking was being continued by Sarah Shakle in Birmingham.[119] Her workshop had an anvil, bellows, tongs and a list of wares for sale or that had been made to order, including 'stock at Bristol'. The inventory listed a kitchen, buttery, shop, chamber over the kitchen, chamber over the shop and finally 'wares', suggesting that they were stored in the house. She was perhaps doing out-work for a larger dealer since William Kettle of Birmingham,

---

[116] WSRO, probate inventory for Widdow Wheggrom, Broadwater, 1670. Our thanks to Nancy Cox for deciphering this list.
[117] LRO, Katherine Daintry, widow, Newcastle under Lyme, 1694.
[118] LRO, Jane Browne, widow, Bridgnorth, 1797.
[119] LRO, Sarah Shakle, widow, Birmingham, 1719.

with a substantial ironmongery business, and Thomas Ainge, a filemaker, were her appraisers.

It was not only the trades with obvious dirt and disorder that could threaten the domestic arrangements of a home. Many women took in washing as a business. Washing clothes and linen in large quantities was time consuming and involved many different processes, from pre-wash soaking to ironing the delicate frills on the neckline of a dress. In addition to the hard work involved, a high level of organisation was required to maintain order when every day was washday. Miss E. Arnsworth did laundry work for other people for a living, and had an inventory made of her home 'for administration' purposes by the Peat firm of cabinetmakers in Chichester in 1844.[120] Her home contents were valued at just £48 15s 6d, which was low for the period. Her home had a modest number of rooms but also contained a number of service areas and outbuildings that helped her to organise her work and keep her home life separate. The list began with the wash house, followed by the scullery and then the ironing room:

Washhouse [in the Midlands this would have been called the brewhouse]
A patent mangle
Deal table & 2 drawers
2 blinds & 4 rope mats
1 Copper & brickwork
4 wash tubs & stools
3 pails & water shoot
1 Cloth horse & 1 hand dish
fire shovel & soap board
2 stools towel roler & steps
Scullery
Cinder sieve & shelves
1 Cloth waggan & barrel
Ironing Room
1 drying stove & tubs
2 [illegible]
3 saucepans 1 pot
5 tin candle sticks & snuffer
[No kitchen was listed so it seems that the 'ironing room' was also the kitchen.]

Then enumerated were the contents of two living rooms, a back parlour used as a dining parlour and a front parlour, with two bedchambers above them. These four main rooms of the house only had the items to be expected for the type of rooms

[120] WSRO, Add. Mss. 2245, Henry and William Peat notebook. Some of the inventories in this notebook can be compared to houses still in existence and this reveals that the Peats were systematic in recording rooms and their contents.

and the usual uses. The inventory ended with clothing and a list of bed and table linen, followed finally by the laundry and garden:

Laundry
1 Doz. Irons
4 iron boards
fender & fire irons
3 cloth horses
4 Cloth baskets
3 coarse pans
Goffering & crimping machine
Coals box & coals

Garden
9 Cloths post
Cloths line & pegs

The careful arrangements in her home and the respectable nature of her household perhaps indicates that she also lived in the central streets of Chichester, where a mixture of trade, retail and domestic dwellings were found. Many of the middle-class customers of the well-established firm of cabinetmakers who made the inventory were located in this area.[121] Similarly, in Shrewsbury in the 1851 census, alongside retired solicitors and clergymen were listed two laundresses as well as a charwoman, all widows.[122] Both towns continued to adhere to the eighteenth-century style of having central areas that had a mixture of wealthy and professional people with some plebeian households alongside which were often supplying services to them. Despite the low value, modest furnishings and humble nature of her home Miss Arnsworth's multitude of goods connected with her work were well organised and in the correct place. A simple listing of items does not capture the house in daily use, with the heat, smells and back-breaking work that she engaged in. However, when her work was done she could sit in her parlour with tables, chairs, carpet on the floor, framed pictures on the wall, ornaments on the mantel, and wine glasses, tea cups and saucers with refreshments. The areas of her life were distinct and 'correctly' ordered, even if they coexisted uneasily in very close proximity.

Most of the single women who lived and worked alongside their occupation, whose inventories were examined, kept a small shop or worked with textiles. For example, the widow Jane Carter (d. 1678) kept a mercer's shop in Derby. The spinster Mary Higgins (d. 1701) was a mercer and haberdasher in Chesterfield. Also in Derbyshire was the home of Margery Johns. She ran a mercer and

---

121   WSRO, Add. Mss. 2239, Samuel Peat day book.
122   1851 census, St Chad's parish, Shrewsbury.

grocer's shop in Matlock until her death in 1683.[123] The shop goods included basic and more expensive items such as calico, Holland, buckram, fustian, vermillion and flaxen [cloth]. Trimmings and made-up items included trousers, children's frocks, caps, gloves, thread, purses, tapes, buttons, laces, points and inkles, bindings and ribbons. A curious mixture is suggested by other items such as wormseed, horse spice, books, caddis, candles, locks, brown sugar, comfits, seeds, Jamaica pepper, nails, aniseed, ginger, loaf sugar, strong waters, tobacco, raisins, currants, oils, hops, sand, copperas, vinegar, soap and starch. All these were listed in the 'Shop' and the house appears to have been purely domestic. It consisted of a houseplace that combined kitchen and living space, and several chambers above. Johns left half of her goods, both household and shop, to Elizabeth Burlowe, her servant. Johns was following a perceptible trend in the wills of single women to provide for other unmarried female friends and relatives. Her bequest would have given Burlowe a chance of independence by continuing a thriving business in Matlock with a great many customers.[124]

The widows Mary Parker (d. 1734) and Ann Roberts (d. 1746) perhaps sold a similar mixture of goods in their shops that both combined textiles and groceries in Alfreton and Madeley.[125] The spinster Ann Heeley and the widow Mary Pritchard both kept a grocery shop in Birmingham when their homes were inventoried in 1764; and Sarah Maddock (d. 1838) had a grocery shop in Stoke-on-Trent.[126] These trades were more readily included in the domestic environment than working with animals and the messier trades such as metalworking. Some other businesses that had traditionally allowed a large degree of overlap were cabinetmakers and upholsterers, who frequently used their homes as showrooms for their wares.[127] For instance Sarah Tipping, the widow of a Birmingham upholsterer, mixed work and domestic items in her home, and although the rooms were not named, she clearly continued her husband's business after his death.[128]

The only inventory consulted of a man working in a trade connected to textiles was the feltmaker George Crudgington (d. 1689) of Bridgnorth.[129]

[123] LRO, Jane Carter, widow, Derby, 1678; Mary Higgins, spinster, Chesterfield, 1701; Margery Johns, widow, Matlock, 1683.

[124] For women leaving bequests to other women, see Maxine Berg, 'Women's Consumption and the Industrial Classes of Eighteenth-Century England', *Journal of Social History*, 30/2 (1996), pp. 415–34, pp. 422–3 and 425; Froide, *Never Married*, pp. 46–9.

[125] LRO, Mary Parker, widow, Alfreton, 1734; Ann Roberts, widow, Madeley, 1746.

[126] LRO, Thomas Heeley, bachelor or widower, Birmingham, 1764; Mary Pritchard, widow, Birmingham, 1764; Sarah Maddock, widow, Stoke-on-Trent, 1838.

[127] For a description of the overlap between home and work in the premises of upholsterer James Eykyn, see Margaret Ponsonby, 'Towards an Interpretation of Textiles in the Provincial Domestic Interior: Three Homes in the West Midlands, 1780–1848', *Textile History*, 38/2 (2007), pp. 165–78.

[128] LRO, Isaac Tipping, Birmingham, 1767; Sarah Tipping, widow, Birmingham, 1768.

[129] LRO, probate inventory of George Crudgington, bachelor, Bridgnorth, 1689.

He had a fairly extensive property over three floors with several outbuildings that contained his trade tools. The main rooms of the house, including three bedchambers, only had domestic items listed that corresponded with the early date of the inventory. There was even a 'Hall House' with a 'Joynd press 4 Joynd Stools 3 Chayers' that appears to have acted as a parlour. However, two attic rooms were multifunctional. These were named as the 'Wool Cockloft' and 'the other Cockloft' and both had several beds together with a 'pack of Wooll' in one and 'Wooll both Washt & Carded' in the other. The shop was integrated with the house, with a bedchamber listed above it, which contained several presses and '4 douzen of Hatts with Bands and Lineings'. Crudgington may well have employed workers in his business and perhaps he even housed them in the attics along with the stored materials of his trade.

Encroachment could be quite subtle, as in the case of Sarah Maddock who ran a grocery shop with her unmarried son.[130] When she died in 1838 an inventory made of her property listed the 'shop bell' in the parlour so that she was always 'on call' to her business. The proximity of retailing to the domestic part of the house was common in the early modern period, the parlour providing a place to sit between customers and also a comfortable and warm place in which to attend to important customers.[131] However, encroachment could take a far more dramatic form – as described by Catherine Hutton. In 1779, she visited Sutton-in-Ashfield and wrote to her brother that she had visited the home of a Mr Unwin. It was a rather grand stone house but she was amazed and disappointed to find that all 'the best rooms are occupied as warehouses and counting houses for the cotton manufactory'.[132] Unwin was sacrificing all his prospects of living a genteel life and engaging in polite sociability to his business concerns.

In already small dwellings, giving over a room or two to business concerns influenced how the home was organised and functioned on a daily basis. Ann and Thomas Heeley were brother and sister who lived together in Birmingham in the mid-eighteenth century. Thomas died in 1764 and a probate inventory recorded the house contents.[133] He was a button- and toymaker and she kept a shop. Both enterprises were run alongside their living accommodation and this affected how they organised their home. Due to their business concerns encroaching on their living space they had just a kitchen and two other domestic rooms, designated bedchambers. No parlour was listed and no doubt the grocery shop was at the front of the building and took up the space that would otherwise have been available to provide a parlour. The kitchen had a table and chairs, but so too did each bedchamber – suggesting that the rooms doubled as private sitting rooms. A brother and sister sharing a home

---

[130]   LRO, Sarah Maddock, widow, Stoke-on-Trent, 1838.

[131]   Claire Walsh, 'Shop Design and the Display of Goods in Eighteenth-Century London', *Journal of Design History*, 8/3 (1995), pp. 157–76; Cox, *The Complete Tradesman*.

[132]   Catherine Hutton Beale, *Reminiscences of a Gentlewoman of the Last Century: Letters of Catherine Hutton* (Birmingham: Cornish Brothers, 1891), p. 22.

[133]   LRO, Thomas Heeley, bachelor or widower, Birmingham, 1764.

meant that two bedchambers were required, whereas a husband and wife would have shared a room, allowing an upstairs room to be made into a parlour. This was a common arrangement in townhouses built on narrow plots.

The furnishings of the Heeleys' bedchambers hint at different ways of using the rooms, and perhaps suggest gendered use. The Back Chamber contained a bureau and bookcase, and the clothes were kept in a chest. The Front Chamber had a swing glass and also a large looking glass and two pictures; here the clothes were kept in a chest of drawers. It is tempting to assume that Thomas's room was the Back Chamber and that Ann had the Front Chamber, but is this imposing an interpretation on the evidence: that Thomas did the bookkeeping and that Ann took more care of her appearance? Beverly Lemire has argued that women often demonstrated their numeracy by keeping accounts in this period.[134]

The small business concerns examined here were neither large nor advanced enough to have employed dedicated showrooms such as Boulton and Watt had at Soho, or as Wedgwood provided at Etruria or the better-known venue in London. Increasingly for larger concerns in the nineteenth century showrooms were used to display goods and the separation between shop and home became more distinct.[135] Skilled artisans, however, even when employing a number of workers, continued to live and work in buildings in close proximity. Although in 1798 James Watt junior, while still a young man, lived for just over a year close to his business concerns, he was soon able to move to more salubrious surroundings. For wealthier entrepreneurs like Matthew Boulton and James Watt senior the centres of towns were too dirty and congested for their home life. Their sons, in line with other successful businessmen on a similar level, were even able to establish themselves as gentlemen with country estates.[136] The tendency for middle-class retailers and tradesmen to remove themselves from the centre of Birmingham increased in the nineteenth century with the growth of Edgbaston, the town's first suburb, which catered only for better-off residents.[137]

Storage: A Place for Everything and Everything in Its Place

The methods employed for the storage of goods were an indication of whether a home was well organised or not. As the home became a more refined space, furnishings became increasingly sophisticated and items of specialised storage

[134] Beverly Lemire, *The Business of Everyday Life: Gender, Practice and Social Politics in England, c.1600–1900* (Manchester: Manchester University Press, 2005).

[135] Clive Edwards, *Turning Houses into Homes: A History of Retailing and Consumption of Domestic Furnishings* (Aldershot: Ashgate, 2005), p. 46.

[136] James Watt junior lived at Aston Hall and Matthew Robinson Boulton purchased a country house in Oxfordshire. Mason, *Hardware Man's Daughter*, pp. 151 and 159.

[137] Davidoff and Hall, *Family Fortunes*, p. 368.

furniture were utilised. The basic premise continued, however, that storage was a good indicator of organisation within the home.

The storage of objects in the home was closely linked to housekeeping methods that were taught to young girls by their mothers or to servants by the mistress or housekeeper. The link with women's work is made clear in the advice book *The Accomplish'd Housewife: or the Gentlewoman's Companion*, with a section on economy in the house being titled 'The Science of the Female Sex'.[138] Organisational skills were needed but also people needed to embrace the idea that it was important to keep order in the home. Such organisation included both short- and long-term storage. In the short term, storage kept living areas free from objects that might get in the way; but at the same time it enabled objects to be to hand for servants or the owner to access them. In the long term, storage kept objects safe and in good condition. Storage could also help to keep work and home life separate. Ceramics and linen might be divided into best and everyday or family and servant use, and stored accordingly. Thus, earthenware would be listed in a kitchen, whereas the china would be kept in a pantry or with the parlour or drawing room items stored in a piece of furniture such as a sideboard or, by the nineteenth century, a chiffonier or in a built-in cupboard in the room. In the case of linen, how it was divided seems to suggest things that were in everyday use and those that were in more long-term storage, as some linen was often listed in a bedchamber whilst a longer list often appeared in a garret. Such organisation was an indication of good 'housewifery' since careful storage preserved items from breakage, damage by moths and spoliation by insects and vermin.

Underlying these practices though are cultural attitudes on how best to run a household. As Mary Douglas has shown, our attitudes to dirt and purity are culturally acquired.[139] While some household skills are based on practical common sense, others stem from habits and customs learnt in childhood and anything that deviates from them would be viewed as negligent or worse, immoral. *The Family Economist* makes this point when it defined the meaning of 'home' and declared at the heart of it was 'order and cleanliness; they generally go together. A disorderly house is a distressing sight, but a dirty house is worse … On daily cleaning and daily ordering mainly depends our home comfort and enjoyment.'[140] Dirt and disorder were banished through cleaning and laundering. For example, table and bed linen needed to be washed completely clean of all marks and stains, despite the huge labour involved before washing machines were available. Long after this period, housewives took pride in their laundry skills, as demonstrated by Judy

---

[138] Anon, *The Accomplish'd Housewife: or the Gentlewoman's Companion* (London, 1745), p. 10.

[139] Mary Douglas, *Purity and Danger: An Analysis of Concepts of Pollution and Taboo* (Harmondsworth: Penguin, 1996). See also Emily Cockayne, *Hubbub: Filth, Noise and Stench in England* (New Haven and London: Yale University Press, 2007), pp. 181–205.

[140] Anon, *The Family Economist: A Penny Monthly Magazine for the Industrious Classes* (London: Groombridge & Sons, vol. 6, 1853), p. 183.

Attfield in her study of housewives in the 1950s, where she concludes that their practices were a reversal of economist/sociologist Thorstein Veblen's notion of conspicuous consumption. Attfield refers to the display of washing on a line as 'conspicuous labour'.[141] An example of this in the period would be the treatment of table linen, which was on display in the public room of the house and therefore it was thought necessary to iron it smooth and then store it in a linen press so that when on the table the definite creases produced by pressing were clearly visible. While this practice is shown in contemporary paintings, it is not discernable from lists in an inventory; but the general attitudes that prevail in a household towards household management, whether they followed the prevailing cultural norms or deviated from them, can sometimes be detected through the implied storage and organisation of goods in the home.

People with better incomes tended to live in houses with designated storage rooms, with sufficient servants to take care of the house. For example, in 1785 an inventory was made of the home of James Wakeman Newport, although the reason for making it is not known since he lived for another 40 years and took over as the first colonel of the Worcestershire militia in 1795.[142] The 21-room house of this bachelor had an extensive service area that included a housekeeper's room, with the linen, china, glass and earthenware stored; a hall for the servants to eat in; a back kitchen and a best kitchen plus a brewhouse and cellars.[143] To some extent the use of specialist storage furniture was also linked to wealth, but not always. Some people were less willing to change their habits and continued to use old styles of furniture despite newer, more fashionable items being available. Therefore, the use of coffers, chests and trunks continued throughout the period despite chests of drawers and wardrobes being available. Such decisions were not only due to wealth but also to lifecycle. Probate inventories were made when people died and therefore predominantly reflect homes many years after they were first set up, and older people were more likely to continue with the methods they were used to. Gender differences with regard to the organisation of the home are more difficult to pin down, and no doubt individual character traits would also have played a part.

Little is said on the subject of storage in any household management books. Even in the comprehensive *The Country Housewife's Family Companion*, William Ellis does not deal with it explicitly despite covering such diverse subjects as food preparation, brewing, managing a dairy, looking after pigs and chickens and

---

[141]   Judy Attfield, 'Inside Pram Town: A Case Study of Harlow House Interiors, 1951–1961', in Judy Attfield and Pat Kirkham (eds), *A View from the Interior: Women and Design* (London: The Women's Press, 1995).

[142]   W. Page and J.W. Willis Bund, *Victoria County History: Worcestershire, vol. 2* (London: James Street, 1906), p. 240.

[143]   Wanklyn, *Inventories*, inventory of James Wakeman Newport, bachelor, Hanley William, 1785.

dealing with a variety of ailments using country-style medicines.[144] The nearest he comes to good organisation in the home is to deal with the correct storage of grain and flour to prevent it going mouldy or being infested with vermin. Similarly, he devoted many pages to the practical aspects of the preservation of seasonal fruit and vegetables.

William Ellis's audience were country people eking out a living on the land. Where servants were employed they were more likely to have been female servants in husbandry and undertaking a range of productive work rather than purely domestic servants.[145] By the early nineteenth century, advice books aimed at wealthier and more genteel middle-class readers, particularly those residing in London and larger towns, implied the importance of a well-maintained interior, although the practical advice was still limited. In *The Footman's Directory and Butler's Remembrancer,*[146] published in 1823, numerous tasks which were usually the province of the male servants, if they were employed, were described in detail. These included cleaning boots and shoes, silver plate, trimming and cleaning lamps, waiting on table and many more. Many of these tasks were dirty jobs that would have made a mess; where and how the work was carried out was crucial to a well-run household. Adequate and appropriate service areas of a house were essential. Even by the mid-nineteenth century in *Beeton's Book of Household Management* the idea of storage was not dealt with explicitly. Mrs Beeton divided work in the home into different areas and the appropriate servant or the mistress of the house was responsible for each area. For example, the housekeeper dealt with linen, including its suitable storage; the valet's day began by seeing 'that his master's dressing room is in order'; and the lady's maid had the duty of putting away the clothes of her mistress.[147] Throughout her household advice Mrs Beeton repeatedly used the words 'in order', thus stressing their importance; but she did not explicitly explain what was required.

Slightly more informative are contemporary books on furnishing the home in the early to mid-nineteenth century. For example, J.C. Loudon recognised the difficulty of storing china, glass and other utensils used in serving food and drink so that objects were accessible without intruding on living arrangements. His advice was to have a large closet or storeroom 'communicating with the breakfast room but so placed that it may be accessible without entering that room'.[148] This arrangement

---

[144]   William Ellis, *The Country Housewife's Family Companion* (London: James Hodges, 1750). Ellis was reprinted many times. See also the reprint with an introduction by Malcolm Thick (Totnes: Prospect Books, 2000).

[145]   Bridget Hill, *Women, Work and Sexual Politics in Eighteenth-Century England* (London: University College London, 1994), p. 70. See also Steedman, 'Servant's Labour'.

[146]   Anon, *The Footman's Directory and Butler's Remembrancer* (London: Hatchard and Son, 1823).

[147]   Isabella Beeton, *Beeton's Book of Household Management* (London: Chancellor Press, 1997; facsimile of 1859–61 edition), pp. 977–9.

[148]   J.C. Loudon, *The Suburban Gardener and Villa Companion* (London: Longman, Orme, Brown, Green and Longmans, 1838), p. 85.

would have allowed the mistress and servants access without interrupting people in the breakfast room – the daytime sitting room of the house. Such considerations show how the refinements of the nineteenth-century home had progressed, with detailed advice being given that had not been thought necessary a century earlier.

Anne Boulton's house in the 1820s had a service area containing the housekeeper's room, the butler's pantry, kitchen, larder and pantry, with an outside yard from which access could be gained to the brewhouse, laundry and stables.[149] This arrangement allowed the house to function in the prescribed way. Servants were able to access everything that they required to serve food and drink, to clean the silver and to put things away after use. This could all be done without inconveniencing the householder, just as Loudon stipulated and as *The Footman's Directory* described, and without making a mess or getting in the way of the important work in the kitchen. This level of refinement went with genteel living. Boulton ensured the smooth running of her household by keeping a careful eye on her servants, prescribing their duties and specifying what was acceptable behaviour.[150] Although she was a wealthy woman, Boulton had many years' experience of managing a household. Thornhill, during her occupation, had the necessary rooms and servants for it to run efficiently and to offer a genteel lifestyle but, as mistress, Boulton also needed to maintain control.

The tendency in large houses from the 1840s onwards was to increase the number of service rooms to cover every aspect of household management, the most ludicrous being a separate small room for ironing the newspapers.[151] This tendency did have the advantage of separating dirty work from areas needed to be clean, especially in food preparation. Earlier arrangements were undoubtedly lacking in hygiene: as an observer of houses in the late eighteenth century, François de la Rochefoucauld, observed, in reception rooms 'cleanliness … pervades everything'; but the kitchens were quite different and he was appalled by the dirtiness.[152]

Even small houses usually had garrets and these were an ideal place to store goods. Many inventories summarise the contents of garrets simply as 'lumber' and give a value for the total, suggesting a miscellaneous assortment of goods. In her garret, Jane Irland was storing numerous items that were of value but surplus to requirements when she died in 1725: 22 pewter dishes, eight pewter plates, 32 pairs of sheets, three dozen napkins and 10 tablecloths variously packed away in chests, a box and a trunk. The value of these items came to the quite considerable sum of

[149]   Drawings of the floor plans at Thornhill are reproduced in Mason, *Hardware Man's Daughter*, pp. 162–3.

[150]   BCA, MBP MS3782/14/83, miscellaneous papers.

[151]   Robert Kerr, *The Gentleman's House or How to Plan English Residences from the Parsonage to the Palace* (London: Murray, 1864).

[152]   David N. Durant, *Living in the Past: An Insider's Social History of Historic Houses* (London: Aurum Press, 1988), p. 33.

£40.[153] Susannah Smith stored old kitchen and dairy implements in her 'Servants Garrets' along with several beds.[154] Many servants must have slept alongside all manner of goods. In a similar way, Smith had an odd mixture of items in a small bedchamber. Along with an old bedstead were various storage chests and boxes, a pillion saddle and its cloth, and trenchers and a knitting frame. Without seeing the items, it is impossible to know whether these goods were discarded in an unused room or packed away carefully for future use or safekeeping. Certainly the storage arrangements contrast with several other chambers that had good-quality furniture, such as bedsteads with moreen hangings, feather mattresses, walnut chests, a pier glass and window curtains, and a similarly well-furnished parlour with only appropriate items present, which suggests some method at work in the use of rooms.

The loss of a spouse might result in changes to household arrangements and these are discernable in the rare instances of two inventories surviving, the first made when the husband died and the second some years later when his wife died. John Marrian a farmer in Bobbington, Staffordshire, died and an inventory was made of his home and farm, dated 16 April 1761. The inventory listed a parlour, kitchen, hall, pantry, best cellar, small beer cellar, dairy, a room over the parlour, a chamber over the kitchen and over the hall, large garret, little garret, brewhouse and, outdoors, grain and livestock. His widow, Susanna, died nine years later and an inventory was made dated 17 June 1770.[155] This inventory covered the same rooms, although in a different order; but it also included a chamber over the pantry and a cheese chamber between the two garret rooms. Presumably there was nothing in this latter room in April so it was not listed, whereas in June there was '14 score pound of cheese at 3d pr lb' – total value £3 10s. On the whole, the contents of the house had not greatly changed during the nine years that separated them. There were however a few subtle alterations. Some small additions had been made and these were listed in 1770. In the kitchen these consisted of window curtains, a Dutch oven and a saucepan; an additional six delft plates had been added to the original six, and some 'tea cups saucers &c 3s'.[156] Missing from the kitchen were 20 trenchers. These old-fashioned wooden plates had presumably been replaced by the small quantity of ceramic wares now listed. A small but perhaps significant addition was a glass case for books in the chamber over the pantry, a room that did not figure at all in John's inventory. The other noticeable addition to Mrs Marrian's inventory was linen ware. In John's inventory, the linen was listed in the chamber over the hall as 'linen of all sorts 12s'. In Susanna's inventory, linen was listed in the chamber over the kitchen and was a

---

[153] WSRO, Jane Irland, spinster, Bury, 1725.

[154] WSRO, Susannah Smith, widow, Old Fishbourne, 1765.

[155] LRO, John Marrian, Bobbington, 1761; Susanna Marrian, widow, Bobbington, 1770.

[156] See also Amanda Vickery, *Behind Closed Doors: At Home in Georgian England* (New Haven and London: Yale University Press, 2009), p. 229.

much longer list, itemised and valued at considerably more than 12s. The linen listed in Susanna Marrian's inventory 1770 was:

3 pair of fine sheets	£1	15s	
15 pair of coarse ditto	£3	15s	
9 old napkins		4s	6d
2 huckaback table cloths		3s	
2 hurden ditto		3s	
1 huckaback table cloth		1s	
new cloth	£2	15s	
a stamp sheet		5s	
a new bed tick and bolster		12s	
5 fine table cloths	£1	3s	
2 pillow bears		1s	

It seems likely that these items did not appear in John Marrian's inventory because they were deemed Mrs Marrian's property, a not unusual situation.[157] These additions and omissions were not huge changes but do correspond with what is to be expected of gender preferences in household goods. The wife taking more interest in window curtains, linen and ceramics can all be seen as 'female' consumption practices. When considering storage and the organisation of the household, the two lists reveal that the same items of storage furniture were employed and in the same locations; yet the use of rooms and storage of items, particularly in the bedchambers, had changed. In John's inventory the chamber with the best-quality bed was the chamber over the hall and it was this room that ended with John's clothes and 'watch and money in pocket', indicating that this was the room in which he slept. Susanna's list showed a change of use since three beds were listed in this chamber in 1770. No other bedchamber was obviously being used as a 'best' bedroom. In 1761, the chamber over the kitchen was used as a bedroom with three bedsteads in it, but nine years later this room was used for storage along with one bed. As well as the linen listed here there was also a store of flax, malt, undressed feathers, a pad of cloth, yarn of different sorts and '5 score and 15 pound of bacon at 5d pr pound'. Some of these differences may have been caused by the inventories being made at different times of the year, as in the case of the cheese chamber that was not listed in the earlier inventory. However, there also seem to be other reasons for organising the house differently, resulting in a former bedchamber becoming predominantly a storeroom and a previously empty room, the chamber over the pantry, later listed with bedroom items. The bedchambers in this house were organised differently, were used differently and would have looked quite different to the inhabitants of the house. While it is impossible to decide whether Mrs Marrian was better organised after her husband's death, it is clear that she made some changes that affected storage and sleeping arrangements.

---

[157] Erickson, *Women and Property*, pp. 144–7.

Perhaps Susanna had now moved into a small room, the bedchamber over the pantry, as this was now all she required as a widow.

Specialist Storage Furniture

At the outset of the period boxes, trunks, chests and the like sufficed for essential needs, but more substantial and fashioned items of storage furniture came into wider currency as the seventeenth century progressed. Alongside the chest of drawers – common across the Midlands sample by 1700 and virtually ubiquitous in the extant records post-1750 – a variety of functionally specialist storage equipment came to be listed in probate documents. Thus, cupboards for display and practical purposes feature as prominent household assets.[158] Similarly, livery cupboards and presses for household linen and napery wares, clothes wardrobes, smaller corner cupboards, dressers, buffets and other prominent personal furniture, like desks and bureaux, start to appear with increasing frequency throughout the eighteenth century – and in increasingly fashionable forms of construction, for example japanned ware and exotic woods.

Investment in storage could be extensive. For example, in 1706 Elizabeth Pershouse had seven chests, three boxes, two arks, 13 trunks, a table cupboard, four livery cupboards, a little chest of drawers, a sideboard in the parlour and a little writing cabinet scattered about her rambling and modishly equipped 21-room house.[159] In addition, the appraisers of Pershouse's home noted both specific storage areas between the main rooms and rooms almost wholly converted to accommodate a miscellany of personal valuables and everyday lumber.[160] Alongside an array of fashionable upholstered furniture and up-market decorative fitments (Spanish tables, window curtains and silver goblets, for instance) Pershouse also possessed the kind of very traditional goods, such as simple hanging shelves and old trenchers, which were somewhat old-fashioned in 1706. This is fitting in that Pershouse's goods were clearly accumulated over a lifetime. Two hair trunks, monogrammed and dated, stored selections of the household's impressive collection of linen and napery. Here storage as practical requirement, functional necessity and repository of wider consumption modes such as affective memory collided.[161]

---

[158]   For a discussion on storage furniture, see Overton et al., *Production and Consumption*, pp. 92–8.

[159]   LRO, Elizabeth Pershouse, widow, Walsall, 1706.

[160]   Both the 'old nursery' and the 'space over the jack house' were used exclusively for stockpiling goods.

[161]   See Kevin Hetherington on the emotional aspects of retaining goods in storage. K. Hetherington, 'Secondhandness: Consumption, Disposal and Absent Presence', *Environment and Planning D: Society and Space*, 22 (2004), pp. 157–73.

The most basic form of storage was the box, trunk, coffer, ark or chest: simple, lidded, often portable devices constructed from vernacular woods that served to store linen, bedding, personal clothing and other household goods. Over 85 per cent of the sample listed at least one of these items among the appraised goods and, as Vickery has argued, even the most materially denuded of inventories often noted a solitary chest or trunk in which the meagre amount of goods deemed worthy of valuation were stored.[162] For example, in 1697 Mary Lunn, a Lichfield spinster and domestic servant, left an estate worth £12 2s 4d, the bulk of which (£10 5s 4d) comprised her wearing apparel and ready money.[163] A simple trunk (5s) and a rather more elaborate and expensive chest of drawers (£1 12s) constituted the remainder of the estate. Characteristically, Lunn willed these small pickings to her immediate female kin. Lunn's experience was probably not unlike many singlewomen in service in that her position was indicative of the main female lifecycle occupation before marriage; but it is notable that in an inventory that clearly indicates the limited living space of the single female servant, personal storage was a key element that secured, however tenuously, an element of self-determination.[164]

Some sixty years after Mary Lunn's death a similar picture of an independent but economically constrained existence was the lot of Martha Byollin, living in Ellesmere, Shropshire.[165] Byollin seems to have been a dressmaker – evidenced by the large numbers of aprons, caps, handkerchiefs, shifts and petticoats, together with 10 gowns valued at 10s each being listed – although typically her probate inventory merely describes her as a spinster rather than specifying a trade. Her meagre belongings amounted to about £12, together with £50 in cash. Apart from her bed and a small table to work at, Byollin owned a chest of drawers, a chest and 'one old box' to store her stock and personal belongings.

For older spinsters and widows their home was often scaled down in their final years. A one-time household might be reduced to one room in the home of a family member. This reduction in space produced a concentration of worldly goods, firstly into one room rather than a house and secondly into a few items of storage furniture that offered security, mobility and perhaps continuity with their earlier life. A profusion of possessions had become abbreviated to a handful of items that must signify the ones that had been distributed, sold or lost over a lifetime – the numerous rooms of a complete household compressed into a token home of a box or chest of drawers. The inventory of Ann Cox of Chilvers Coton in Warwickshire, for instance, when proved in 1744 revealed an estate dominated by an interest-bearing bond of £120. Household goods – often described as 'old', and wearing apparel, which was itemised in full – reveal the remnants of an independent lifecycle. Cox possessed only three boxes at death, presumably sufficient to store her limited collection of linen and old but serviceable clothes; it

---

162   Vickery, *Behind Closed Doors*, pp. 25–48.
163   LRO, Mary Lunn, spinster, Lichfield, 1697.
164   Froide, *Never Married*, pp. 90–92; Erickson, *Women and Property*, pp. 208–9.
165   LRO, Martha Byollin, spinster, Ellesmere, 1761.

is clear from her will that she had been living at the house of her nephew, William Wagstaffe, for some considerable time.[166]

A similarly reduced home life is evident from the probate evidence of the spinster Sarah Carles.[167] Earlier in her life she was clearly mistress of a substantial home, with fine-quality furnishings and a good income. By the time of her death in 1794, however, she had distributed or used up most of her wealth and belongings and now lived with her nephew and his family in Birmingham. Within this family home her world had shrunk to just a single bedchamber with the necessary bed furniture, a few mahogany chairs, an oak pillar and claw table, a looking glass, a 'Portrait of a Lady in black frame and seven small drawings in black lead'. In addition, Sarah was able to arrange her personal possessions – jewellery, papers and books, linen and wearing apparel – in a mahogany bureau and bookcase and a small, mahogany chest of drawers.

For most people old age resulted in a contraction of their home life, partly due to their reduced circumstances and for the widowed the return to singleness after married life. Anne Chandler was able to retain her home after she was widowed, but her living arrangements were severely contracted and she therefore illustrates a not uncommon experience of widows in straitened circumstances.[168] Two rooms in her small house were let out to a lodger and she inhabited just a kitchen and a parlour that doubled as a bedroom. Within this room she had a great many possessions, small items, many of which indicated that formerly she had enjoyed a more extensive material existence. Among the china, silver, books and family portraits she had a chest of drawers for her clothing and linen and a locked chest for her valuables. Widows in particular wanted to retain reminders of their former life and to demonstrate their competence as managers of a household. However, instead of complete household effects their belongings were often reduced to the meagre contents of a chest of drawers and a locked chest, to be organised and preserved and finally bequeathed to the next generation after their death.

Inappropriate Arrangements

While Susanna Marrian adapted her home to meet her requirements as a widow, other homes displayed inappropriate storage methods and disorganised modes of housekeeping, perhaps resulting from the lack of a housewife. For example, Richard Price, a miller who died in 1802, had saddle bags listed in his bedroom.[169] Were the saddle bags particularly valuable or did they contain money at the time of his disease and therefore were kept where he could keep an eye on them?

---

166   LRO, Ann Cox, spinster, Chilvers Coton, 1744.
167   LRO, Sarah Carles, spinster, Han[d]sworth, 1794. In her will, made in 1768, she had left considerable sums to family members but little of this money survived at her death.
168   LRO, Anne Chandler, widow, Shrewsbury, 1814.
169   LRO, Richard Price, bachelor, Allum Bridge, 1802.

Rural homes were more likely to display objects 'out of place' but that was to some extent due to the tendency of farmers to allow work-related items to encroach on their living space so that a clear distinction between home and work was less discernable than in homes in urban areas. The home of Thomas Lovatt, a yeoman farmer, and his sister Jane in rural Shropshire displayed some of these tendencies. When Thomas died in 1786,[170] their farmhouse had two parlours but neither of them functioned purely as a living room. The first parlour listed in the inventory contained a table and chairs, along with two spinning wheels, a saddle, a bridle, two wagon ropes and some hemp. For Jane to be using the parlour to spin yarn in her 'leisure time' was not unusual. Ann Simpson, in Broseley, Shropshire, also had '17 slippings of linen yarn, and some hemp and flax tow' in her parlour in 1750, although her spinning wheels were listed in a garret.[171] However, in the Lovatt household the saddle, bridle and rope were completely out of place for a parlour in the late eighteenth century. Their second parlour, designated the 'little' parlour, was being used as a multipurpose room too. The presence, in this room, of a bed and one for a servant perhaps only dated from Thomas's last illness. The room contained parlour items, namely two small tables, a couch and three chairs; but it also had two 'market baskets', again suggesting that storage was rather randomly organised. As Caroline Herschel was unable to curb her brother's monopolisation of their home with his astronomical equipment, perhaps Jane Lovatt was also not in control of the furnishing of the parlour in the farmhouse she occupied with her brother.

Another rural home that was particularly idiosyncratic in its organisation was that of James Mullock, who died in 1804.[172] His lifestyle was formed by a number of influences: as a farmer and butcher in rural Shropshire, by advanced age and by his bachelor status. The items out of place in this house included bed linen and numerous books in a houseplace that was clearly used as a kitchen. A pillion saddle and a butcher's pad were in a chamber used as a bedroom; six riddles, another butcher's pad, together with old furniture and lead weights were in the upstairs lobby; parts of a bedstead and a 'two panel door' were in a chamber used as a bedroom; and in the closet of this room was a kitchen grate. James Mullock's own bedroom had another room leading off it and in this room, along with a bed and the usual items, was a large oak chest which contained all manner of items stored there for safekeeping. These items included jewellery, money, a number of silver tankards and other silver items, a pistol, two tablecloths (perhaps used to wrap the silver items) and a pair of money scales.

The idiosyncratic storage arrangements in James Mullock's home hint at his lifestyle but do not reveal his day-to-day life or how he used the rooms of his farmhouse. Even homes with the appropriate rooms and furnishings might be used

---

[170]   LRO, Thomas Lovatt, bachelor, Claverley, 1786.

[171]   HRO, Ann Simpson, widow, Broseley, 1750.

[172]   SA, 6000/12167 Auctioneer's notebook, James Mullock, bachelor, Whitchurch, 1804.

in ways that would have been judged odd or even objectionable if viewed by outsiders. The basic rituals of life – preparing and cooking food, washing and caring for the body, laundering and maintaining clothing and linen, cleaning the inhabited space – have all become increasingly sophisticated over time and expectations have risen with better access to plumbed water and other modern conveniences.[173] The homemaking of single people who were not wealthy enough to rise above the problems of organising and managing their households was particularly prone to makeshift arrangements. The diary of impoverished printer and occasional newspaper reporter George Gitton in Bridgnorth provides an example of this.[174] Although his house had a parlour, rarely was a fire lit there. Instead, most evenings Gitton economised and sat by the fire in the kitchen – the room also used by his servant, Susan. He recorded one evening that he was 'Drove out owing to Susan's boiling down beeve's cheek & fire taken up.'[175] Reading and drinking a variety of alcoholic drinks occupied most of his evenings at home. Every few months, however, Gitton recorded an important event: on 17 May 1866 for example his diary entry concluded with 'Sausages for supper. 2 pints ale. Washed feet & cut toe nails this night & got to bed by 11 o'clock.'[176] An inventory of Gitton's house might have recorded a reasonably well-appointed home with appropriate furnishings but would not reveal where he washed his feet and clipped his toenails.

A less extreme suggestion of a man unable to organise his home is the painting by John Edward Soden entitled *Man Smoking in a Parlour*, dated 1862 (see Figure 3.3).[177] This painting is densely packed with visual messages about the man and his parlour. Although the room appears superficially comfortable, with the major ingredients in place, clearly all is not well. The man is contravening domesticity in a number of ways: firstly by smoking in a parlour, but also with his muddy trousers and shoes on the fender before the fire; his discarded tankard and cards on the floor; and a tobacco or snuffbox on the table. A book entitled *The Turf* and a print of a hunting scene provide further evidence of 'masculine' interests. On the wall, top left, is a print of Hogarth's *Marriage a la Mode*, a series about a fashionable but deeply dysfunctional marriage. The man's posture, slumped in a chair, mimics the husband in the Hogarth print and the playing cards, showing the king and queen, lie crossways – perhaps suggesting a couple at odds with each other. The Soden painting is clearly a comment on marriage but the man's marital status is not certain. Was he meant to represent a bachelor, a widower, a deserted husband or simply a

---

[173]   See Norbert Elias, *The Civilising Process* (Oxford: Blackwell, 1978).

[174]   See David Hussey, 'Guns, Horses and Stylish Waistcoats? Male Consumer Activity and Domestic Shopping in Late-Eighteenth- and Early-Nineteenth-Century England' in Hussey and Ponsonby, *Buying for the Home*, pp. 67–8.

[175]   Malcolm Wanklyn (ed.), *The Diary of George Gitton of Bridgnorth for 1866* (Keele: Centre for Local History, University of Keele, 1998), p. 110.

[176]   Wanklyn, *Diary of George Gitton*, p. 27.

[177]   John Edward Soden, *Man Smoking in a Parlour*, 1862, The Geffrye Museum, London.

Figure 3.3   John Edward Soden, *Man Smoking in a Parlour*, 1862, uses symbolic disarray to comment on the domesticity of a single man. *Source*: The Geffrye Museum, London.

Figure 3.4   William Redmore Bigg, *A Cottage Interior: An Old Woman Preparing Tea*, 1793, depicts poverty common to aged widows and spinsters but with numerous domestic 'comforts'.

Source: © Victoria and Albert Museum, London.

man whose wife has gone away for a few days; although his reddened face suggests habitual alcohol consumption? Perhaps Soden did not wish to be specific but rather wanted to make a humorous comment, with a more serious underlying message that men were not able to create or sustain a domestic set-up as a true home without a woman. Home was not 'home' under masculine superintendence.

The homes of unmarried men examined here were more prone to inappropriate arrangements. Although it is generally assumed that widows and spinsters were worse off than widowers and bachelors since they were marginalised by society and usually had less earning power than men, they were perhaps better placed for homemaking. The skills that they had acquired for organising and managing a home stood them in good stead when their lives dictated retrenchment. These skills included the most basic aspects of cleaning a home. This situation was described by Charlotte Brontë in *Shirley*, when Caroline Helstone visited an 'old maid':

> Ushered into Miss Mann's little parlour, Caroline found her, as she always found her, surrounded by perfect neatness, cleanliness, and comfort; (after all, is it not a virtue of old maids that solitude rarely makes them negligent or disorderly?) no dust on her polished furniture, none on her carpet, fresh flowers in the vase on her table, a bright fire in the grate. She herself sat primly and somewhat grimly-tidy in a cushioned rocking-chair, her hands busy with some knitting.[178]

Miss Mann was an unattractive person with severe manners and Caroline had needed to summon up her courage to visit her. Although Miss Mann's home was clean and bright it presented rather sterile conditions. Brontë presents an ambivalent picture of elderly singleness. While her portrayal of young governesses in her other novels is wholly sympathetic, her treatment of Miss Mann adheres somewhat to contemporary ideas of the 'old maid' with a crabbed nature and empty life. Brontë suggests, however, through her description of Miss Mann's natural affinity to homemaking that she deserved respect and consideration and, indeed, Caroline revised her opinion of the elderly spinster after this visit.

Ascertaining whether homes were clean and tidy is impossible from inventory evidence alone. However, what is clear is that many of the single or widowed women in the sample had acquired and retained minor items of decorative display. For example, the spinster Sarah Dudley's (d. 1746) effects only amounted to £13 6s but included two pictures, window curtains, a drinking glass, six jelly glasses and a flower pot.[179] The poor widow Ann Devey (d. 1767), whose goods were granted to a grocer and cheese factor – her principal creditors – had sufficient furniture, cooking equipment and a few decorative items in her house in Bridgnorth to warrant the name 'home', although all her goods and chattels only amounted to £19 6s 2d.[180] Ownership of such meagre but prized possessions is portrayed in the

---

[178]   Charlotte Brontë, *Shirley* (Harmondsworth: Penguin, 1985 [1849]), p. 193.
[179]   WRO, Sarah Dudley, spinster, Rowley Regis, 1746.
[180]   LRO, Ann Devey, widow, Bridgnorth, 1767.

genre picture painted by William Redmore Bigg (Figure 3.4),[181] thought to have originally been exhibited as 'Poor old woman's comfort'. The painting includes a wealth of detail in the many items of material goods in this poor cottage interior. A simple tripod table has ceramic tea wares, and a clock and brass warming pan hang on the wall. A few books and some decorative and useful items are also on shelves and on the mantelpiece.[182] Bigg specialised in depicting the 'virtuous poor' and hence their hard work and frugal habits has resulted in their acquiring and managing to retain small comforts in the form of material possessions. The common occurrence of such possessions in the homes of widows and spinsters in the inventory sample hints at a desire for enhancing the home environment not only through material goods but also through domestic practices.

A quite different picture emerges from the inventory of John Clay, a bachelor and yeoman farmer. Clay was worth far more than Sarah Dudley or Ann Devey and occupied a better position in society; his 'Goods, Chattels, Credits and personal Estate' came to £138 15s 0d. However, the majority of that sum was made up of a bond and other investments. Clay's worldly goods at his farm in Loscoe near Heanor, Derbyshire, seem pathetically meagre and yet the inventory maker stressed twice that the following list included all the goods owned by John Clay when he died in 1781.[183] The total goods listed for John Clay were:

The deceased's Wearing Apparel of all sorts being very old			
	1	0	0
One Bed and Bedding thereto belong which the deceased lay upon himself being very old and decayed	1	0	0
One chest	0	4	0
Two old tables	0	2	6
Fire Irons	0	2	6
An iron Pott	0	1	6
Five old chairs and two Buffets	0	1	6
A little Parcel of Hay	0	6	0
Potts and Platters	0	1	0
An old Leather Pad	0	0	6
An old flesh Beam and Ropes	0	1	6
A Warming Pan	0	1	0
A Barrel	0	1	0

---

[181] W.R. Bigg, *A Cottage Interior: An Old Woman Preparing Tea*, 1793, Victoria & Albert Museum, London, VAM 199-1885.

[182] No ceramic plates are present in the painting. A pewter plate and wooden trencher are displayed on the shelf behind her. This combination of goods was often found in the inventory sample.

[183] LRO, John Clay, bachelor, Heanor, 1781. Consistory court inventories were made due to a dispute, hence the careful wording.

While many reasons can be put forward for inventories not being complete, in the example of John Clay the admission that he slept on a 'very old and decayed' bed reveals that this was a life with few physical comforts. A warming pan and a barrel of beer may have been the extent of them. The furniture was almost certainly locally made and of rough construction in a regional style, and the 'Potts and Platters' suggest rudimentary methods for serving food. And yet this household catered for all John Clay's immediate needs, with a pot to cook his food, a bed, a table and chairs. Storage was provided by a chest for his old clothes. The inclusion of the hay and the butchering equipment amongst the other household effects may have been the result of a forgetful inventory maker, but may equally indicate that here was a hopelessly disordered 'home' that contained the barest necessities to warrant that name. John Clay's nephew came forward to claim his uncle's estate but perhaps in life he had left him to go his own way on that farm in Derbyshire.

Conclusion

While single people of the level of Anne Boulton and James Watt junior, examined at the outset of this chapter, were able to establish independent households with sufficient servants to maintain their homes in comfort and propriety, others lived in desperate conditions of poverty and want. Homemaking was a luxury they could not afford. In between, however, the middling sort were a large section of the population and single people within this group juggled economy, respectability, frugality and propriety.

Heading a household was a burden and for this reason many single people, whatever their social and economic position, chose to live with someone, usually a sibling. This arrangement allowed the practical burden of household management and organisation to be shared. However, setting up a home in the long eighteenth century was not solely about economic and practical considerations. A home also had symbolic meanings that were understood by contemporaries. These meanings evolved over time and if anything became more onerous, again putting the single homemaker at a disadvantage. This is the subject of the next chapter.

Chapter 4

Social and Symbolic Uses of the Homes of Single People

The Reverend William Cooper, when a young curate in Thaxted, Essex in1759, spent his mornings administering to his parishioners and trying to do some good for the poor people in his care.[1] The afternoons he spent furthering his own career by making the acquaintance of people 'whose Integrity and good Sense might be of service to me in my further progress through ye World'. This often meant visiting them in their homes and although he never described his own abode, he was extremely conscious of the houses he visited. Among them was Easton Lodge, home of Lord Maynard, which was impressively large, with its own deer park – 'from ye diningroom Windows you have a most noble and delightful prospect: ye romantic Tilty [Abbey, in ruins] … adds not a little to ye grandure of ye scene'. The house had a library with 'a very fine collection of books' and its own chapel. Cooper was rather envious of Lord Maynard's two chaplains, especially the Rev. Mr Forester, who had a house within the park which commanded the same views as the main house. In its garden Forester had a 'very pleasant Arbour in which he sometimes reads a piece of Divinity, a [sic] sometimes a News-paper; also a fish-pond well supply'd with Tench, which however he is not remarkably expert in catching. His House contains six Bedrooms, a Parlour, Drawing-Room, Hall, Kitchin, and other conveniences.' Cooper also visited Sir William Maynard's house near Cambridge, where he admired the 'splendid' furniture, the pictures and the 'finest India paper, I ever saw'. Cooper was a connoisseur of fine interiors and since he eventually became Archdeacon of York, presumably he achieved an elegant home of his own which poor curates might visit and envy.

The home environment was first and foremost created for its occupants. However, the physical elements of building, decoration, furniture and furnishings were a powerful statement about who you were and your position in society. While wealth was important, it was not the only element considered when a home was judged by contemporaries. The material culture of the home expressed a person's judgement, taste and moral and religious outlook. Observing the correct procedure for furnishing and using the home was important for establishing a person's position in society when communities were tight-knit and unchanging. An understanding of what was correct and desirable in home furnishings and how the home and its

---

[1] Cooper's diary is reproduced in A.F.J. Brown (ed.), *Essex People 1750–1900: From their Diaries, Memoirs and Letters* (Chelmsford: Essex Record Office Publications No. 59, 1972), pp. 50–55.

contents should be used was acquired in large part by visiting the homes of others. Homes offered the opportunity for the householder to display their status and gentility; for their guests to observe and absorb ideas; and for both to demonstrate their understanding of correct behaviour in the rituals of sociability.

Unmarried 'Apprenticeships' in Homemaking

For young single men and women of the middling sort still living with their parents, visiting the homes of family and friends was an important part of growing up. Diarists in the eighteenth and nineteenth centuries make frequent references to such visits although, unlike William Cooper, they rarely refer to interiors and their furnishings in any detail, if at all. The two examples of Sarah Hurst and Thomas Jordan to be examined here were chiefly concerned with meeting their friends and observing others and forging their own relationships with the opposite sex. The homes of friends, with parents providing hospitality, were an important venue for young unmarried people to meet and for relationships to develop. However, the material culture of interiors would no doubt have been consumed along with the refreshments against the time that they would establish their own homes.

Sarah Hurst began her diary when she was 22 years old and recorded her daily activities during the few years that led up to her marriage.[2] Her father was a tailor in the small town of Horsham in Sussex and Sarah worked in the shop and helped with the sewing. On several occasions, she went to London to see suppliers and place orders, and dined with the tradesmen and their family. Much of her time was taken up with the family business but Sarah participated in a full if rather narrow social life, with friends of her own age or members of her family. Although a small-town tailor was a rather humble position the family were well connected through marriage and Sarah was exposed to a range of interiors when out visiting, including on one occasion Goodwood House, the home of the Duke and Duchess of Richmond. Apart from long walks with endless discussions of their love lifes, with her great friend Sally Sheppard Sarah visited the homes of friends or relatives on an almost daily basis. Amusements recorded included playing at cards, music making and dancing, occasionally dining with her hosts. For example, on 16 April 1759 she recorded: 'Dine at Mrs Seyton's with my Aunt Waller, Aunt Tasker & Graham, the Supervisor and his wife, she is a very pretty behav'd woman, he by all accounts a vile fellow to her.' More gossip and some moralising were included on 29 August 1759: 'At Mrs Bridger's all the evening, play at quadrille, how passionately she loves cards. Gives us an account of her dining at Lord Irwin's, nothing but made dishes. I am difficult & doubt I shou'd be starv'd in such a family. Luxury is I think as little excusable as any vice.' Sarah's observations of people's behaviour reveals how she was sizing up good and bad conduct and

    [2]   Susan C. Djabri (ed.), *The Diaries of Sarah Hurst 1759–1762: Life and Love in Eighteenth-Century Horsham* (Stroud: Amberley, 2009).

comparing them with herself and Harry Smith, the man she hoped to marry. On 1 May 1759 she recorded a happy evening that turned sour due to bad behaviour: 'Walk to see Mr Nathaniel Tredcroft, with Mrs Wicker, Miss Powell, Mrs Tasker and Miss Tredcroft. We play at Matrimony, are excessively merry & then dance. Nat was very drunk, sure nothing is a greater deprivation of human nature than this shocking vice.' Sarah perhaps felt more at ease in all-female company, and such visits were frequently summarised as simply 'drink tea' at a particular house. On 16 January 1759 for example is the entry: 'At home. Work afternoon, drink tea at Aunt Grace's, just remov'd to their new house. Plan many subjects for poems but fear I shall never have time to finish them. Call on Betsy Sheppard, laugh at her going to be married but am really much concerned about losing my dear companion.'[3] It is difficult to imagine that Sarah, so observant of behaviour and manners, did not also take note of the tea wares she drank from or the decoration of the various parlours in which she sat against the time when she and her 'Dear Harry' might set up home together.

Some 75 years divide the diaries of Sarah Hurst and Thomas Jordan but a remarkably similar picture emerges of the lives of young people hoping for the fulfilment of romantic attachments and for a successful and happy life. Thomas Jordan's diary for 1835, the year in which he reached the age of 22, is interesting for its reflection of the social activities of a young unmarried man.[4] He was religious but not so devout that he avoided all leisure pursuits and was able to enjoy both male and female company with surprisingly little supervision in both public and private spaces. The presence of chaperones seems less than in Sarah Hurst's accounts. This is probably due to Jordan reflecting life from the male perspective and because he was of somewhat lower status than Sarah rather than a relaxing of conduct, since the need for chaperones increased for middle-class girls in the nineteenth century.[5] Jordan lived with his parents and sisters in Birmingham and worked for Mr Lucas 'in the shoe trade'. Lucas was listed in trade directories as a shoemaker, although whether Jordan did manual work or was employed in the shop is not clear. On several occasions, he recorded taking care of things while Mr Lucas travelled the area in pursuit of orders. Jordan was a sociable young man who was constantly out most evenings and on Sundays. His main leisure activities were going on long walks with either a male or female companion or calling to see a friend at their home, where he met both male and female unmarried friends in his circle. Jordan was less forthcoming about his feelings than Hurst and only made fleeting and rather coded references to a young lady that he liked and admired.

Jordan's other activities included visiting the Bazaar in New Street; exhibitions of plants at the Botanical Gardens; evenings at the Birmingham Vauxhall; visits to

---

[3] Betsy was the sister of Sally Sheppard; she married Sarah's uncle and therefore became her 'Aunt Tasker', which put their friendship on a more formal footing. Djabri, *The Diaries*, p. 20.

[4] Birmingham Central Archives (BCA), MS805 Diary of Thomas Jordan.

[5] Leonore Davidoff, *The Best Circles* (London: Croom Helm, 1973), p. 50.

the theatre with a female friend; and seeing new technology in the form of a steam coach and the newly opened Birmingham and Liverpool Railway. He was a religious young man, going to church twice every Sunday. On only one occasion did Jordan mention alcohol: on 11 September he and two friends went to the George Hotel 'to have a glass'. His other 'transgression' was horseracing and making bets; he belonged to the St Leger Club that met once a month and on 2 September he 'drew the horse Pilgrim'. He made only a few references to eating food away from his home, such as on 9 February when he had 'Supper [at] Miss Price's in the evening.' On only two occasions did he record eating in a public place. Once was on 31 October when he went with two friends 'to Foxalls to have tripe in the evening'. Rather grander was the occasion of 6 July when he went to the Birmingham Vauxhall for the day. There was a horse raffle in the evening and 'about 40 sat down to supper'.

While food and drink must surely have figured in the entertainment provided when Thomas Jordan visited the homes of friends he did not comment on the fact, perhaps for the very reason that it was a common occurrence. Like Sarah Hurst, he spent much of his leisure time with friends in the homes of their parents. These homes provided the backdrop to the entertainments, a setting for the action, although more often than not the action was limited to conversation and drinking tea. The furnishings, along with the correct behaviour, were absorbed for future reference when each anticipated setting up a home of their own. Sarah did indeed marry her dear Harry although the details of their home are not known, and Thomas Jordan's subsequent life is even more of a mystery. For the majority of young people the aim in life was to marry and establish their own home. For a large number this was either not to be or they found themselves widowed at a later stage in their lives and thus returned to a single life. For a minority of singletons an independent home was possible. The ideas they had gleaned during their apprenticeship in life stood them in good stead for establishing homes that was as much like those of their married peers as possible.

Taste and the Single Homemaker

Rather than seeking highly individual expressions of personality, people in the early modern period wanted their homes to conform to what was deemed appropriate so that visitors and observers understood the symbolic message contained in its material possessions. In the early modern period and into the later nineteenth century people, with very few exceptions, wanted to create a home that was an expression of who they were – namely respectable and if possible genteel. It would not have occurred to them to go against the tide of what was regarded as acceptable behaviour and sensibility in this respect, although a few eccentric individuals have always done so.[6] It would not have been desirable to create a

---

[6]   The lack of organisation in some homes as seen in Chapter 3 may be examples of this but also the homes of antiquarians sometimes broke the rules of domesticity in their

home that diverged from the taste displayed in everyone else's home. Linda Young expresses this attitude to personal taste as a desire for 'genteel taste [that] was an expression of adherence to middle-class values; it was not, as the modern meaning has it, a style of individual choice'.[7] However, that did not exclude homes from expressing individual personalities. A home inevitably does that since every item in the home was chosen for inclusion or retention with an individual outcome. Since single people often occupied a slightly awkward position in polite society their homes were particularly open to judgement and this probably made them more conscious of being inconspicuous and conforming to general practice.[8]

Throughout the period, the notion of 'taste' was conveyed through material possessions. Having 'taste' automatically meant good taste; the alternative was no taste at all. The concept depended on education and therefore was obliquely linked to wealth. Apart from displaying lineage and a classical education, taste also embraced unwritten rules that caught out the uninformed. Opening the home to the scrutiny of outsiders could confirm a person's position in society, whether that was elevated or otherwise.[9] Entertaining in the home was therefore a risky but necessary exercise. For independent single people there was the added risk of being judged inadequate due to the absence of a family and, as the nineteenth century progressed, this became particularly relevant with the growth of importance of domestic ideology that dictated that the home should be a physical expression of family life.[10] While the evidence of how individual homes were used for entertaining outsiders is only rarely accessible, the ingredients for entertaining are often revealed through inventory evidence. Some homes were well equipped – even excessively so for such small households – and therefore suggest that some entertaining probably occurred. Other homes were totally inadequate by contemporary standards and suggest that either no entertaining was conducted or that in some circumstances such inadequacy was acceptable. Commentaries in

---

arrangements. See Clive Wainwright, *The Romantic Interior* (New Haven and London: Yale University Press, 1989).

[7] Linda Young, *Middle-Class Culture in the Nineteenth Century: America, Australia and Britain* (Basingstoke: Palgrave Macmillan, 2003), p. 155.

[8] On the marginal position of single women's homes see Anna Lepine, '"Strange and Rare Visitants": Spinsters and Domestic Space in Elizabeth Gaskell's *Cranford*', *Nineteenth-Century Contexts*, 32/2 (2010), pp. 121–37.

[9] Maxwell Hutchinson, *Number 57: The History of a House* (London: Headline, 2003), p. 28.

[10] See for example Deborah Cohen, *Household Gods: The British and their Possessions* (New Haven and London: Yale University Press, 2006); L. Davidoff and C. Hall, *Family Fortunes: Men and Women of the English Middle Class 1780–1850* (London: Hutchinson, 1987); Thad Logan, *The Victorian Parlour* (Cambridge: Cambridge University Press, 2001); Jane Hamlett, *Material Relations: Domestic Interiors and Middle-Class Families in England, 1850–1910* (Manchester: Manchester University Press, 2010).

diaries can also help to fill the gaps of inventory evidence and provide a notion of the kind of sociability that some single people felt was acceptable and desirable.

Entertaining in the Homes of Single People

While the provision of food and drink to outsiders was always an important mark of civility and hospitality, the tendency during the period was for more emphasis to be put on this activity. The evolution of sociability at this time was often expressed through the material culture of the home and the increased refinement of the domestic interior.[11] The coffee house and inn were important for male sociability. Whether this space is drawn as a Habermasian 'public sphere' wherein the constructs of urbane yet respectable masculinity were enacted is, however, debatable.[12] Indeed, the notional exclusion of women to a confined and surveyed domestic 'separate sphere' does not translate quite so seamlessly to historical experience,[13] and recent scholarship has begun to repopulate such distinctly male enclaves as the coffee house and alehouse with the presence and voices of women.[14] However, all-male gatherings were important throughout the period for political and business meetings and robust sociability. Increasingly though, the home provided a more comfortable and genteel environment for impressing business associates. The increased emphases on material goods, more elaborate meals and the use of carefully trained servants to wait at table, and the presence of women to provide genteel company and perhaps musical entertainment all increased during the eighteenth century. By the nineteenth century, the middle class had ritualised such entertaining even more. Access to these codes was an important badge of politeness and respectability, and the refined nature of the domestic environment reflected upon the wider credit of the household.

---

[11]   Amanda Vickery, *Behind Closed Doors: At Home in Georgian England* (New Haven and London: Yale University Press, 2009), p. 18.

[12]   Woodruff D. Smith, *Consumption and the Making of Respectability, 1600–1800* (London: Routledge, 2002), pp. 140–61.

[13]   Amanda Vickery, 'Golden Age to Separate Spheres? A Review of the Categories and Chronology of English Women's History', *The Historical Journal*, 36/2 (1993), pp. 383–414; Robert B. Shoemaker, *Gender in English Society, 1650–1850: The Emergence of Separate Spheres?* (London: Longman, 1998).

[14]   See Brian Cowan, 'What was Masculine about the Public Sphere? Gender and the Coffee House Milieu in Post-Restoration England', *History Workshop Journal*, 51 (2001), pp. 127–57; Helen Berry, 'Rethinking Politeness in Eighteenth-Century England: Moll King's Coffee House and the Significance of "Flash Talk"', *Transactions of the Royal Historical Society*, 6th Series, 11 (2001), pp. 65–81; and Brian Cowan, *The Social Life of Coffee: The Emergence of the British Coffeehouse* (New Haven and London: Yale University Press, 2005), pp. 243–54.

For the wealthy, entertaining in the home might be the opportunity to show off with lavish feasts; but for the middling sort at the outset of the period providing a clean room and simple, basic food was sufficient. Not being able to provide this was a sign of poor housewifery and a household that was ignominious or in distress. Entertaining guests could cement friendships and further business deals. Entertaining outsiders in the home took different forms according to the usual variables of time, status and location but also according to gender. For the full range of sociable activities appropriate for a period and within a particular status group to take place a family home with both a husband and wife were needed, although both were not expected to be present at all events. It is this division according to gender that is useful to consider when thinking about how single people heading a household might have used their homes for entertaining.

Broadly, the opportunities for women to socialise in the home increased during the period while their public role outside the home decreased. However, this oversimplifies a complex situation that changed and evolved, and in ways that we do not fully understand. We cannot rely on 'the polarised picture of relations between men and women presented by prescriptive literature' to understand how men and women used domestic space.[15] It is clear though that men and women were expected to have different roles in the home and outside it. Whereas men in the seventeenth century were able to visit taverns and alehouses, it would not have been acceptable to take their wives with them. 'Keeping at home' was a common theme that was well established in the mid-seventeenth century and continued throughout the period. In the early nineteenth century, Mrs Taylor was warning her female readers that a husband was likely to stray if his wife was out of the house too much.[16] Status was a consideration and women from the labouring class were permitted more freedom, although their reputation might suffer as a result. Visiting the homes of friends, family and neighbours and welcoming the same into their own homes was safer and seen as a necessary part of a woman's social obligations and as a means of showing hospitality. Even then prescriptive literature and satirical prints warned of the dangers of assignations and gossiping. A fine balance was required.

Entertainment in the home was most often presided over by married women.[17] Unmarried men hardly ever hosted social events in their own homes, partly because

---

[15]   Amanda Flather, *Gender and Space in Early Modern England* (London: Royal Historical Society, The Boydell Press, 2007), p. 31. This point also made by Shoemaker, *Gender in English Society*.

[16]   Mrs Taylor, *Practical Hints to Young Females: On the Duties of a Wife, a Mother, and a Mistress* (London, 1822).

[17]   Flather used evidence from 330 court depositions involving 806 people that recorded home-based social activities and found that married women were the most likely to host such occasions, followed by married couples and then married men. Very few (only 2.9 per cent) were hosted by unmarried women and none by unmarried men (although the marital status of some men was unknown). Flather, *Gender and Space*, pp. 96–7.

they were more likely to be in lodgings but perhaps also suggesting that their homes were seen as inadequate in some way.[18] However, there was a significant minority of men – particularly those in the professions, such as clergymen and lawyers – who were better placed to entertain, if only all-male company. The situation for unmarried women was more precarious both financially and socially, but again there were exceptions; and in some circumstances their homes could be used in a social way, perhaps finding a stronger position by the mid to late eighteenth century, in towns where informal 'spinster clusters' existed[19] and through the popularity of tea drinking. Certainly, by the mid-nineteenth century and beyond, all-female gatherings took place because of charity work practised by women, and for some a more determinedly single but collective existence was pursued through careers such as teaching or the civil service, including working for the Post Office – all of which required women to remain single to retain their positions. How such life choices impacted on homemaking is beyond the scope of this book.[20]

For most middling sort people in the seventeenth century entertaining in the home took a rather basic form of providing food and drink that was simply prepared and served on pewter or wooden plates with a knife and spoon. Simple food was necessitated by most houses having nothing more sophisticated that an open fire to cook on. An iron pot hung over the fire was the usual way of cooking much of what a household ate and was ubiquitous in even the meanest home. Meat was either boiled or roasted using a spit.[21] Overton et al. make the point that the simply cooked meal went with basic forms of serving and consuming food, on a wooden

---

[18]   Vickery's chapter on bachelors suggests that they were always wanting to be invited to someone's home in order to get a good meal. Vickery, *Behind Closed Doors*, pp. 49–82.

[19]   For the example of Ludlow see Mark Girouard, *The English Town* (New Haven and London: Yale University Press, 1990); David Lloyd, *Broad Street: Its Houses and Residents through Eight Centuries* (Birmingham: Ludlow Research Papers, No. 3, 1979); S.J. Wright, 'Sojourners and Lodgers in a Provincial Town: The Evidence from Eighteenth-Century Ludlow, *Urban History*, 17 (1990), pp. 14–35.

[20]   For the later nineteenth century, including photographs of female students having tea in their rooms, see Hamlett, *Material Relations*, chapter 4. For examples of women involved in philanthropy, charity work and increased education opportunities leading to careers, see Christina de Bellaigue, *Educating Women: Schooling and Identity in England and France, 1800–1867* (Oxford: Oxford University Press, 2007); Marina Benjamin (ed.), *Science and Sensibility: Gender and Scientific Enquiry, 1780–1945* (Oxford: Basil Blackwell, 1991); Clarissa Campbell Orr (ed.), *Women in the Victorian Art World* (Manchester and New York: Manchester University Press, 1996); Gerry Holloway, *Women and Work in Britain since 1840* (London: Routledge, 2005); Philippa Levine, *Victorian Feminism 1850–1900* (Gainesville: University Press of Florida, 1994); Claire Midgley, *Women Against Slavery* (London: Routledge, 1992); Joan Perkin, *Women and Marriage in Nineteenth-Century England* (London: Routledge, 1989).

[21]   Many of the Midlands inventories consulted listed a variety of paraphernalia associated with spit roasting, including cranes and dog wheels.

trencher with a spoon. The adoption of knives and forks, and the use of plates rather than trenchers to eat a meal, was associated with changes and refinements to how food was cooked.[22] The use of saucepans is therefore indicative of the changes to cooking methods. Saucepans were flat-bottomed and either placed on a tripod over the open fire or used on a range. They were ideal for cooking small amounts of food quickly but required more skill than boiling. The use of sauces made meals more interesting but required skill and instructions in cookery books, and was often popularly associated with 'French' ways. For a variety of reasons, saucepans only gradually gained favour in the early eighteenth century, mostly with wealthier people and those living in London – and to a lesser extent in other major cities – but hardly at all in rural areas until much later.[23] Hannah Glasse published *The Art of Cookery Made Plain and Easy* in 1747 and this widely read book, among others, introduced wealthier households to new ideas, including sauces. By 1845, Eliza Acton's *Modern Cookery for Private Families*, aimed at a middle-class audience, devoted an entire chapter to savoury sauces. Other refinements connected with serving and eating dinner included the move to place food on the table in courses rather than all at the same time, but again this came about slowly and made little impact away from the capital and amongst the middling sort until at least the end of the eighteenth century.[24]

While more sophisticated meals were possible for the wealthy, for most people simple cooking arrangements lasted throughout the eighteenth century and beyond. The cooking range was introduced into middling homes gradually in the later eighteenth and early nineteenth century, but even then very few middling sort people had one that included an oven for baked dishes. By the nineteenth century, serving dinner in wealthier homes became still more elaborate and required specialist equipment, suitable spaces within the home and the knowledge to participate in the associated rituals that were linked to both fashion and to notions of polite social behaviour.

Dining and 'Masculine' Entertaining

Throughout the eighteenth century, the main meal was eaten in the middle of the day; by the 1780s the meal started at two or three in the afternoon. For wealthy

---

[22]   Mark Overton, J. Whittle, D. Dean and A. Hann, *Production and Consumption in English Households, 1600–1750* (London and New York: Routledge, 2004), p. 106.

[23]   Lorna Weatherill, *Consumer Behaviour and Material Culture in Britain, 1660–1760* (2nd edn, London and New York: Routledge, 1996), p. 77. See also Karin Dannehl, '"To Families Furnishing Kitchens": Domestic Utensils and their Use in the Eighteenth-Century Home' in David Hussey and Margaret Ponsonby (eds), *Buying for the Home: Shopping for the Domestic from the Seventeenth Century to the Present* (Aldershot: Ashgate, 2008), pp. 27–46.

[24]   Weatherill, *Consumer Behaviour*, p. 152.

people, eating might go on for hours. Indeed, taking a long time over dinner showed that you were a gentleman and did not need to earn a living, but for the middling sort with long working hours this was not an option.[25] For them the midday meal was perfunctory, and only gradually as the main meal was deferred until the evening did this become a possible occasion for entertaining. Serving dinner to guests with any degree of refinement required more elaborate equipment than most middling sort homes often possessed. The sample of inventories was used to gauge the spread of two key items, namely saucepans and knives and forks (see Table 2.1). In line with Weatherill and Overton et al.'s findings, saucepans remained rare in provincial towns and almost non-existent in rural areas: only 7 per cent of homes in the Midlands were found with saucepans up to 1724, most in the homes of relatively wealthy widows. Between 1725 and the end of the eighteenth century, ownership of saucepans increased – although remaining uncommon. Most were found in the homes of widows rather than spinsters, although the respectable home of Catherine and Hannah Poyner in Bridgnorth had two listed.[26] Similarly, the well-furnished home of Miss Lamprey in Canterbury had several saucepans listed in the sale catalogue of her house.[27] In both of these examples from the 1760s, the women still only had an old-fashioned grate rather than a range to cook on. However, both homes had a brewhouse/washhouse with a furnace and it was here that the saucepans were listed. By the nineteenth century the ownership of specialist equipment associated with newer ways of cooking, serving and eating meals had increased. Virtually all the later inventories listed such items. For example, Celia Parker had a 'small range' and a saucepan listed in her kitchen in Chichester, while the wealthy widow Alithia Newland had a range, five saucepans and a fish kettle, along with numerous items for baking bread, pastry dishes and cakes.[28]

A similar pattern in the ownership of knives and forks was found in the eighteenth century inventories. Only 7 per cent of single people had these items listed before 1724. Of these two were the gentlewomen Anne Dowdeswell (d.

---

[25] Hutchinson, *Number 57*, pp. 30–35. For the laborious nature of the rituals of dining and toasting, see Johanna Schopenhauer, *A Lady's Travels: Journeys in England and Scotland from the Diaries of Johanna Schopenhauer*, translated and edited by R. Michaelis-Jena and W. Merson (London: Routledge, 1988), pp. 154–9. For an account of wealthier dining habits and utensils see Philippa Glanville and Hilary Young, *Elegant Eating: Four Hundred Years of Dining in Style* (London: V&A Publications, 2002).

[26] Lichfield Record Office (LRO), Catherine and Hannah Poyner, spinsters, Bridgnorth, 1765.

[27] Catalogue of all the household goods of Miss Lamprey, Canterbury, 1764. *Eighteenth Century Collections Online (ECCO)*, http://gale.cengage.co.uk/product-highlights/history/eighteenth-century-collections-online.aspx. Gale document number CW107372180.

[28] Both inventories were made by the Peat firm of cabinetmakers in Chichester, Celia Parker in 1848 and Alithia Newland in 1852. West Sussex Record Office (WSRO), Add. Mss. 2245, Henry and William Peat notebook.

1681) and Elizabeth Pershouse (d. 1706) – both fairly wealthy widows – and the bachelor Francis Thompson (d. 1705), a *rentier* and farmer.[29] Thompson had little by way of household goods and the total inventoried value of his estate, £90, was mostly made up of debts. The cutlery he owned may have been merely a set for his own use. After 1800, ownership of knives and forks in the sample became common and only incomplete households tended not to have them listed. Between these two dates, knives and forks only gradually became more common in the inventories for women, although their acquisition was slightly more common amongst the more limited sample of men. The opposite trend was true of silver, with far more women having silver items listed than men. However, this was due to silver often being regarded by women as an investment to be turned into cash when necessary rather than an indication that they were using silver items for serving meals, or even showing them off on a sideboard or buffet.[30] Doubtless most of these items were packed away for safekeeping. In the eighteenth century middling sort plates were usually made from pewter, and all the single men and over half of the women had them listed throughout the period up to the 1790s, when ceramic plates became more usual.

The increase in the ownership of ceramic dinner wares and knives and forks suggests that serving and eating food was becoming more elaborate and refined. However, far more was required than knives and forks for serving dinner to guests with real gentility. Multifunctional rooms that had been common and acceptable in the seventeenth century were less acceptable amongst the wealthy by the end of the century, and the dissatisfaction spread to polite society during the eighteenth century. A house with only a general-purpose parlour, which had been not only adequate but desirable, seemed unfashionable by the nineteenth century for the better-off middle-class home. A room dedicated to dining was deemed necessary so that it could be furnished in the appropriate manner and equipped with specialist items. A clear idea of what dining rooms should be like comes from the numerous descriptions in advice literature; and while not everyone could accomplish the levels of furnishing specified, and even those who could may have deviated somewhat, the prevalence of the description suggests that the authors were describing the accepted notion of what was thought correct. D.R. Hay developed a theory of colour values, including the

---

[29]   Malcolm Wanklyn (ed.), *Inventories of Worcestershire Landed Gentry 1537–1786* (Worcester: Worcestershire Historical Society, New Series, vol. 16, 1998), inventory of Ann Dowdeswell, widow, Bushley, 1681; LRO, Elizabeth Pershouse, widow, Walsall, 1706; LRO, Francis Thompson, bachelor, Kingsbury Whateley, 1705.

[30]   Silver items often appeared in the wills of unmarried and widowed women: see Maxine Berg, 'Women's Consumption and the Industrial Classes of Eighteenth-Century England', *Journal of Social History*, 30/2 (1996), pp. 415–34. On comparisons of male and female ownership of silver see Lorna Weatherill, 'A Possession of One's Own: Women and Consumer Behaviour in England, 1660–1740', *Journal of British Studies*, 25 (1986), pp. 131–56, 149.

notion that the main living rooms should have distinct characters, and influenced many other writers of the period. He stressed that in 'a drawing-room vivacity, gaiety, and light cheerfulness, should characterise the colouring', whereas the 'dining-room should be warm, rich, and substantial'.[31] Mrs William Parkes gives a gendered slant to the furnishings: 'The furniture most usual in the dining-room is of a substantial kind; for instance, mahogany chairs, tables, and side-boards; curtains, frequently of moreen, and sometimes of crimson or scarlet cloth, but never, I think, of a lighter kind, such as chintz. A solid simplicity generally characterizes the style of the dining room'.[32] Therefore, the use of a room that was multifunctional – and that did not include the necessary ingredients or create the right ambience – put the householder at a disadvantage, and to some extent precluded certain forms of entertaining. The supposed masculine nature of the dining room was meant to be a reflection of whose presence would hold sway there: the dining room was masculine; the drawing room was meant to be feminine to contrast with it. An additional parlour or morning room/breakfast room might be included in larger houses as a daytime sitting room for the women of the house, and be decorated and furnished accordingly. Apart from the attractiveness and comfort of such interiors, the specialist items also signalled more strongly than the sparsely decorated parlours of the previous century that these rooms were places for entertaining and that work-related activities were out of place.

Dedicating a room specifically to dining was a luxury and did not spread throughout the middling sort until at least the late eighteenth century, and designating the room as a 'dining room' took even longer. In the examples of inventories consulted, only one person, Sarah Greaves, had a dining room listed before the nineteenth century.[33] This scarcity is partly explained by the sample consisting almost exclusively of middling sort living predominantly in rural and small town locations, and the fact that in some inventories rooms were not named. However, it is clear that the term 'dining room' came into use slowly. The 'Little Dining Room' in Sarah Greaves's house in Bradwall, Derbyshire, was far from being a smart room with only basic furniture consisting of a table with two forms and, rather strangely, a clothes horse. How this room differed from the rooms used for dining in other homes is difficult to say.

Rather than a designated dining room it was far more common to have several parlours with one used as a dining parlour, even in homes of high status. One such example is the home of bachelor Henry Wakeman Newport, who lived in a large house in rural Worcestershire.[34] No dining room was listed in

---

[31] D.R. Hay, *The Laws of Harmonious Colouring* (Edinburgh and London: William Blackwood and Sons, 1847 [1836]), pp. 167–8.

[32] Mrs William Parkes, *Domestic Duties* (London, 1828), p. 173.

[33] LRO, Sarah Greaves, widow, Bradwall, 1711.

[34] Wanklyn, *Inventories*, inventory of James Wakeman Newport, bachelor, Hanley William, 1785.

the house but it seems that the 'Large room' served this purpose, whereas the 'Drawing Room' was a formal reception room and the 'Little Parlour' probably doubled as an informal parlour and dining parlour. The Large room contained 'Twelve mahogany chairs open banisters hair seats brass nailed, [a] pair large mahogany square leaf dining tables, [a] large mahogany side board carved frame, [a] pair brass sconces double branches, [a] brass stove, [a] grate and fender'. This room therefore had the necessary specialist equipment for a smart dining room. Mahogany was the fashionable material for furniture by this period and woven horsehair was a practical and popular choice for upholstery since it could easily be wiped clean. A more luxurious alternative would have been leather seats. In a separate list that suggests they were the contents of cupboards in the housekeeper's room were quantities of china, glass and earthenware. Again, specialist items were noted – such as wine decanters, cut glass syllabub dishes, a set of stands for pickles and a pair of sauce boats.[35] Other china consisted of several sets of cups and saucers but the only plates listed were 'six small desert plates blue'. The only other plates listed for this house were all pewter: 'thirteen pewter plates, one dozen hard pewter plates, twenty three old plates, five hard soup ditto'. While pewter plates were still commonly used by many middling sort people at this time, they were becoming old-fashioned and would certainly have been seen as such amongst the wealthier people whom James Wakeman Newport might be expected to have entertained to dinner.

A number of other men in the sample also had several living rooms listed, one or both of which might have been used as a dining parlour. The home of Edward Baldwyn (d. 1700), a gentleman farmer in Worcestershire, provides an example of several multipurpose rooms where food could be served wherever it was convenient, depending on the numbers or status of visitors.[36] The house had a Great parlour, and a Little parlour, each with a table and a variety of chairs listed. There was also a Hall, which seems to have served its traditional function, with three tables, two forms and 14 chairs. Perhaps his servants or farm workers used this room. Certainly, the furnishings of the parlours – with the seating incorporating leather and Turkey work upholstery and a couch – suggest better-quality furnishings and surroundings that were more comfortable.

Combining dining rooms and parlours in multifunctional living rooms continued throughout the period, although specialist dining rooms had become commonplace in the homes of the wealthy. The scarcity of dining rooms in the sample is partly an indication of the status of the homes, but it also reveals that the householder did not provide formal dining for guests. Many homes in the first half of the nineteenth century that were in other ways comfortable, well equipped and even fashionable were still lacking in this respect. For example, before she died in 1848 and an inventory was made of her goods, Celia Parker

---

[35] One small saucepan was listed in his 'Back Kitchen'.

[36] Wanklyn, *Inventories*, inventory of Edward Baldwyn, bachelor, Longdon in Tredington, 1700.

in Chichester had a drawing room and front parlour.[37] Neither room had a dining table, only smaller ones such as a Pembroke table, and several chairs were present in each room. The front parlour had a mahogany cellaret sideboard with knife case and decanters, suggesting that it was a dining parlour. However, both rooms also had comfortable seating – a *chaise longue* in the parlour and a sofa in the drawing room – that confirms that these were in practice multifunctional rooms.

For a single man, eating and drinking were important pastimes and the dining parlour would have been central to his home. The gendered nature of the dining room meant that he would feel 'at home' and could relax. If he was on his own or with male friends, drinking to excess was acceptable, as was using a chamber pot kept in a special compartment of many sideboards.[38] While polite society might dictate certain levels of decorum and specify a growing number of specialist items and furniture, for men on their own the situation was more easygoing. Male sociability in the home could continue to centre on the serving of basic meat, bread purchased from a baker and beer or wine, and therefore did not require any new equipment that would be revealed in an inventory. Men could entertain other male friends and business associates in their home with somewhat inadequate equipment. An older man might even entertain mixed company if the situation was right and no impropriety could be inferred. As Miss Matty declares when she, Miss Pole and Miss Smith visit the bachelor Mr Holbrook in *Cranford*, 'It is very pleasant dining with a bachelor … I only hope it is not improper; so many pleasant things are!'[39] The Cranford ladies did not know which room to choose to sit in since none of the rooms seemed 'appropriate', but then far less in the way of home comforts and refinements were expected of men. They were shown into a room of uncertain character with:

> oak dressers and cupboards all round, all over by the fireplace, and only a small Turkey carpet in the middle of the flag floor. The room might have been easily made into a handsome dark-oak dining parlour, by removing the oven, and a few other appurtenances of a kitchen, which was evidently never used.

The ladies reject this 'ugly apartment' and instead sit in Mr Holbrook's counting-house, which had a pleasant outlook and was filled with books that covered the walls but also spilled onto the table. Clearly, Mr Holbrook also favoured this room. Mrs Gaskell was conveying the message that Mr Holbrook's shortcomings were only superficial. Indeed, the shortcomings would not have been present if Mr Holbrook and Miss Matty had married as they had intended. He would then have had a wife to make him a proper home. The women of Cranford would not

---

[37]   WSRO, Add. Mss. 2245, Henry and William Peat notebook.

[38]   Hutchinson, *Number 57*, p. 32. See also Glanville and Young, *Elegant Eating*, pp. 74–5.

[39]   Elizabeth Gaskell, *Cranford* (Harmondsworth: Penguin, 1976 [1851]), pp. 72–82.

have been so forgiving if one of their number had entertained them in a dusty and disorganised parlour.

Men offering hospitality in their own homes to an all-male gathering could obey rather different rules from those governing a mixed group, as the occasion of what came to be known as the 'Immortal Dinner' demonstrates.[40] The artist Benjamin Robert Haydon knew a great many artists and writers and they often called to see him, sometimes to sit for him – providing the characters in his large biblical scenes – but also sometimes staying for dinner. On one notable occasion, 28 December 1817, his rented rooms provided the backdrop for a distinguished gathering. His guests included Wordsworth, Keats and Lamb, plus a cousin of Mrs Wordsworth. As dinner progressed they discussed Homer, Shakespeare, Milton and Virgil. The serious nature of the discussion was lightened by humour, particularly since Lamb got 'tipsey' and was 'excessively merry and witty'. Charles Lamb suffered from 'mental instability', which manifested itself in mood swings from depression to the use of 'outrageous puns and hysterical fits of gaiety on solemn occasions'. He enjoyed drinking alcohol but did not have a good head for it and became intoxicated quickly.[41] Therefore, his contribution to the proceedings can easily be imagined.

As the evening went on other guests arrived – including Joseph Ritchie, who was a surgeon and African explorer. The conversation moved on to discussing the African continent. Although Haydon did not describe the rooms or list how many he rented, he seems to have had at least one living room beyond his painting room, which also doubled as a living room. The company moved between the rooms, taking tea in a different one from where they had dined. Food was never mentioned, but alcohol was apparently plentiful. He summed up the happy occasion by saying: 'There was not the restraint of refined company, nor the vulgar freedom of low, but a frank, natural license, such as one sees in an act of Shakespeare, every man expressing his natural emotions without fear.' The only dampener was the presence of the comptroller of the Stamp Office, who did not drink alcohol, remained serious throughout and, to Wordsworth's embarrassment, became the brunt of Lamb's excessive humour.[42]

Such high spirits and relaxed atmosphere was probably only possible for Haydon and other men of his outlook in an all-male gathering. Their shared literary and artistic interests were important to their friendships, but so too was their shared homosociability. For wealthy men in the nineteenth century London club culture catered for such gatherings, providing 'an extension of the homosocial network

---

[40]   See Penelope Hughes-Hallett, *The Immortal Dinner* (Chicago: New Amsterdam, 2002). This event was some years before his marriage.

[41]   Helen Ashton and Katharine Davies, *I Had a Sister* (London: Lovat Dickson Limited, 1937), pp. 54–5.

[42]   Wordsworth held the office of distributor of stamps in Westmoreland. The dinner is described in Haydon's diary; see Willard Bissell Pope (ed.), *The Diary of Robert Haydon* (Cambridge, MA: Harvard University Press, 1960), vol. 2, pp. 173–5.

of the public school system that groomed gentlemen' and where 'a gentleman-bachelor spins his orbit through a world of men'.[43]

For Haydon and his friends, the presence of women would have required 'unnatural' restraint rather than the 'frank, natural license' possible amongst male friends.[44] A similar dissatisfaction was no doubt often the reaction of women to 'mixed company', although perhaps having a rather different ideal in mind. Sarah Hurst commented on this problem. For example, one evening she recorded: 'Reflect on the trifling conversations generally found in mix'd company that never tends to improve and seldom to divert the mind.' On the occasion of a friend's marriage she lamented that there was 'A great deal of company but no conversation, this is always the case in mix't companies, the converse of one dear friend is infinitely preferable.'[45] The perception of mixed male and female company being a constraint on behaviour and conversation indicates how the sexes were divided by manners and cultural interests.

Within the conjugal home the everyday entertaining of guests of mixed sex to a meal accompanied by beer could be conducted in a parlour or even in a houseplace for the lower-status middling sort. Women were needed to provide the right setting, and to order the food but were expected to leave so that men could smoke and talk without inhibition. The same situation prevailed throughout the long eighteenth century. Women on their own perhaps only rarely served dinner to guests beyond their immediate family, especially to mixed company. Serving a polite dinner required specialist equipment and ideally a room to be set aside specifically for dining. It was not just having the right equipment that prevented women participating in such activities, but rather society's expectations of what was correct behaviour. Single men, on the other hand, could entertain people to dinner with less than perfect equipment and, despite the increase in formality associated with dinner, this need not be observed in an all-male gathering. While not having a wife to cook and preside over serving the meal might have been a slight disadvantage to them, single men with sufficient income could employ an efficient housekeeper to meet these requirements, or they sufficed with a valet or good manservant.

Men could also entertain friends and business associates outside their homes. They could leave all the food, preparation, utensils, furniture and a convivial atmosphere to be provided by an inn or similar establishment. This was a common

[43]   Barbara J. Black, 'The Pleasure of Your Company in Late-Victorian Clubland', *Nineteenth-Century Contexts*, 32/4 (2010), pp. 281–304, pp. 281–2. See also A. Milne-Smith, 'A Flight to Domesticity? Making a Home in the Gentleman's Clubs of London, 1880–1914', *Journal of British Studies*, 25/4 (2006), pp. 796–818. On male bonding in schools, universities and clubs, see Richard Dellamora, *Masculine Desire: The Sexual Politics of Victorian Aestheticism* (Chapel Hill and London: University of North Carolina Press, 1990), p. 195.

[44]   Pope, *Diary*, p. 175.

[45]   Djabri, *The Diary*, pp. 67 and 75.

occurrence in London and other large towns, although less common in smaller urban locations. As Johanna Schopenhauer observed: 'the Londoner prefers to take his friend to a tavern rather than to entertain him at home. There, tête-à-tête or in a larger, but always private circle, they indulge in wine, politics and light-hearted banter.'[46] It is a common assumption that men, as agents of Enlightenment rationality, were the primary actors in fostering sociability beyond the confines of the household and this important part of male life. Diarists such as Woodforde, Holland and Oakes attest to the amount of time middle-rank men devoted to such activities.[47] In practice, this was probably more amplified when singlehood made polite forms of domestic social diversion problematic either as a direct result of compromised or shared living arrangements, or accusations of possible indecorous or rather indelicate association when entertaining. Many inns also offered a quasi-domestic space and were at the forefront of consumption, acquiring luxuries and new types of furnishings before individual homes. In 1782, the German traveller Carl Philip Moritz stayed at an inn in Derby and reflected in his diary on the decoration in inns that he had visited:

> Usually you find that the pictures and copperplate prints hung in English inns are portraits of the Royal Family in a group assembled round their father the King, or a map of London. The portrait of the King of Prussia I have found to be very popular in this district. Scenes by Hogarth are often to be found.

Moritz was on a strict budget and liked to stay in 'homely' inns, but doubtless many other single men enjoyed the additional comforts and material benefits afforded them by such establishments.[48]

A flavour of male behaviour can be gleaned from the diary of John Lush in 1836. Lush was a bachelor and working artist in Chichester who subsisted on an erratic supply of portraits, repair jobs, artistic instruction and other petty and infrequent commissions.[49] However, whilst Lush clearly affected an air of gentility identified from his careful sartorial bearing to the cigars he smoked and distributed to clients and would-be customers, home was not a happy site of entertainment and sociability where the sentiments of polite masculinity were located. Like many lower-rank artisans, home was firmly associated with work;

---

[46] Schopenhauer, *A Lady's Travels*, p. 153.

[47] See Margot Finn, 'Men's Things: Masculine Possession in the Consumer Revolution', *Social History*, 25/2 (2000), pp. 133–55; pp. 137–42 for the habits of these male diarists.

[48] Carl Philip Moritz, *Journeys of a German in England in 1782*, translated and edited by Reginald Nettel (London: Jonathan Cape, 1965), pp. 31 and 157.

[49] WSRO, Add. Mss. 19026, Diary of John Lush; David Hussey, 'Guns, Horses and Stylish Waistcoats? Male Consumer Activity and Domestic Shopping in Late-Eighteenth- and Early-Nineteenth-Century England' in Hussey and Ponsonby (eds), *Buying for the Home*, pp. 47–69.

and composition, far from being an artistic oeuvre, was viewed merely as labour: 'at home painting' is a regular refrain from the pages of the diary. Elsewhere and outside the confines of his domestic situation, Lush was clearly more animated. He was a regular and vigorous impromptu singer at local inns; enjoyed attending cricket matches, dinners and clubs with a host of clients, Chichester worthies and assorted friends; and, where propriety permitted, was keenly interested in gallant dalliances with female company when in the process of visiting or undertaking local excursions. Chichester offered many diversions, including a dinner club for men to which Lush belonged, and various inns hosted all-male dinners to celebrate such events as the racing at nearby Goodwood, and local MPs hosted dinners for their supporters.[50] To Lush the separation of work and home – a process that was well advanced in the bourgeois home of the early nineteenth century – was thus somewhat inverted. In this context, Lush's rented rooms were not a bastion of the self or much of a refuge from the commercial intrusions of the outside world, but rather a dystopic arena characterised by the quotidian pressures of work.

Tea and 'Feminine' Entertaining

While the dining room and the dinner table had a distinctly male flavour in the long eighteenth century, the tea table was loaded with feminine symbolism. Serving hot drinks – in particular tea, but also coffee and chocolate – became a key method of offering sociability and was a popular alternative to serving a meal from the later seventeenth century onwards. Tea drinking took place after dinner, the main meal of the day, and also as independent refreshment – although the notion of a 'tea time' at about four o'clock in the afternoon did not evolve until the nineteenth century when the hour for dinner was pushed further back into the evening.[51]

The importation of tea began in the mid-seventeenth century at the outset of the period under consideration here.[52] The specialist equipment needed to make and serve tea was first imported and later made in Britain and both the tea and the equipage gradually became more readily available, although it took most of the eighteenth century for the price to come down sufficiently for tea to become commonplace. However, by the eighteenth century tea was overtaking coffee and chocolate as the most popular hot drink. Coffee and chocolate needed more preparation and servants did this in the kitchen. Tea, on the other hand, was made

---

[50]   Such events were regularly covered in the local newspaper: see for example an account of a dinner to honour a visiting dignitary hosted by William Charles Newland, *Sussex Agricultural Express*, 8 July 1843.

[51]   Davidoff, *Best Circles*, p. 49.

[52]   Carole Shammas, 'Changes in English and Anglo-American Consumption from 1550–1800' in John Brewer and Roy Porter (eds), *Consumption and the World of Goods* (London: Routledge, 1993).

in the parlour or drawing room by the lady of the house[53] and therefore lent itself to genteel rituals and encouraged the acquisition of specialist equipment, the spread of which is readily discernible in inventories of the period.[54] Many of the single women in the sample of inventories examined were well equipped to socialise in this way, certainly by the mid-eighteenth century.

Some items were essential for making and serving tea and other hot drinks, namely a tea kettle and ceramic wares. Other items were desirable and added to the ritual – such as tea caddies, mote spoons, slop bowls, tea trays and tea tables. These items might also incorporate attractive materials with display qualities such as silver and mahogany. A suitable room for sitting and receiving guests was also needed. The emergence of the parlour as a room separate from work activities and gradually free from sleeping arrangements happened at the same time that tea became a popular drink and tea drinking a polite way to entertain guests. Lorna Weatherill has likened this use of the parlour in the presentation of self to others using Goffman's 'front stage' concept. While there are flaws in the analogy, the parlour did function as a polite space. Before 1699 barely 11 per cent of women in the sample had earthenware listed and these items were not necessarily all tea wares; a further 3 per cent had porcelain (china) listed, and these were amongst the wealthier homes. By 1700–24 the numbers had risen slightly so that 22 per cent had earthenware listed; but china continued to be rare, with only 4 per cent owning such items (see Table 2.1).

Among the early examples of ownership of ceramic wares is Dame Mary Wintour, a widow living in Huddington in Worcestershire who died in 1697 and who had a large house with fine furnishings that were both luxurious and following fashion with a number of new commodities. Apart from the earthenware and china, she also owned glassware, window curtains and looking glasses; but the carpets in the house still seem to have been placed on tables rather than the floor. Somewhat less wealthy but still living in some comfort were Elizabeth Pershouse and Hannah Bradley from Staffordshire, who both died in 1706.[55] Pershouse was a gentlewoman living in Walsall and Bradley was a rural *rentier* living in the village of Wordsley, near Kingswinford – and both had small quantities of ceramic wares for tea drinking. Another woman with ceramics listed by this date was the widow Sarah Greaves.[56] She was a Derbyshire grocer and lived in a substantial house, the contents of which – together with stock, cash and debts – amounted to £712 when she died in 1711. None of the single men from the sample owned any ceramics by this date. Between 1750 and 1774 about half of the female sample acquired

---

[53]   Anon, *The Footman's Directory and Butler's Remembrancer* (London: Hatchard and Son, 1823), p. 112.

[54]   Weatherill, *Consumer Behaviour.*

[55]   Wanklyn, *Inventories*, inventories of Dame Mary Wintour, widow, Huddington, 1697; Elizabeth Pershouse, widow, Walsall, 1706; LRO, Hannah Bradley, widow, Kingswinford, 1706.

[56]   LRO, Sarah Greaves, widow, Derby, 1711.

earthenware ceramics; and between 1800 and 1850 virtually all inventories for single women listed utensils required for hot drinks, including ceramics, tea kettles and tea caddies – the exceptions being the poorest examples, and most were in rural locations. Porcelain remained rare although becoming more widespread after 1800, at which time porcelain production was increasing in England.[57]

The serving of tea and other hot drinks was closely linked to contemporary ideas of politeness.[58] The correct ingredients and paraphernalia were required and the hostess needed to know how to use the equipment correctly. She was demonstrating her knowledge of polite society as well as her ability to purchase the goods.[59] House visiting to drink tea and have polite conversation with friends and associates was a particularly female activity, as evidenced by the many entries relating to this in Sarah Hurst's diary. During the year 1759 she made explicit references to drinking tea when visiting others on 26 occasions and served tea to visitors 17 times. In addition, a great many other social occasions were recorded where tea drinking was probably involved.[60] Such activities were sufficiently common by the early eighteenth century for men to be worried that it encouraged gossiping and perhaps other bad habits amongst women. As early as 1701 Charles Burnaby's play *The Ladies Visiting Day* lampooned the gossip and intrigue that went on over the teacups. By 1800 the practice of paying calls was such a central plank in polite association that it could support a guide that promised to 'reduce to a system' how best to deliver visiting cards and save on postage.[61] The ritual of female visiting became ever more codified and observed a strict hierarchy of who was invited and the level of hospitality that was offered. Throughout the nineteenth century offering tea to guests continued, particularly as a female custom.[62]

While tea drinking and the equipage have been strongly associated with female practices,[63] contemporary sources suggest that men took an interest in this form of consumption too. The examples of inventories for single men examined here revealed a similar pattern of ownership of these commodities despite no single men having ceramics before 1724. After that date about half acquired hot-drink utensils and most had them after 1800. The few who did not have such items recorded either had incomplete households for one reason or another, or they were old-

---

[57] See Hilary Young, *English Porcelain, 1745–95: Its Makers, Design, Marketing and Consumption* (London: V&A Publications, 1999).

[58] Rachel Kennedy, 'Taking Tea' in Michael Snodin and John Styles (eds), *Design and the Decorative Arts: Britain 1500–1900* (London: V&A Publications, 2001), p. 253.

[59] Clive Edwards, *Turning Houses into Homes: A History of the Retailing and Consumption of Domestic Furnishings* (Aldershot: Ashgate, 2005), p. 78.

[60] Djabri, *The Diaries*.

[61] Patrick Boyle, *The Ladies Complete Visiting Guide* (London, 1800).

[62] Davidoff, *Best Circles*, p. 74. See Margaret Ponsonby, *Stories from Home: English Domestic Interiors, 1750–1850* (Aldershot: Ashgate, 2007), pp. 142–9.

[63] Elizabeth Kowalski-Wallace, *Consuming Subjects: Women, Shopping and Business in the Eighteenth Century* (New York: Columbia University Press, 1997).

fashioned rural households such as that of James Mullock, the unmarried farmer of Whitchurch, Shropshire, who died in 1804.[64] As the disorder of his home clearly indicated, Mullock wanted no involvement with genteel consumption practices or with offering any form of polite hospitality beyond peremptory or casual business association.

Of course, single men of substance were likely to invest in the requirements of a polite household. Here, the entertaining of colleagues, business associates and fellow worthies ensured that the imbalanced nature of the non-marital household towards notionally masculine spaces and pursuits was lessened. For example, Henry Woollcombe, the Plymouth attorney, invested heavily in fashionable dinner equipment and ceramics as well as more gender-specific items such as a well-stocked wine cellar. As a private household inventory revealed in December 1841, Woollcombe had an extensive array of domestic silver and plate – over 350 individual items, some of which were either sold or later dispersed through lack of use. In addition, Woollcombe possessed some 101 items of glassware, mostly wine glasses and tableware, and over 220 pieces of china – divided between a 'best set' (143 items, of which there were 56 dinner plates) and a more everyday 'blue set' of 79 pieces. As befitted his status as a prominent figure in the administrative and literary circles of Plymouth, Woollcombe – who had effectively retreated into semi-retirement by this time – had the capability, if not perhaps the inclination, to entertain on the grand scale.[65]

An indication of potentially different attitudes to the household, and in particular the ownership of ceramics, is demonstrated by comparing the inventories of two couples where the husband died a few years before his wife and the inventories suggest that the wife had increased the ceramic wares for the household. In both these instances, the ceramic items may have been omitted from the earlier inventories for a host of reasons. In both cases, the women had been married before and therefore some of the goods could well have been excluded since they were legally or informally considered to belong to the wife under the law of coverture.[66] None the less, the increased presence of ceramics imply that both of these women had closer associations with ceramics than their husbands and that they were perhaps able to modify the rituals of serving and eating food and drink in their homes after they had been widowed.

The inventories and administrations, dated 1728 and 1735, of Thomas and Anne Creswell of Tideswell in Derbyshire reveal a number of differences.[67] It is in

───────────

   64   Shropshire Archives (SA), 6000/12167, Auctioneer's notebook, James Mullock, bachelor, Whitchurch, 1804.

   65   Plymouth and West Devon Record Office (PWDRO), 710/398 Henry Woollcombe, inventory of wine, silver, plate, glass ware and china, December 1841.

   66   Erickson outlines a number of cases where such informal agreements separated household goods: Amy Louise Erickson, *Women and Property in Early Modern England* (London: Routledge, 1993), pp. 144–7.

   67   LRO, Thomas Creswell, Tideswell, 1728; Anne Creswell, widow, Tideswell, 1735.

the decorative and expressive goods that the two inventories differ. In particular, Anne's inventory listed a range of additional domestic niceties – including a 'tea table, 3 hand boards, a set of blue and white china, 6 coffee pots, 5 plates, slop bason, milk jugg, [and] 2 sugar dishes' – that were entirely absent from the marital home.[68] A similar pattern of ownership is apparent in the less affluent home shared by John and Susanna Marrian in Bobbington, rural Shropshire. The farmhouse was somewhat lacking in ceramics when John died in 1761.[69] The couple and their children had relied heavily on pewter and wooden plates, with a just a few delft ware items. When Susanna died nine years later the wooden trenchers were missing from the kitchen list and the delft ware had doubled in number.

Social rituals connected with tea drinking changed over time, but location was also a factor in people's participation. Tideswell was a small village and Bobbington was an agricultural hamlet and therefore both Ann Creswell and Susanna Marrian would have had limited access to company to entertain in their homes. The town of Bridgnorth in the early to mid-eighteenth century was a more promising venue since it was a busy market town that attracted gentry families to live, or at least to shop at the numerous retailers and tradesmen catering for luxury trades, such as cabinetmakers and upholsterers.

The unmarried sisters Catherine and Hannah Poyner shared a home in Bridgnorth until they both died, in their mid-50s, in 1765.[70] The Poyners were a well-established family in the town where their father had been a successful timber merchant and had held the office of both burgess and churchwarden. Their position in Bridgnorth, their well-appointed home in the centre of town and the extensive array of goods that it contained offered them ample opportunities to entertain local ladies in comfort and with appropriate gentility. Their parlour was simply furnished with a Japanned tea board and two mahogany trays, a tea chest with canisters, and several tables and chairs. While the pewter and common earthenware were stored in the kitchen, the Poyners' porcelain was listed separately either for convenience (the house contents were to be sold off to pay their brother's debts) or because it was stored in a different place suited to its delicate nature. The detailed listing of Catherine and Hannah's china provides ample evidence of their interest and pleasure in having a well-equipped tea table. As well as several teapots, sets of both plain china, and blue and gold cups and saucers, there was also a sugar dish with a cover, a china tea canister, several slop basins and a boat for spoons.

While undoubtedly a genteel and polite ambience could be achieved in the Poyners' parlour, their home lacked really smart elements. They had no large items of furniture in mahogany or walnut, and there were no gilded mirrors or even window curtains. Bridgnorth was a busy market town on the Welsh border and was therefore somewhat limited in the fashionable consumption that was either possible or desired

---

[68]   For a wider discussion of the Creswells see Chapter 2.

[69]   LRO, John Marrian, Bobbington, 1761; Susanna Marrian, widow, Bobbington, 1770.

[70]   LRO, Hannah and Catherine Poyner, spinsters, Bridgnorth, 1765.

by its residents. The city of Canterbury, by contrast, was a hive of commercial and manufacturing enterprise. In addition, the city boasted many places of entertainment as well as the social activities connected with an important cathedral and these facilities attracted the elite in society. The possibilities for entertaining in homes there were almost limitless. As Overton et al. have indicated,[71] people residing in Kent were generally well placed to acquire and use new commodities and therefore Canterbury would have been a particularly good location to live for fashionable consumption. An example is provided by the home of Miss Lamprey, who lived in Canterbury until her death in 1764, when an extensive catalogue was produced and which included all the paraphernalia required for serving tea politely in a refined ambience in the mid-eighteenth century.[72] The parlour contents included a mahogany tea table, mahogany tea board, coffee mill, a tobacco dish, a cribbage board, a mahogany tea chest, two Japan tea boards and one waiter. The decorative elements further included a large square looking glass, two pairs of crimson checked window curtains and a small pier glass. These items were followed by a list of china and glass, perhaps stored in a built-in cupboard in the parlour. The extensive list included: 'Thirteen blue and white china plates, Ten blue and white cups and eight saucers, Six blue and white coffee cups, Six coloured coffee cups, One coloured tea pot, one milk pot, two tea spoon boats, Five tea cups and fifteen saucers'. The blue and white china was either imported porcelain or made by one of the English makers, such as Worcester. Porcelain ceramics were highly prized at this period, especially before Wedgwood perfected his creamware – a refined version of earthenware which became a cheaper and fashionable alternative in the mid-1760s.[73] However, Miss Lamprey's coloured or enamelled wares were even more impressive than the blue under glazed china, being more expensive to purchase. The teapot and other items would have been an attractive sight on her mahogany tea table, just as they were pictured in many conversation pieces of the period. Her walnut and wainscot furniture was perhaps not as fashionable as the mahogany items, and crimson checked curtains were not especially grand. For 1764, however, Miss Lamprey had everything to serve hot drinks in a refined, genteel and polite interior; and the quantities of the ceramic wares suggest that at least occasionally she had entertained guests with these hot drinks and with genteel pastimes such as playing cribbage.

Individual Tastes and Interests

The homemaking practices examined so far in this chapter have dealt with singletons who had learnt sociability and seem to have desired to relate to other

[71]   Overton et al., *Production and Consumption.*

[72]   Catalogue of all the household goods of Miss Lamprey, Canterbury, 1764. *ECCO*, Gale document number CW107372180.

[73]   See Sarah Richards, *Eighteenth-Century Ceramics: Products for a Civilised Society* (Manchester: Manchester University Press, 1999).

people in ways that conformed to the principles dictated by society at large. This society favoured the marital home containing a husband and wife. However, an independent life did offer stronger possibilities for diverging from the usual patterns of home life. Some singletons chose not to be sociable. Indeed, some perhaps had never acquired this skill and this in part accounted for their remaining single. Different lifestyles might also be reflected in the way that a home was furnished and used. As their life progressed, the unmarried homemaker might indulge special interests, acquire collections of objects, use rooms to suit individual preferences and generally be more selfish in their domestic practices. As Mary Wollstonecraft expressed it in a letter to a friend: 'It is a happy thing to be a mere blank, and to be able to pursue one's own whims, where they lead, without having a husband and half a hundred children at hand to tease and control a poor woman who wishes to be free.'[74] How such wishes might find expression in the material culture of the home is an intriguing point, particularly with regard to gendered differences. The remainder of this chapter looks at sometimes slender and in some cases more substantial evidence of single people indulging their individual preferences in their homemaking.

In the plethora of home furnishing advice books that were published in the nineteenth century a common theme was explaining and demonstrating the gendered nature of different types of sitting room in the home, chiefly the 'feminine' drawing room and the 'masculine' dining room.[75] By the 1880s Jane Ellen Panton, a writer of a number of such books, argued for the third sitting room, if a house should run to more than two, to be a feminine morning room (also described as a breakfast room) rather than a masculine study or library. A morning room would have provided an informal daytime sitting room with lighter colours often employing naturalistic flower patterns and lighter wood or perhaps cane furniture. Not only women but also the children of the household would have used such a room. By contrast, a study or library may well have been considered a private sanctum by the man of the house, in which he could escape his family duties.[76] The choice of types of sitting room by single people who were in a position to please themselves reveals something of the gendered nature of homes and how people wished to express their preferences in homemaking. Such choices would have been reflected in the decoration and contents as well as the function of living rooms. Despite the pressure to conform, some single people broke the rules

---

[74]   Quoted in Bridget Hill, *Eighteenth-Century Women: An Anthology* (London: Allen & Unwin, 1984), p. 129.

[75]   Juliet Kinchin, 'Interiors: Nineteenth-Century Essays on the "Masculine" and the "Feminine" Room' in Pat Kirkham (ed.), *The Gendered Object* (Manchester: Manchester University Press, 1996), pp. 12–29.

[76]   Jane Hamlett, 'Managing and Making the Home: Domestic Advice Books' in Jeremy Aynsley and Charlotte Grant (eds), *Imagined Interiors: Representing the Domestic Interior Since the Renaissance* (London: V&A Publications, 2006), pp. 184–5.

and used their homes in ways that would have been seen as different and even eccentric by contemporaries.

The association between women and drawing rooms was firmly established by the early nineteenth century. Loudon stated: 'The furniture for the drawing-room being generally chosen by the lady, a tolerably fair opinion of her taste and good sense may be formed from the manner in which it is displayed and arranged.'[77] As Disraeli also observed, 'Woman alone can organize a drawing room; man succeeds sometimes in a library.'[78] So, for example, the gendered nature of the homemaking of James Watt junior and Anne Boulton is shown by their choices of living room. While Watt spent quite lavishly creating a small library at Thornhill House with bookshelves commissioned from the cabinetmaking firm of George Bullock, spending enough to warrant taking them with him when he moved to Aston Hall, Boulton made the same room into a breakfast parlour.[79]

A library contained more than books. This was where collectors would keep their prints, coins, medals, antique busts and other classical, antiquarian or natural history items – depending on taste, interests and income. *Practical Economy* in 1822 observed that 'even the economical amateur may venture upon a few specimens to complete the arrangements of his library'.[80] Although other parts of the book assume a female reader, this section was clearly addressing a masculine audience.

Thomas Sheraton, in *The Cabinet Dictionary* (1803), warned against introducing items into a drawing room that would detract from conversation, the main function of the room. Such items included books and globes.[81] However, a few years later Mrs Parkes, in her advice manual, suggested the opposite: that some well-chosen ornaments would stimulate conversation, although cautioning against making the room too fussy.[82] Nineteenth-century prescriptive literature was constantly offering advice that probably left the reader more confused than enlightened, for example that rooms should be rich but not gaudy. However, the difference of opinion between Sheraton and Parkes coincides with the idea of making libraries into general living rooms, especially as a kind of morning room, in family homes by the early nineteenth century rather than the all-male preserve that they had been in the previous century. Libraries had originally held a marginal position in the house, tucked away with the gun room and other parts of larger houses given over to masculine pursuits. It was not counted as one of the public

---

[77]   J.C. Loudon, *The Suburban Gardener and Villa Companion* (London: Longman, Orme, Brown, Green and Longmans, 1838), p. 101.

[78]   B. Disraeli, *Coningsby* (1844), cited in P. Tristram, *Living Space in Fact and Fiction* (London: Routledge, 1989), p. 59.

[79]   Shena Mason, *The Hardware Man's Daughter: Matthew Boulton and his 'Dear Girl'* (Chichester: Phillimore, 2005).

[80]   Anon, *Practical Economy* (London, 1822), p. 115.

[81]   See Edwards, *Turning Houses*, p. 79.

[82]   Parkes, *Domestic Duties*, p. 194.

rooms of the house until the seventeenth century, when gradually it took on more social and cultural importance. This physical change of location also meant that the library became a fashionable room suited to its greater exposure to the gaze of visitors to the house.[83] As the library was claimed as a general living room the studious reader was forced to escape to a *sanctum sanctorum*, usually a private study where peace and quiet could be guaranteed. Sir Walter Scott needed to create such a room at Abbotsford for writing his novels since his impressive library adjoined the drawing room and the two rooms were used together to accommodate large gatherings of people in the house.[84] This general trend perhaps had less effect on the homes of unmarried people who could continue the use of gender-specific rooms.

One man who succeeded in furnishing his library with every comfort and refinement was the Rev. Robert Norgrave Pemberton, who lived in a roomy rectory in Church Stretton, Shropshire. Pemberton had a dining room and drawing room that were correctly furnished for the period when he died in 1848. Next to the drawing room, however, was the room that perhaps most expressed his personality and that he enjoyed spending time in, his library. This room had the most extensive list of any in the inventory of his home and was itemised in some detail.[85] Pemberton's library contained:

2 pair Chintz draperies over Window & Cornice
Brussels Carpet on floor & Hearth Rug
Mahogany Glazed bookcase opposite fire
Ditto Glazed Bookcase opposite windows
Ditto Ditto side of fire
Ditto Ditto Ditto
Ditto Ditto in Pier
Library Table with drawers Desk on top
Pembroke Table & small ditto Table
Mahogany Whatnot
Pedestal of drawers
Folding Screen & Chair Back Screen
Couch in Chintz cover
Easy Chair in leather
Mahogany Carved Arm Chair

---

[83]   T.A. Birrell, 'Reading as Pastime: The Place of Light Literature in Some Gentlemen's Libraries in the 17th Century' in Robin Myers and Michael Harris (eds), *Property of a Gentleman: The Formation, Organisation and Dispersal of the Private Library, 1620-1920* (Winchester: St Paul's Bibliographies, 1991), p. 129.

[84]   Clive Wainwright, 'The Library as Living Room' in Myers and Harris, *Property*, p. 19.

[85]   SA, D3651/B/9/6/2/5 Auctioneer's inventory of Rev. Robert Norgrave Pemberton, Church Stretton, 1848.

6 Mahogany Chairs in Coloured Hair Cloth
Mahogany Stool in Needlework
Footstool ditto under Desk
Door Porter, Tea Caddy and Book Tray
Indian Box
4 Varnished prints black frames
Portrait Crayon
Oil Picture 'Heads'
View of Millichope[86]
1 Plaster bust, 6 Ditto Figures
Vase, 4 Other Casts, & 2 marble Vases
Pastille Burner & 2 Spill Cups & large medallion & Oval hanging Glass
Flower Vase & marble Vase
2 letter Weights & Bronze Candlesticks
Silver Ink Stand & 2 Glasses
2 Earthen flower Pots
bronze fender Set Fire irons
Guard, Coal Hod, Hearth Brush & pr Bellows

This precise listing reveals that Reverend Pemberton's library had two windows, the fire was at right angles to the window wall and that each wall had bookcases lining them. Surrounding the fireplace some wall space was free to display seven pictures and a looking glass. Some of the plaster busts and marble statues and vases must have sat on top of the bookcases or above the door, and a few items were on his desk along with the writing paraphernalia. The presence of sculptures was entirely appropriate for a serious library. The pedestal of drawers might indicate a collection of some sort, such as coins or medals or natural curiosities – again appropriate for someone with a wish to use the library in a serious and studious manner. According to Wainwright's observations, the only things missing are a set of library steps to facilitate reaching books on the higher shelves, but this was a country vicarage not a grand country house.[87] Pemberton had a mahogany chair drawn up to the desk with a stool beneath it to protect his feet from draughts. A folding screen and one on his chair back took care of draughts in the room more generally. The floor was covered in carpet and curtains draped the two windows. When he wanted to relax he could choose between a chintz-covered couch and a leather-covered easy chair, the latter being ubiquitous with a gentleman's library.

---

[86]   Millichope Park was the property he had inherited from his father in 1832 and which he rebuilt in the 1840s as a grand country house. Although an absent clergyman in his later years he seems to have retained his rectory with all the furnishings complete. See G.C, Baugh, *Victoria County History of Shropshire* [*VCH Shropshire*]. *Vol. 10: Wenlock, Upper Corve Dale, and the Stretton Hills* (Oxford: Oxford University Press for the Institute of Historical Research, 1998), pp. 112–14 and 159.

[87]   Wainwright, 'The Library as Living Room', p. 22.

Here was a room of physical comfort that provided Pemberton with the practical items necessary for him to write letters and sermons, it also expressed his identity as a university educated and land-owning gentleman.[88] What are missing from the inventory are the books that lined the shelves. Pemberton amassed over 900 books in his library and their tooled leather bindings would have added considerably to the serious and masculine luxury of the room.[89]

A library or study could provide a private space for a man to escape from domestic pressures. For example, Oliver Heywood, a non-conformist minister, recorded an argument with his wife; and to escape her 'peevish' mood he 'withdrew myself into my study'.[90] However, a private sanctum was not necessarily a luxury and could produce a cell-like environment. Such was the case in the home of the clergyman John Skinner in Camerton, Somerset, who obsessively collected material on Roman Britain.[91] After his young wife and his favourite child died, Skinner mentally retreated into his studies and physically retreated into his library. By the time of his death, at his own hand, he had accumulated 98 volumes of manuscripts dealing with his research that filled three iron chests. For Skinner the return to being a singleton provided the opportunity for his melancholic mind to be indulged and his ill-founded obsession to prove the importance of Camerton in Roman Britain to take over his domestic life.

The closest any of the Midlands examples came to creating an antiquarian interior was James Watt junior. Watt rented Aston Hall on the outskirts of Birmingham between 1818 and 1848. It was a huge house for a bachelor living alone and he only lived in one section. Watt had previously commissioned furniture from George Bullock but he had died in 1818 so Watt used Richard Bridgens, who had worked with Bullock. Bridgens designed some individual pieces of furniture in Greek Revival style but also produced a number of items in a heavier Jacobean style, including a chair using earlier panelling. In the 1820s, the antique furniture trade was still in its infancy and there were none of the worries about authenticity that became important later. The grandest room at Aston Hall was the long gallery, followed by the 'great dining room', with an elaborate plasterwork ceiling and wooden panelling. This panelling had been 'modernised' at some point by painting it white. Perhaps James reacted to it in the same way that Mrs Radcliffe's heroine, Emily, did in her Gothic novel *The Mysteries of Udolpho* (1794) when she was 'distressed to find the beams and wainscot of the Gothic hall at Epourville painted white'.[92] Watt had the paint removed to restore its appearance. This is the room that became his library. Watt enhanced the period details of the room, although

88 He owned land and properties including the Fox Inn at Church Stretton that was run by tenants; this was before inheriting the Millichope estate. SA, 1045/522 will of Pemberton dated 1834.

89 *VCH Shropshire*, vol. 10, p. 114.

90 Quoted in Flather, *Gender and Space*, p. 59.

91 Wainwright, 'The Library as Living Room', p. 21.

92 Quoted in Tristram, *Living Space*, p. 166.

Figure 4.1   The library at Aston Hall by A.E. Everitt, 1854. James Watt enhanced the Jacobean style decoration to make a suitable setting for a gentleman's serious library, including the addition of blinds painted with knights in armour to match the plaster decoration. *Source:* © Birmingham Museums and Art Gallery.

some were only in a Jacobean style carried out in the eighteenth century (Figure 4.1).[93] For example, he used a sympathetic paint treatment on plasterwork friezes and panels depicting knights in armour. A sombre colour scheme of dark reds and blues and bookshelves and furniture 'with curly strapwork and split baluster ornament' all gave the room the appropriate 'historical' ambience.[94]

While filling a home with antiquarian objects and displaying them remained rare in the eighteenth century, collecting minor items of antiquarian interest or specimens of geological or natural history was quite common. *The Servants' Guide and Family Manual* recommended making collections of shells but only if the collector found out about them; otherwise they would be 'mere baubles' and to 'display a collection under such circumstances is to emblazon ignorance'.[95] These interests seem to have appealed particularly, although not exclusively, to men and a number of the single men examined here had such collections in their homes. Such 'masculine' interests were expressed by, among others, the Rev. Henry Nussey when he moved to a remote coastal parish in West Sussex. He recorded walking in the countryside and on the seashore, taking some comfort in the scenery and changing weather conditions, to offset the alienation he felt from living in such a remote spot as well as his lack of success in finding a wife. He described collecting things on the beach and on one occasion even discovered a skeleton, which he and a friend dug up. He took the bones home, 'where they form a fine but melancholy addition to my small stock of curiosities collected at the beach amongst which are some very large teeth, supposed mammoth's'.[96] These objects became a talking point for Nussey and his few male friends in Sussex. This was in 1839 and long before Darwin's shock revelations; but interest in palaeontology and archaeology was growing and the discovery of fossils and dinosaur bones was already stimulating debate into the age of the Earth.

Numerous learned societies and associations were founded in the first half of the nineteenth century to pursue research into archaeology, geology and natural history. Among them was the Natural History Institution of Hereford, founded in 1836, which later became known as the Woolhope Naturalists' Field Club.[97] Men overwhelmingly populated such societies. Amongst the members were many

[93] Birmingham Museums and Art Gallery, 1946p20. Although dated 1854, Glenn's research suggests that preparatory sketches were made at the time of the sale in 1849 following Watt's death. See Virginia Glenn, 'George Bullock, Richard Bridgens and James Watt's Regency Furnishing Schemes', *Furniture History*, 15 (1979), pp. 54–67.

[94] Glenn, 'George Bullock', p. 56.

[95] Anon, *The Servants' Guide and Family Manual* (London, 1830), p. 96. The advice on collections continued with the comment that collections of china were a waste of money since they merely collected dust in 'some dark closet'.

[96] British Library, Egerton MSS 3268A, Diary of Henry Nussey, 14 February 1839.

[97] F.C. Morgan, 'Woolhope Naturalists' Field Club: An Outline of Its History 1851–1951' in *Herefordshire: Its Natural History, Archaeology, and History* (Gloucester: The British Publishing Company, 1954), p. 2.

clergymen and others in the professional class. Field trips of the Woolhope club always ended with dinner at a local inn. At just this period, the British Archaeological Association came into being and helped to formalise the discoveries being made. Henry Wace, an unmarried solicitor in Shrewsbury, became a member, serving on the local committee of the society.[98] His interests inspired him to make a journey to Egypt and he wrote about his experiences and paid for them to be published as a slim volume entitled *Palm Leaves from the Nile* (1865).[99] However, despite these interests, his home was probably furnished in a conventional manner since he purchased carpets and furniture from the fashionable and conservative Birmingham furnishing draper, Eld and Chamberlain.[100]

Similarly, Henry Nussey's rectory in rural West Sussex seems to have been conventionally furnished. He and his sister Anne were sharing the accommodation in 1844 when an inventory was made of the contents prior to the house being packed up and removed to Derbyshire, where Henry had been appointed vicar at Hathersage. There were two living rooms described with the conventional titles of dining room and drawing room. However, from the listing of contents it seems that Henry used the dining room as a study-cum-library since the rectory did not have any additional rooms to serve this purpose. The main items in the dining room were mahogany bookshelves and some chairs. The furniture in the drawing room combined both dining and parlour-type items, with an easy chair, a chiffonier, dining table and eight chairs present. No books were listed but a large number are indicated by Henry's diary entry in March 1839, a few months after his arrival in this remote area. He was overjoyed when his books arrived, coincidently on his birthday, recording: 'On Thursday ... received my boxes of books etc from York, Six men req'd to lift chest, cost only 5s 6d carriage ... Thank God for their safe arrival.'[101] Presumably his books, papers and 'small stock of curiosities' were housed in the room listed as the 'dining room', and could be viewed there by his male visitors.

A general interest in natural history, technology and history was in evidence throughout the home of Jonah Bissell,[102] an unmarried metalwares manufacturer in Birmingham in 1842. The ornaments in his front parlour and rear sitting room consisted of:

Parlour
Time piece in a spar frame
Pair of glazed medallions of George III, with small shell ornaments
Stuffed pheasant in glazed case

---

[98] Wace was listed in a printed leaflet of the 17th Annual Meeting of the Shrewsbury branch of the British Archaeological Association in 1860. SA, Watton Cuttings, volume 8, p. 175.

[99] A copy is in the Shropshire Archives.

[100] BCA, MS1081/1–8 Eld and Chamberlain catalogue and receipts for Wace.

[101] British Library, Egerton MSS 3268A, Diary of Henry Nussey, 1 March 1839.

[102] BCA, MS 319/6 Auctioneer's leaflet for Jonah Bissell, 1842.

Pigeon and bantam cock in glazed cases
Two paintings by the Woodman
Capital wheel barometer by Pedretti

Sitting room
Spar ornaments
Two stuffed woodcocks, in glazed frames
Capital eight-day clock, in polished mahogany case, with day of the month, minute hand dial, &c
Small wheel barometer

Bissell's books included 'Smith's Map of England and Wales, Dugdale's Antiquities of Warwickshire, in 1 vol. folio, with plates, 1745, Dugdale's Correspondence and Life, 1 vol. 4to., Chamber's Encyclopaedia of Arts and Sciences, fine plates, in 4 vols. Folio, strong calf'. Further evidence of his being drawn to antique curiosities was listed in the bedrooms. An 'Antique carved oak linen chest' and a 'Curious antique musical chime clock, by Wentworth, of Sarum' were highlighted by the catalogue.

The above section on personal interests and specialised taste expressed through home furnishings is limited to people who kept their interests confined to a modest expression and only indulged their interests in a restrained manner that did not disrupt the domestic nature of their homes. Some people, however, knew no bounds when their interests reached epic proportions, and in the homes of unmarried people there was no spouse to keep interests in check – or at least confined to the early modern equivalent of a shed in the garden. Such individuals allowed their special interests to change their homes quite dramatically. For example, before his marriage, Andrew Crosse inherited Fyne Court in the Quantocks. Interested in 'spontaneous life forms', and possibly an influence on Mary Shelley's *Frankenstein* (1818), Crosse created a 'huge, chaotic laboratory' in what had been the ballroom.[103] Tastes in interiors could be taken a stage further than merely a room devoted to study and a collection of antiques and geological or natural history specimens. Some homes became what Wainwright has termed 'Romantic Interiors', where the collections of antiquarian objects took over and dictated the entire ambience of the interior. Where such passionate interests dominated the material culture of homes they invariably affected domestic routines.

The freedom to arrange the home to suit personal preferences was an advantage enjoyed by single people who had sufficient income to be independent. Will Fellows argues that 'gay' men have been particularly prone to such homemaking practices. He suggests that they have been particularly active as 'keepers of culture'. Fellows defends the use of the term 'gay' to apply to earlier periods than our own and across cultures since his definition of 'gay identity' requires looking 'at a person's

[103]   Richard Holmes, *The Age of Wonder: How the Romantic Generation Discovered the Beauty and Terror of Science* (New York: Pantheon Books, 2008), p. 420.

nature beyond the scope of his sexual orientation per se'. Thus, Fellows looks for certain traits in behaviour as well as biographical details to identify men who displayed the characteristics of gay identity although their sexual orientation is not known. Fellows summarises gay identity as 'gender atypicality, domophilia, romanticism, aestheticism, and connection- and continuity-mindedness'.[104] While the use of the term 'gay' is problematic and the attribution of gayness to historic figures is controversial,[105] still we cannot ignore the fact that some singletons chose to remain unmarried due to gender 'atypicality', even if not acted upon or acknowledged. The earliest example that Fellows quotes is of the Reverend William Bentley, who was a great collector of objects connected with the history of the area of Massachusetts where he lived. In his diary, Bentley lamented the death of an elderly bachelor in 1796, wishing that he could purchase his home and its contents in order to preserve them intact as an historical document. Fellows goes on to give numerous examples of the traits that he has identified – including Henry Davis Sleeper, who created a house in Gloucester, Massachusetts, in which each room expressed a different historical theme. One room was called Strawberry Hill, inspired by the Gothic house of Horace Walpole, and Sleeper also founded the Walpole Society in 1910 for like-minded collectors and preservationists.

Horace Walpole certainly corresponds to Fellows' criteria. He has been described as 'an interpreter and preserver of the past … a re-creator of the cultural inheritance who manipulates past and present for his own aesthetic purposes'.[106] During his formative years, Walpole created his aesthete persona at the same time as acquiring the taste that resulted in his extraordinary house, Strawberry Hill in Twickenham. Walpole was a huge influence on his friend Richard Bateman, claiming to have converted him 'from a Chinese to Goth' or from chinoiserie to Gothic.[107] Bateman rented a fairly humble dwelling in Windsor called Grove House and in the 1740s he had enhanced it to create a Chinese fantasy of temples and pagodas. However, after his conversion, Grove House was added to and transformed into a cloistered 'mock-monastery' and renamed The Priory. Mrs Delany visited him and claimed that the house had 'changed its religion'.[108]

---

[104]   Will Fellows, *A Passion to Preserve: Gay Men as Keepers of Culture* (Madison: University of Wisconsin Press, 2004), pp. 13 and 25. See also Dellamora, *Masculine Desire.*

[105]   Although controversial, Fellows' project is not unique. For example, in November 2010 Birmingham Museums and Art Gallery staged an exhibition entitled 'Queering the Museum' to reinterpret some of their collection.

[106]   Brian Louis Pearce, 'Horace Walpole: The Creation of a Persona' in *A Tribute to Horace Walpole and Strawberry Hill House: On the Occasion of the Bicentenary of his Death on 2 March 1797* (London: Borough of Twickenham Local History Society, paper no. 74, 1997), p. 3.

[107]   Nikolaus Pevsner, *The Buildings of England: Herefordshire* (Harmondsworth: Penguin, 1963), p. 288.

[108]   David Nash Ford, 'Royal Berkshire History, http://www.berkshirehistory.com/castles/priory (accessed 19 January 11).

Bateman was wholehearted in this endeavour and created a museum in the house for his collection of curiosities that included 'a piece of the True Cross', and the collection spilled over into the parlour and library. The dining room was designed by John Henry Muntz in a Gothic style.[109] Even the bedchambers had curious items of furniture and rather funeral furnishings. The influence also flowed in the opposite direction: when Walpole saw Bateman's collection of stained glass he ordered some for himself; and after Bateman's death, Walpole purchased at the subsequent house sale a large number of ancient chairs and took them back to Strawberry Hill. Bateman had collected some of these chairs at farmhouses in Herefordshire near his family's country seat. Bateman was a younger son and when his brother John became the Second Viscount Bateman and took over the family estate at Shobdon he allowed Richard to remodel the parish church. This unfortunately involved the demolition of an important Romanesque building, but the new church was a delicate and light creation similar in style to Strawberry Hill.[110] Richard Bateman had been disappointed in love and before reaching the age of 40 he seems to have given up on the idea of matrimony. An unmarried sister was given a home in a building called The Hermitage in the grounds of The Priory and Bateman devoted his life to his friends and to his collection and building enterprises.

Not all of Walpole's circle were as wealthy as Bateman. Others were academically inclined men whom he had first met at Cambridge. During this period he made friends with, among others, the poet Thomas Gray[111] – who accompanied him on his tour of Europe – and William Cole. Cole accords with the less wealthy, professional antiquarian of which there were a great many in the eighteenth and early nineteenth centuries, many of whom did not marry. Cole entered the Church and became a curate in Suffolk, although retaining his rooms at King's College as well as a small country property. When he became a vicar in Buckinghamshire in 1753 he gained his own rectory and finally gave up his college rooms. Since Cole did not agree with clergymen getting married he depended on servants to look after his home and tellingly wrote to Walpole that his collections were his 'only delight – they are my wife and children'. His life work was historical research, in particular the history of Cambridgeshire. He amassed a huge collection of books, prints and stained glass at his home, many of which he bequeathed to the British Museum.[112]

---

[109]   Teresa Sophia Watts, Johann Heinrich [John Henry] Müntz, *Oxford Dictionary of National Biography* (*ODNB*) online, http://www.oxforddnb.com (November 2004).

[110]   John Andrews, 'The Churches of Shobdon' in *A History of Shobdon Church*, booklet, n.d.

[111]   See R.L. Mack, *Thomas Gray: A Life* (New Haven and London: Yale University Press, 2000).

[112]   John D. Pickles, William Cole (1714–1782), antiquary, *ODNB* online (October 2004).

Similar to William Cole was the parson described by Washington Irving in *Bracebridge Hall*. Irving made several trips to Britain during which he visited Scott at Abbotsford and Aston Hall near Birmingham, the home of James Watt junior. The central house in *Bracebridge Hall* was loosely based on Aston Hall. Irving suggested that many 'poor scholars', such as this parson, met wealthier patrons when they were students together at university. The parson he described:

> lived almost entirely among books, and those, too, old books ... his taste for literary antiquities was first imbibed in the Bodleian Library in Oxford; where, when a student, he passed many an hour foraging among the old manuscripts. He has since, at different times, visited most of the curious libraries in England, and has ransacked many of the cathedrals.[113]

He is 'quaint' and a 'dark, mouldy little man' but he comes alive when talking on his favourite subject of rare books and particularly enjoys viewing them in a dusty room with Gothic furniture: 'At his suggestion, the squire has had the library furnished in this antique taste, and several of the windows glazed with painted glass, that they throw a properly tempered light upon the pages of their favourite authors.' Although Irving is clearly delighting in painting a caricature of an antiquarian, it was also a type that his readers would recognise; and the physical attributes and obsessive learning of the unmarried clergyman were set against a suitably antique backdrop.[114]

Limitations on Female Expression in the Home

For women there was no possibility of going to university or taking up a profession that would give them an independent income with which they could establish a home and scholarly collection. Katherine Sharp has argued that the 'New Learning' meant that women were able to take an interest in 'mathematics, science and natural history, collecting and arranging specimens to assist their observations', and that these interests and collections influenced domestic interiors.[115] It is still the case that examples of women creating extraordinary interiors that were dominated by their interests are few and far between and most are drawn from aristocratic and wealthy families. For example, the Parminter cousins, Jane and Mary, designed and built a 16-sided house called A la Ronde, in Exmouth, Devon. It was filled

---

[113] Washington Irving, *Bracebridge Hall* (London: Macmillan, 1882 [1822]), pp. 91–4.

[114] For a further literary example see Walter Scott, *The Antiquary*, first published in 1816.

[115] Katherine Sharp, 'Women's Creativity and Display in the Eighteenth-Century British Domestic Interior' in Susie McKellar and Penny Sparke (eds), *Interior Design and Identity* (Manchester and New York: Manchester University Press, 2004).

with curious objects collected on their travels in Europe and decoration that they devised incorporating feathers and shells. The cousins did not marry and stipulated in their wills that the house should pass down through the female line.[116]

Eleanor Butler and Sarah Ponsonby were almost as famous for creating an antiquarian interior at their home in Llangollen as for their 'elopement' and 'romantic friendship'. When they set up home together in Llangollen both women were escaping from unsatisfactory home lives.[117] Eleanor Butler's family were trying to force her to become a nun since she refused to marry. Sarah Ponsonby was an orphan and dependent on a cousin whose husband made unwelcome advances. While homosexuality in men was outlawed and condemned by society at large, homosexuality in women was largely unrecognised since it was seen as an impossibility. However, it was not entirely ignored. In 1789 Mrs Piozzi published an article in which she referred to Sapphists as 'the latest unnatural vice'.[118] According to Elizabeth Mavor, in the later eighteenth century, romantic friendships used the word 'romantic' to mean extravagant and fanciful and therefore was applied to intense friendships between women that occurred due to the cultural gulf that generally existed between men and women: 'A glance at the more notable correspondence of the period will show that what we would now associate solely with a sexual relationship; tenderness, sensibility, shared tastes, coquetry; were then very largely confined to friendships between women.'[119] While such friendships were generally accepted and thought normal by society[120] in some cases the attachments were felt to be dangerous when the feelings involved knew no restraint. Eleanor Butler and Sarah Ponsonby, the 'Ladies of Llangollen', were criticised by some for these tendencies and Mrs Siddons suggested that Bath was 'a cage of these unclean Birds'.[121]

The Ladies of Llangollen were exceptional since they were from an aristocratic background, which perhaps gave them the confidence to pursue their individual taste and lifestyle. Although chronically short of money, and living on a few hundred pounds a year, they embarked on ambitious schemes at their small cottage, called Plas Newydd – adding a kitchen and brewhouse and making various alterations.[122]

---

[116]   Siân Evans, 'Houses of Character: Eccentric Personalities in National Trust Houses', *The Royal Oak Newsletter* (Fall 2006), pp. 1 and 9–11. A la Ronde is now a National Trust property and open to the public.

[117]   For an account of their lives, see Elizabeth Mavor, *The Ladies of Llangollen* (London: Penguin, 1971).

[118]   Quoted in Mavor, *The Ladies*, p. 78.

[119]   Mavor, *The Ladies*, p. 81.

[120]   See Sharon Marcus, *Between Women: Friendship, Desire, and Marriage in Victorian England* (Princeton: Princeton University Press, 2007).

[121]   Mavor, *The Ladies*, p. 81.

[122]   They only rented the cottage until the early nineteenth century, when their faithful housekeeper Mary Carryll died and left them her savings and they used the money to purchase it.

Most ambitious and remarkable was the 'Gothicisation' of the cottage, particularly the additions of carved oak decoration. In true eighteenth century style, they made a collage effect of carved panels from a variety of sources attached to the walls of rooms and the staircase. They were not afraid to combine different styles of carving; nor presumably were they worried about plundering items of old furniture for their panels of decoration. Likewise, fragments of stained glass, some pieces found at the nearby ruins of Valle Crucis Abbey, were inserted into windows to make a patchwork of colours and patterns. The downstairs accommodation consisted of a dining room and library, no parlour or drawing room. This might be construed as a 'masculine' choice of living rooms since both dining rooms and libraries were designated as such in the later eighteenth century. The library was lined with Gothic-style bookcases and was described by the unmarried poet and friend of the Ladies, Anna Seward, as a 'saloon of the Minervas'. Upstairs was their bedroom and dressing room. From their written accounts, the dressing room was small and cosy but was in reality the large room above the library. The Ladies retired here at nine each evening in order that their servants might go to bed. Here they continued their daytime activities of writing letters, reading and playing backgammon. Although this room was being used as a sitting room, due to its position, upstairs, accessed through their bedroom and designated a 'dressing room' it was effectively made a private room not available to visitors.

Having won their freedom the Ladies were determined to live their lives in the way that they chose. They developed a 'Plan' by which they would fill every minute of their day with studying languages, philosophy and literature, Eleanor often reading aloud while Sarah did fine needlework, embroidery and netting purses. Their home was famous and influential; their many visitors included illustrious people of the time, many of whom brought an antiquarian gift to increase the ornamentation and decoration of the cottage. The exterior grounds at Plas Newydd were also ornamented to match with rustic bridges, a temple and even the font from Valle Crucis Abbey.

Catherine Hutton recorded visiting 'the cottage of Lady Eleanor Butler and Miss Ponsonby' in 1796[123] but made no further mention of her reactions to the way that the cottage was furnished or to the gardens, perhaps because much of the Gothicisation took place after this date. She had already taken an interest in gardening and indeed had sampled cottage living. After the Birmingham riots of 1791 had almost destroyed their country house, called Bennett's Hill, they lived in a cottage while the house was repaired. She commented: 'My inexhaustible fund of amusement is the garden; there I sow and plant, and weed and water without end, and it does as well as anything else.' Catherine's outlook on life was similar to the Ladies of Llangollen in that she believed in self-improvement and always having something to do. At the age of 89 she claimed: 'I never was one moment

---

[123]   Catherine Hutton Beale, *Reminiscences of a Gentlewoman of the Last Century: Letters of Catherine Hutton* (Birmingham: Cornish Brothers, 1891), p. 118.

unemployed when it was possible to be doing something.'[124] Her employments
included reading, drawing, studying English and foreign clothing, which along
with autographs she collected and pasted into books and carefully indexed. She
was also a great needlewoman and, like Sarah Ponsonby, took great 'delight
in netting purses'. She wrote to a friend in 1829: 'You will laugh at me but the
contrast of colours, and variety of patterns, please and interest me. I believe I was
intended by nature for a needle-worker.'[125] However, her letters gave no indication
that she developed the same taste for Romantic and Gothic interiors so beloved by
the Ladies, although she knew and corresponded with the Birmingham antiquarian
William Stamper.

For many women indulging in the acceptable interests of reading, sewing,
painting or collecting china, the amount of equipment required was negligible
and therefore would not be listed in an inventory of a home's contents or, if of
a personal nature, they had been dispersed prior to death. It was not until the
mid-eighteenth century that specialist equipment became available, and indeed
began to be thought necessary. In the case of needlework, this equipment took
the form of sewing tables made by cabinetmakers in attractive designs with
silk bags on the underside to hold all the threads and work in progress. Such
worktables were found in the inventories of many of the single women's homes
in the sample in the early to mid-nineteenth century. Miss Mayor in Meole Brace
near Shrewsbury, for example, had 'Mahogany Lady's Work Tables' listed in the
auctioneer's advertisement for her home in 1831[126] and Mary Ann Livingston had
a total of four such tables listed in her drawing room after her death in 1843. The
decorative possibilities of these objects are revealed by the various descriptions
of Livingston's worktables. Two were made in mahogany, one was on a black
stand and one was a painted table on a tripod stand.[127] Such worktables could also
be used as side tables for placing teacups and refreshments and were therefore
perfectly at home in parlours and drawing rooms.

Fewer women than men created highly individual interiors or allowed obsessive
collections to take over their domestic lives. As Virginia Woolf argued in *A Room
of One's Own*, there were good reasons for this:[128] a lack of education available to
most women; the inability of women to generate and control a sufficient income
for independence; and, similarly, their insufficient command of space in their
home to devote to their own interests whatever form this took – whether writing,
collections or scientific experiments.[129] Nor were there professional occupations,
so prevalent in the male examples quoted above, for women in the long eighteenth

[124]   Beale, *Reminiscences*, p. 215.
[125]   Beale, *Reminiscences*, p. 202.
[126]   *Salopian Journal*, 20 December 1831.
[127]   WSRO, Add. Mss. 2245, Henry and William Peat notebook.
[128]   Virginia Woolf, *A Room of One's Own* (Harmondsworth: Penguin, 1995 [1929]).
[129]   Jane Hamlett suggests that some female students went against 'feminine' style
decoration in their college rooms in the later nineteenth century. Hamlett, *Material Relations*,

century. The possible exception was that of governess and they lived in the homes of others and did not command income or space sufficient to mould their domestic lives in a significant way.

A few exceptional women overcame the obstacles. Caroline Herschel was unusual in that she was as passionate as her brother in his scientific interests, and her research was even published by the Royal Society – a rare accomplishment for a woman. Equally rare was the pioneering photographic work of Lady Lucy Bridgeman and her sister Charlotte, although remaining largely unknown beyond their family circle.[130] Lucy and Charlotte were the daughters of the 2nd Earl of Bradford of Weston Park in Shropshire and they acquired a camera in the early 1850s.[131] This would almost certainly have been a sliding-box camera, which preceded the folding bellows model. The process of early wet-plate photography was difficult to master and Lucy's early experiments were not particularly successful. One setback was recorded in Charlotte's diary on 27 November 1855, for example:

> the stuff we made for sensetising [sic] the paper proved to be in anything but a clean bottle and we had the whole trouble of filtering it all over again and we still have to do the paper tomorrow. It certainly is very puerile work at present but I hope we shall get the swing of it soon.

They persevered and achieved striking results. Most of Lucy's subjects were family and friends with a country house backdrop. On 16 February 1856 Charlotte wrote: 'We photographed in the diningroom the upper servants in a group and then me. Both successful. We also did Miss Hope after luncheon before going out.' They thus fitted in their hobby between social obligations. The portrait of Charlotte shown here was probably the one she noted in her diary (Figure 4.2).[132] The pose she adopted prefigures the seated husband and standing wife convention and instead a picture is positioned on the chair, possibly one of their own paintings since they were both accomplished artists.

Lucy and Charlotte pasted their photographs into albums to be viewed by family and friends. Such albums were given decorative borders to set off the

---

pp. 159–63. For a wider discussion on the command of space see Shirley Ardener, *Women and Space: Ground Rules and Social Maps* (Oxford: Berg, 1993).

[130]   Both sisters experimented with photography but Lucy seems to have been the most proficient.

[131]   Information about Lucy and Charlotte Bridgeman was kindly provided by the curator at Weston Park. Charlotte's diary is in a private collection. Lucy and Charlotte died in tragic circumstances in 1858, when they were 32 and 31. Their dresses caught fire in the library at Weston Park and they both died a few days later. See also C.S Sykes, *The Country House Camera* (London: Weidenfeld & Nicolson, 1980).

[132]   Lady Charlotte Bridgeman photographed by her sister Lucy, c.1855. The Trustees of the Weston Park Foundation.

Figure 4.2   Lady Charlotte Bridgeman photographed by her sister Lucy, c.1855.
               These pioneer photographers couched their efforts in homely
               domesticity despite the scientific nature of photography at the time
               or the artistry of their output. *Source*: The Trustees of the Western
               Park Foundation.

photographs and were drawing room artefacts rather than seen as scientific objects
or artistic productions to be displayed in an exhibition. The domestic rooms at
Weston Park were not disrupted by being turned into a darkroom to house the
chemicals required for the photographic processes. Instead, Lucy and Charlotte
confined their work to the cellar of the Temple of Diana in the grounds. Their self-
deprecating view of their work is captured by Charlotte's entry in her diary for 7
November 1855: 'shuttered myself up in the Temple to see if the stone parlour
would do for photograph messing in'.

Many other women must have been frustrated in not being able to pursue their
interests due to considerations such as education, propriety and income. Richard

Holmes suggests that women needed 'supportive or (even better) dead husbands, or private incomes' if they were to progress in science.[133] By the later nineteenth century this situation had improved a little as more career and educational opportunities opened to women. Such professions as teaching stipulated that women were not allowed to marry and therefore women who pursued them were out of necessity lifelong singletons. Some no doubt created homes that reflected their interests but they are beyond the scope of this book.

Conclusion

Women gained some ground for entertaining in the home due to the popularity of tea drinking, and the growth of the idea of comfort favoured their homemaking practices. Men had other opportunities for entertaining, especially at all-male gatherings for meals in the home or elsewhere in the public arena. Men were more likely to have strong interests that changed the domestic nature of their home interiors – they had the financial freedom to do this or it was linked to their work. A small minority of women were able to live independently and they were to some extent able to please themselves in their domestic arrangements; but even they seem to have been less likely to have created a 'gendered' room for self-absorbed interests that disrupted the essential domestic nature of the home.

Many of the examples dealt with in this chapter held relatively privileged positions due to financial security. Most singletons in the period were not so fortunate. Most lived more dependent lives, although, even within the confines of dependency, many were able to carve out a degree of individual homemaking. These compromised homes warrant extensive consideration and are the focus of Chapter 5.

---

[133] Margaret Bryan, Priscilla Wakefield, Jane Marcet and Mary Sommerville all being examples of successful scientists in the later nineteenth-century. Holmes, *The Age of Wonders*, p. 179. See also Claire Brock, *The Comet Sweeper: Caroline Herschel's Astronomical Ambition* (Cambridge: Icon Books, 2007), p. 157.

Chapter 5

Compromised Spaces: Lodgers, Boarders and Shared Domestic Space

In July 1828, Thomas Giordani Wright, a 20-year-old trainee doctor of some social standing, was required to move to the newly refurbished practice of his master, James McIntyre, in salubrious Eldon Square, Newcastle. The change of domicile from his previous situation – 'a dirty smoky hole with a black ceiling' surrounded by 'walls which could not upon a moderate computation have been papered or cleaned within the last century' – was a cause of some delight as it permitted Wright to enjoy a more congenial working and domestic environment. As Wright reported in his diary:

> Now at any rate I have a comfortable rush bottomed arm chair to sit down in (one or two to spare for a friend also) and the light of heaven and sunshine to enliven me. A pair of globes, pray take notice, ornament my sanctum, and all bears an air of comfortable usefulness. I must not omit to add that a good genteel set of fire irons and fender with a respectable grate and black marble chimney piece form part of our arrangements; and that good inside folding window boards have assumed the place of a queer dingy, black-brown, quondam green gauze blind with sundry rents and peep holes, which was all the protection our last settlement afforded. The new surgery, though, like the room above it small, is at last conveniently arranged; and when *it* gets its finishing coat of paint and I get my room *papered*, this part of the great house will have a genteel appearance not unworthy of the rest of the building.[1]

Whilst Wright eulogised about a fondly imagined and newly acquired status – his room, complete with new oil-cloth flooring befitted, in his words, both the '*dedication* of the place, and the *gentleman* who inhabits it' – it remained, that as an apprentice, his situation was largely circumscribed by the requirements (and material provision) of McIntyre: the comparative sophistication of the grand urban practice could easily be substituted for one of McIntyre's basic surgeries in a dingy colliery outpost. True to form, Wright was dispatched to Backworth, 'in the very midst of inclines, coal pits, wagon ways & steam engines', two days later. Yet for Wright, the creation of a domestic space over which some element of control and direction could be exercised was a key aspect in establishing

---

[1]   A. Johnson (ed.), *The Diary of Thomas Giordani Wright, Newcastle Doctor, 1826–1829* (Surtees Society, 206, 2001), 24 July 1828, pp. 276–7.

personal independence, status and distinction. Even for a comparatively callow youth, Wright's apprehension of his putative status as a nascent gentleman-professional was expressed physically through rooms and goods. Home in its many guises became increasingly a vehicle for freighting a sense of individuality and taste for men and women of the middling sort, although this was expressed within the boundaries of polite expression and mediated by economic necessity.[2] For single households, as indeed for the marital home, maintaining these spaces in both their cultural and material representations denoted a careful adjustment to the demands of respectability and propriety that informed acceptable behaviour. As recent scholarship has outlined, home became equated with a site of comfort, harmony and the performance of distinctive gendered behaviour as the period progressed. Similarly, attitudes to the domestic tended to become more encoded and less flexibly interpreted as the concern for replicating an idealised template intensified.[3] The trend towards homemaking was not lost on those households headed by single men and women, whether widowed or never married; and, where financial and economic circumstances permitted, the single householder was arguably less encumbered than their marital counterparts in the direction of domestic affairs. Certainly, established households like that of parson Woodforde, the more unusual mother–son ménage of the Purefoys or, somewhat later, James Watt junior had a far greater latitude of personal input into the material culture of their homes than other contemporaries whose choices and predilections were naturally mitigated by concerns for spousal approval. In these often exceptional and economically robust instances, single householders could clearly suit themselves.

What then of those single homemakers whose opportunities for inhabiting let alone furnishing these spaces were considerably curtailed? As we have discussed in previous chapters, the immediate constraints of lifecycle rendered the single existence almost inevitable and a period away from the familial home in extended apprenticeship or service formed a common experience for many young men and women in the period. Similarly, old age and the onset of infirmity encouraged many single people who were insulated from the depredations of poverty by accumulated wealth, *rentier* income or annuities to consider living with kin or

---

[2]   See, for example, P. Carter, *Men and the Emergence of Polite Society, Britain, 1660–1800* (Harlow: Longman, 2001); J. Tosh, 'The Old Adam and the New Man: Emerging Themes in the History of English Masculinities' in T. Hitchcock and M. Cohen (eds), *English Masculinities, 1660–1800* (London: Longman, 1999), pp. 219–20, 223; and L. Davidoff and C. Hall, *Family Fortunes: Men and Women of the English Middle Class 1780–1850* (London: Hutchinson, 1987), pp. 17–18 and chs 4 and 7.

[3]   This is discussed more fully in J. Tosh, 'Gentlemanly Politeness and Manly Simplicity in Victorian England' in J. Tosh, *Manliness and Masculinities in Nineteenth-Century Britain* (Harlow: Pearson, 2005), pp. 83–102 and J. Tosh, *A Man's Place: Masculinity and the Middle-Class Home in Victorian England* (New Haven and London: Yale University Press, 1999), pp. 27–50.

engaging in genteel boarding arrangements. Of course, straitened circumstances could throw erstwhile sole heads of households into the kinds of temporary, transient and ultimately insecure types of accommodation that characterised the 'economy of makeshift' endured by the resident poor.[4] This was an ever-present spectre for both the single person without or estranged from the wider support networks of family and near kin and the dependent widow, for whom the death of the spouse was often compounded by debt and the dispersal of the estate.[5] For both these groups, old age was not a site of comfortable retirement, but an altogether more abrasive encounter with the steely rigours of an increasingly prescriptive poor law.[6] In this chapter, we examine the situation of these single agents and the adjustments they made in relation to sharing or letting spaces over which they had restricted control. Were there, for example, opportunities in these compromised areas and, as Marcus has argued, 'fluid spaces' for individual contribution; and could the requirements of the discrete household – security, privacy and choice – be negotiated through the reduced means of the single room?[7]

A Room of One's Own? Lodging in Context

Lodging was commonplace and, from the later eighteenth century, the requirements of a large and increasingly mobile population undoubtedly encouraged the development of both ad hoc arrangements within established households and specialist, semi-formal lodging and boarding houses often

---

[4]   See the chapters contained in Steven King and Alannah Tomkins (eds), *The Poor in England, 1700–1850: An Economy of Makeshifts* (Manchester: Manchester University Press, 2003), especially Heather Shore, 'Crime, Criminal Networks and the Survival Strategies of the Poor in Eighteenth-Century London', pp. 137–65. T. Hitchcock, *Down and Out in Eighteenth-Century London* (London: Hambledon, 2004), pp. 1–22 and S. Hindle, *On the Parish? The Micro-Politics of Poor Relief in Rural England c.1550–1750* (Oxford: Clarendon, 2004), pp. 15–26 also discuss this concept.

[5]   Death was always a time of reckoning for businesses, and widows often found it difficult to maintain the viability of their husband's trade: B. Hill, *Eighteenth-Century Women: An Anthology* (London: Allen & Unwin, 1984), pp. 166–7.

[6]   See, for example, K. Wrightson and D. Levine, *Poverty and Piety in an English Village: Terling 1525–1700* (2nd edn, Oxford: Oxford University Press, 1995), pp. 73–109, 110–41; T. Wales, 'Poverty, Poor Relief and the Life-Cycle: Some Evidence from Seventeenth-Century Norfolk' in R.M. Smith (ed.), *Land, Kinship and Life-Cycle* (Cambridge: Cambridge University Press, 1984), pp. 351–404; W. Newman-Brown, 'The Receipt of Poor Relief and Family Situation: Aldenham, Hertfordshire 1630–90' in Smith (ed.), *Land, Kinship and Life-Cycle*, pp. 405–22; L. Bothelo, *Old Age and the English Poor Law, 1500–1700* (Woodbridge: The Boydell Press, 2004), pp. 18–79; and Hindle, *On the Parish?*, pp. 405–33.

[7]   S. Marcus, *Apartment Stories: City and Home in Nineteenth-Century Paris and London* (Berkeley: University of California Press, 1999), pp. 3, 104–7.

located in the less salubrious areas of provincial market towns.[8] For example, the 1851 census for the central parishes of Worcester reveals that a cluster of lodging houses entirely occupied by unmarried men in their twenties and thirties were located in Lich Street, St Helen's parish, a poor area of closely built timber-framed buildings at the top of High Street. In common with many towns, a great many Worcester households routinely accommodated unrelated individuals alongside the nuclear family. Servants and extended kin were only part of this pattern; assistants associated with the head of household's trade also lived in. Thus, out of 104 households in or near Worcester High Street, 34 households contained apprentices, assistants or lodgers whose occupation was associated with that of the head of household. Most of these individuals were examples of early lifecycle singleness – single men and women who would no doubt go on to marry – whilst it is also clear that some heads of household were widows or widowers adapting to the other imperative of later lifecycle singleness, the need to rent rooms to supplement diminished income. This is consonant with the picture in other urban settlements: Anderson's analysis of the 1851 census indicates that lodgers were present in around 23 per cent of Preston households and that just under half of these lodgers (48 per cent) were unmarried.[9] In addition, at Worcester bachelors were also prominent as heads of households containing co-domiciled assistants. For instance, William Wales, a 26-year-old ribbon and fancy mercer and bachelor, accommodated four unmarried female servants – a milliner, two assistants and the house servant – aged between 20 and 25. Similarly, George Clarke, a bachelor of 27 and a draper, housed four unmarried (male) draper's assistants aged 16–27. The house was looked after by two single female servants aged 17 and 39. This type of lodging arrangement was also, as Trinder argues, not merely confined to urban locations.[10] Although it was a less common feature of village life, lower-status resident labourers and migrant workers comprised a noticeable lodging presence. In Strensham village

        [8]   See P. Sharpe, 'Population and Society, 1700–1840' in P. Clark (ed.), *The Cambridge Urban History of Britain: Volume 2, 1540–1840* (Cambridge: Cambridge University Press, 2000), pp. 513–18 and P. Clark, 'Migrants in the City: the Process of Social Adaptation in English Towns, 1500–1800' in P. Clark and D. Souden (eds), *Migration and Society in Early Modern England* (London: Hutchinson, 1987). For lodging houses, see B. Trinder, *The Market Town Lodging House in Victorian England* (Leicester: Friends of the Centre for English Local History, 2001); M. Glazier, 'Common Lodging Houses in Chester, 1841–71' in R. Swift (ed.), *Victorian Chester: Essays in Social History, 1830–1900* (Liverpool: Liverpool University Press, 1996), pp. 53–83; J. Emerson, 'The Lodging Market in a Victorian City: Exeter', *Southern History*, 9 (1987), pp. 103–13; L. Woolley, '"Disreputable Housing in a Disreputable Parish"? Common Lodging-Houses in St. Thomas', Oxford, 1841–1901', *Midland History*, 35/2 (2010), pp. 215–36.

        [9]   M. Anderson, *Family Structure in Nineteenth-Century Lancashire* (Cambridge: Cambridge University Press, 1971), pp. 46–7, 53.

        [10]   Trinder, *Market Town Lodging House*, pp. 52–3. Transient agricultural labourers and seasonal workers were also often housed in urban lodging houses.

near Worcester, for example, there were a number of homes where this seems a likely explanation for the make-up of the household. For example, in 1851 a 67-year-old widower housed four unmarried male lodgers ranging in age from 13 to 24; all five men were listed as agricultural labourers.[11]

For much of the period, apprenticeship and service defined the experience of young singletons and clearly impacted upon their subsequent material status. For example, in 1688, having completed a copybook apprenticeship to the satisfaction of his erratic but benevolent master, William Stout of Lancaster embarked on his career as an independent dealer in ironmongery and general grocery wares. Acquiring a suitable shop and fitting it out with appropriate fixtures and stock, however, was only one aspect of becoming a sole trader. Stout, who had hitherto boarded with his master, was forced to reappraise his domiciliary arrangements. His solution was to take:

> of[f] the shop a smal room, for a bed, table and a smal light, where I lodged. And … I went to bord with Alderman Thomas Baynes at the price of five pounds a year, victuals and washing. But lodged in the shop, so was seldom in the house, which was adjoining to my shop, but at victuals, summer or winter; for in my apprintiship, and some time after, we were frequently caled up at altimes of the night to serve customers, [which] obliged us to have a bed in the shop.[12]

His subsequent move into independent housekeeping was explained in part by a desire to ring-fence this business autonomy: hitherto the hospitality of his close neighbours permitted him 'to set … boxes of candy and confectioner goods by their fire, which I could not so safly do in a publick house where [I] borded' – but this was clearly an unsatisfactory and temporary arrangement.[13] In general, Stout's aversion to domestic comforts, in contrast to his personal frugality and the joys of business, would become a leitmotiv of the *Autobiography*. As an old man, he shied away from the conviviality of the parlour of his nephew and de facto landlord with its social gatherings of the local urban hierarchy; and throughout his life he never failed to reproach his apprentices, housekeepers and fellow traders on keeping 'wasteful' and 'evil company'. For Stout, commercial relations were not determined by the operation or vicissitudes of the market but by the manner and conduct of a trader's bearing and, thereby, probity. To this extent,

---

[11]   In some households this kind of residence may have been due to seasonal work or transitory labour.

[12]   J.D. Marshall (ed.), *The Autobiography of William Stout, 1665–1752* (Manchester: Manchester University Press for the Chetham Society, 1967), p. 90.

[13]   Marshall (ed.), *Stout*, p. 102. Over 100 years later, another Quaker merchant, Daniel Eccleston of Lancaster, faced similar issues as a young and single trader: C. Downs, 'The Business Letters of Daniel Eccleston of Lancaster (1745–1821): Trade, Commerce, and Marine Insurance in Late-Eighteenth-Century Liverpool, Lancaster, and Whitehaven', *Northern History*, 41/1 (2004), pp. 129–48: 133–4.

Stout was following well-worn Quaker mercantile precepts; but his repugnance of 'the conversation of ... persons who were of no good repuit' and the material outlay on entertainment required to lubricate deals revealed a failure to engage with the subtleties of an increasingly sophisticated transaction-based economy.[14] As Cox, Dannehl and others have argued, the blurring of the boundaries between the shop – gated linguistically by its commercial language and physically by its stock and counter – and the cultural licence afforded to the select guests permitted access to the domestic interior enabled astute traders to utilise household spaces to maximise business opportunities.[15]

If Stout's encounter with the domestic aspects of lodging was partial, other single men regarded such accommodation with more equanimity. As we have seen, Julius Hardy, the Birmingham button-maker, was quite content to board at his brother's house not merely because it was adjacent to his manufactory, but moreover because it obviated the onerous necessity of keeping house himself. As Hardy was to learn, such a task would prove to be far more vexatious than he imagined, and his inability to negotiate appropriate domestic arrangements rather than any romantic attachment actively propelled him into marriage.[16] In a similar fashion, Henry Woollcombe, the Plymouth attorney, experienced a range of semi-permanent lodging accommodation throughout his early career. Whilst completing his legal training at Lincoln's Inn in 1797, he took 'comfortable' but unspecified lodgings in the capital.[17] However, whereas the sights and distractions of the metropolis rather turned the bookish young man's head, Woollcombe was practically silent as to the quality or even the location of his living arrangements. Even so, on securing a lucrative preferment at Plymouth in July 1798, Woollcombe appears to have engaged a series of rather temporary lodging arrangements. Despite the fact that his brother William, the eminent local physician, resided in town, in 1802 Woollcombe finally fixed on lodgings suitable for a young, professional man with rather high Anglican predilections.[18]

---

[14]   For Quaker mores regarding business, see J. Walvin, *The Quakers: Money and Morals* (London: John Murray, 1997), pp. 5–8; A. Raistrick, *Quakers in Science and Industry: Being an Account of the Quaker Contribution to Science and Industry during the 17th and 18th Centuries* (Newton Abbott: David & Charles, 1968); and Marshall (ed.), *Stout*, pp. 103–4.

[15]   N.C. Cox and K. Dannehl, *Perceptions of Retailing in Early Modern England* (Aldershot: Ashgate, 2007), ch. 8, but especially pp. 168–74. See also M. Ponsonby, 'Towards an Interpretation of Textiles in the Provincial Domestic Interior: Three Homes in the West Midlands, 1780–1848', *Textile History*, 38/2 (2007), pp. 165–78: 170.

[16]   Birmingham Central Archives (BCA), 669002, MS 218 Diary of Julius Hardy, Button-Maker of Birmingham, 11 December 1788.

[17]   Plymouth and West Devon Record Office, 710/391–7 Diaries of Henry Woollcombe II, 1796–1828 (hereafter Woollcombe, *Diary*), 5 July 1797. Woollcombe occasionally lodged at an inn.

[18]   Woollcombe, *Diary*, 10 September 1802.

Writing in 1806, Woollcombe revealed that 'after a residence of four years & upwards' he was to quit his current situation for a newly purchased private dwelling that was more befitting to someone of extensive cultural interests and pretensions of high civic office. Tellingly, his assessment touches upon the conditions of what was a more exclusive boarding arrangement than that, for example, described by Stout – and indeed that which was commonly available in the commercial inns and boarding establishments in Plymouth. Woollcombe revealed that he had 'passed my time very pleasantly here, with my few rubs infinitely less than I expected; the owners have been invariably sivil & attentive to me, indeed so much so at times as to be troublesome'.[19]

Here Woollcombe implies an invasion of personal space suffered as the result of a too solicitous rather than blithely negligent landlord. None the less, Woollcombe's real reasons for leaving were painfully apparent. Whilst his new house occupied much of his time – so much so that 'no child can be more fascinated with a new rattle than I am with my revived notions of change'[20] – he admitted that: 'I was to think that I should not leave my lodgings until I married but that event being apparently as far removed now as when I first entered this House, it is in vain to wait.'[21] However, as the novelty of keeping house wore off and the grinding banality of a financially overstretched legal practice bit deeply into Woollcombe's cherished leisure time, he revealed that the large dwelling – and indeed his status as an independent householder – offered him but 'little enjoyment'.

In contrast, for many men the move from lodgings, with all the implied notions of impermanence and cultural inferiority, to sole householder held little of the emotional angst experienced by Woollcombe. For example, in 1808 the artist Benjamin Robert Haydon lived as a lodger at 41 Great Marlborough Street, London. Here he occupied a single, somewhat confined room that sufficed for a studio, parlour and bedroom. The multiplicity of function resulted in Haydon having to paint recumbent to accommodate the large canvases he was wont to produce, whilst eating and sleeping in an environment fouled by paint and solvent fumes. In 1817, however, Haydon quit his lodgings to rent a suite of rooms in 22 Lisson Grove North, Paddington. Here, Haydon's workspace and living quarters were quite discrete and, for the first time, Haydon provided his own furniture, furnishings and servants.[22] This change of status was recorded in his diary, Haydon noting that: 'when I think from what pestiferous air I have escaped and from what agonies I have escaped, as my apartments were so full, air could not circulate … had I not removed I should have died in six months, I am perfectly convinced … I dined & Breakfasted & slept in this air,' None the less, decamping to a more salubrious environment was not without problems:

---

[19]   Woollcombe, *Diary*, 12 October 1806.

[20]   Woollcombe, *Diary*, 16 March 1806.

[21]   Woollcombe, *Diary*, 12 October 1806.

[22]   William Bissell Pope (ed.), *The Diary of Robert Haydon* (Cambridge, MA: Harvard University Press, 1960), p. 129.

27 September 1817

> I left my old Lodgings this day, after living in them 9 years and ¾ I lingered about the rooms with fondness, recalled every action, every thing that I had done, painted, thought, or said. Every place, corner, teemed with associations, and after praying God to bless my worthy Landlord and accept all my gratitude for his infinite mercies to me during my stay, I left the place, musing on the awful nature of change.

Such romantic associations with place – the mark of the modern hedonist – were not lost on the artist. His new and decidedly more bourgeois existence 'was strange to me. I had no associations with it. All was in the future, a wild abyss, untrod, unknown!' Needless to say, Haydon's poetic apprehension of change was leavened by the comfort of material possession. The following day he reported that: 'I breakfasted for the first time in my life on my *own* tea cups and saucers. I took up my *own* knife. I sat on my *own* chair. It was a new sensation!' By the following month, the once struggling artist was clearly at home with the novelty of domestic ease: his 'new rooms' had 'every comfort' and he was, somewhat smugly, 'really & truly happy'.[23]

As these examples demonstrate, both lodging and boarding reflected a variety of situations for middling sort men that closely tracked their economic status and other lifecycle considerations.[24] For example, lodging could be a temporary station on the road to adulthood and, often married, independence. In addition, it represented a rite of passage wherein important pecuniary and housekeeping skills were learned or where the quotidian drudgery of running an efficient household was put off or delegated to others at a time when businesses were being developed and long hours expended in the securing of wider mercantile credit. In the case of William Hickey, this time was spent entertaining soon-dissipated juvenile pleasures beyond the cares of simple household management.[25] Alternatively, lodging accommodation could represent a nest of disagreeable company, a drain on the resources of the naive and unwary and an unwanted intrusion into personal privacy and the autonomous direction of one's affairs.[26] Such considerations formed the backbone to an increasingly moral examination of the lodging economy. By the mid-nineteenth century, the lassitude and wastefulness of the single estate was a stock reference point in comparison to the picture of married domestic rectitude. In

---

[23]   Pope (ed.), *Diary of Robert Haydon*, pp. 130–32.

[24]   For middle-class lodgings in the later nineteenth century, see Jane Hamlett, *Material Relations: Domestic Interiors and Middle-Class Families in England, 1850–1910* (Manchester: Manchester University Press, 2010), pp. 163–70.

[25]   P. Quennell (ed.), *Memoirs of William Hickey* (London: Routledge & Kegan Paul, 1975), pp. 43–55.

[26]   See H. Barker, 'Soul, Purse and Family: Middling and Lower-Class Masculinity in Eighteenth-Century Manchester', *Social History*, 33/1 (2008), pp. 29–30.

the *Economy for the Single and Married* (1845), for example, the expenses of the (male) singleton were unfavourably compared to that of the marital household (see Table 5.1). Here the marital economy was effectively cross-subsidised by letting out a presumably more up-market furnished room than that apportioned to the singleton. In contrast, the single economy was defined by the necessary profligacy of eating out: it was imagined as a public, almost anti-domestic existence.

Table 5.1   Annual expenditure for single and marital households (1845)[27]

£50 Single (p. 11)			
Bedroom (5s/wk)	£12	0	0
Breakfast (coffee house) coffee, roll & butter 4d = 2/6 wk	5	12	0
Dinner – small plate boiled beef @ 4d, potatoes & bread @ 2d = 6d	8	8	0
Tea-room, bread & butter 3d	4	4	0
Supper occasionally (a-la-mode beef, etc.)	2	10	0
Washing	5	0	0
Clothes	5	0	0
Church	0	15	0
Extra	2	1	0
Surplus	4	10	0
	£50		
£50 Married (p. 12)			
House rent & taxes	£24	0	0
Let off a furnished room	18	0	0
	6	0	0
Coals, candle, wood	7	0	0
Tea & sugar	8	0	0
Butter	3	0	0
Meat	12	0	0
Vegetables	5	0	0
Church	1	0	0
Dress, Extras, & washing at home	8	0	0
	£50		

However, describing the accommodation of these rented rooms, and indeed the similar quarters of singlewomen lodgers, has proved problematic: diarists and other contemporaries remained terse when recounting the everyday interaction with the domestic aspect of their lives favouring the bombast of extraordinary events or the quiet introspection of personal, often spiritual reflection. The material culture of

---

[27]   Anon, *Economy for the Single and Married* (c.1845), pp. 11–12, quoted in J.M. Robson, *Marriage or Celibacy? The Daily Telegraph on a Victorian Dilemma* (Toronto: University of Toronto Press, 1995), p. 289.

everyday domestic life, almost by its sheer, banal solidity and omnipresence, escapes record.[28] Depicting this space is also fraught with problems. Pictorial constructions of elite and even middling sort homes are frequent; and the conversation piece, for all its stilted formality and stagey artificiality, offers us glimpses into domestic interiors, albeit carefully reified, abstract interiors.[29] However, the lodging sector remains largely overlooked and only shades into view when, as Styles rightly argues, it is used as a didactic *mise en scène* for studies of degradation and moral decomposition.[30] Beyond these charged, metaphoric devices there are occasional depictions of the kind of everyday lodgings available to the single. One such as these is reproduced in Figure 5.1. Here the sculptor Francis Leggatt Chantrey sketches himself confined to his rented rooms with a severe attack of the mumps around 1805. Chantrey's self-portrait – wistfully titled *Sketch from nature (a bachelor)* – was a drolly imagined cartoon of the artist as invalid, surrounded by restless pets and the bottles of his doctor, Merryman. The interior is comfortable but not lavish, homely but still with a sense of transience. The furniture is serviceable if somewhat old-fashioned and the floor is uncovered by carpet or rug. There is some decoration, although the miniatures on the wall and over the fireplace may well have been examples of Chantrey's own hand; he still subsisted on small-scale commissions as a portraitist at this time. Most striking are the hob, grate and kettle that indicate that Chantrey was able to provide for his culinary needs and extend some refreshment for limited company, if only in an ad hoc way.[31]

If lodgings were overlooked and only infrequently captured in such casual artistic representations, other documentary sources, most notably probate records, can shed an oblique light on the material culture of these impermanent spaces. Firstly, it is clear that lodging was widespread. As Hill, Erickson and Spicksley have demonstrated, widows were especially likely to offer rooms in the once-nuptial house for rent and, just as businesses were often liquidated, downsized or sold on to apprentices and other traders, widows and also spinsters retreated into such culturally acceptable forms of subsistence as leasing property.[32] In certain towns – the spa and

---

[28]   For example, Woollcombe only described the layout of his grand residence in Plymouth when fire threatened to engulf his and adjoining properties: Woollcombe, *Diary*, 9 February 1818.

[29]   See K. Retford, 'From the Interior to Interiority: The Conversation Piece in Georgian England', *Journal of Design History*, 20/4 (2007), pp. 291–307.

[30]   J. Styles, 'Lodging at the Old Bailey: Lodgings and their Furnishing in Eighteenth-Century London' in J. Styles and A. Vickery (eds), *Gender, Taste and Material Culture in Britain and North America, 1700–1830* (New Haven and London: Yale University Press, 2006), pp. 63–4.

[31]   See M. Rogers, *Master Drawings from the National Portrait Gallery* (London: National Portrait Gallery, 1993), p. 84.

[32]   B. Hill, *Women Alone: Spinsters in England, 1660–1850* (New Haven and London: Yale University Press, 2001), pp. 43–52; A.L. Erickson, *Women and Property in Early Modern England* (London: Routledge, 1993), pp. 187–203; J.M. Spicksley, '"Fly with a

Figure 5.1   Francis Leggatt Chantrey self-portrait, *Sketch from nature (a bachelor)*, c.1800. Chantrey's self-deprecating sketch shows the artist holed up in his London lodgings. His room is more comfortable than smart and clearly functioned as both a reception and a rather elementary kitchen. *Source*: © National Portrait Gallery, London.

leisure towns, for example – catering for the lodging or seasonal sojourning market was a lucrative option. In Ludlow, the influx of gentry and the relatively vigorous health of the casual trades also offered opportunities for female employment.[33]

Duck in thy Mouth": Single Women as Sources of Credit in Seventeenth Century England', *Social History*, 32/2 (2007), pp. 187–207. See also H. Barker, *The Business of Women: Female Enterprise and Urban Development in Northern England 1760–1830* (Oxford: Oxford University Press, 2006), pp. 157–65.

[33]   S. Wright, '"Holding up Half the Sky": Women and their Occupations in Eighteenth-Century Ludlow', *Midland History*, 14 (1989), pp. 53–74. See also R.S. Neale, *Bath 1680–1850: A Social History, or, a Valley of Pleasure, yet a Sink of Iniquity* (London: Routledge &

Indeed, for those widows squeezed by meagre settlements or lacking the security of annuities or substantial sums of ready money upon which a *rentier* existence could be comfortably built, letting out the family home to genteel boarders appears to have been preferable than, for example, actively pursuing a husband's trade. As we have seen, Anne Creswell of Tideswell devolved the running of the bulk of her husband's ironmongery business to John Cromwell, who was occupying the shop at the time of her death in 1735. Much of this evidence is, however, more inferential than explicit: Alice Williamson, a well-to-do spinster of Frodswell in Staffordshire, had chambers identified by personal names in her well-appointed farmhouse when her estate was appraised in 1735; and a similar situation was to be found in the widow Sarah Brookes' house in Derby in 1714.[34]

Yet, without corroborative information there is no way of knowing whether this represented lodging arrangements or simply a more personalised approach to service or the co-residence of kin. Similar brief references reveal the presence of lodgers in the homes of widows across the Midlands sample. For example, the probate of Elizabeth Jeffries of Bridgnorth, proved in 1768, revealed a fairly large and well-appointed house which included a 'Lower lodging room'. In her will, Jeffries left John Anderson the bedsteads and bedding from this room, suggesting that he had been her lodger since all her other goods – including clothing and jewellery – were itemised minutely and bequeathed to named members of her wider family.[35] Likewise, Anne Chandler left a four-room house in Shrewsbury. When she died in 1811 the two upstairs rooms were occupied by a lodger who was renting a bedstead, feather bed, pillow and blankets directly from Anne. Chandler's own living accommodation was squeezed into a kitchen and adjoining parlour that also contained her bed.[36]

Rather more information exists on the living arrangements of spinsters. These singlewomen were likely to have been in service and thus occupied a single room at best within the host household, or more probably shared their accommodation with other female servants. For example, in 1676 Sarah Jackson – a spinster nominally of Chester – left a not inconsiderable inventory of over £174, the bulk of which represented ready money.[37] Household goods were notably limited for such a monetarily well-endowed estate: Jackson possessed only the basic accoutrements of domestic living – two tables, a cupboard, a kettle, a cupboard press, a bed and its furniture, a trunk, some napkins, a flaxen tablecloth, six joined stools, a box, a

---

Kegan Paul, 1981), pp. 39–52 and P. Borsay, 'Health and Leisure Resorts' in P. Clark (ed.), *The Cambridge Urban History of Britain: Volume 2, 1540–1840* (Cambridge: Cambridge University Press, 2000), pp. 775–804.

[34]   Lichfield Record Office (LRO), Alice Williamson, widow, Frodswell, 1735; Sarah Brookes, widow, Derby, 1714.

[35]   LRO, Elizabeth Jeffries, widow, Bridgnorth, 1768: probate inventory and will.

[36]   LRO, Anne Chandler, widow, Shrewsbury, 1814: probate inventory and will.

[37]   LRO, Sarah Jackson, spinster, Chester, 1676. The estate was appraised at £174 8s, with £151 15s 6d in money to hand and £6 in wearing apparel forming the principal items of the schedule.

chest and a gold ring. Such a threadbare assortment, and the key lack of kitchen goods beyond the solitary kettle, is explained in the will. Jackson, it is revealed, had been sent into service, albeit at an establishment of superior status consonant with the education of a young woman of such dispensable wealth and, as her will lists, fashionable clothes. Jackson bequeathed the standard funerary gift of a pair of gloves to her 'loveing Master & Mistris' and to 'every one of my fellow servants'. However, the rest of her goods were clearly split between two sites, at neither of which did she exercise much domestic control. Thus the two tables and flaxen tablecloth remained 'in her father's house' in Whitchurch, Shropshire, whereas the 'bed and bed furniture, & my trunke, & all my napkins in it' were at Chester.

The experience of Sarah Jackson is echoed in a host of unmarried women who died in formal and informal service or occasionally at the house of family or near kin. Many singlewomen had very little in the way of material goods, but enough liquid capital accrued from wages and savings to engage probate. For instance, in 1697 Mary Lunn, a spinster of Lichfield, bequeathed a trunk and a chest of drawers – perhaps the sole requirements of personal storage in servants' accommodation – alongside a more substantial sum of £10 5s 4d in clothes, wearing apparel and money. The estate was distributed amongst kin and other servants. In these cases, the presence of highly descriptive allied testamentary material enables a more rounded picture of the domestic situation of singlewomen. Without such material, the task of embedding the deceased into a wider consideration of age and lifecycle is difficult. Thus, it is tempting to regard Margaret Jones, variously described as 'singlewoman' and 'spinster' of Ludlow, in this light. Jones's estate, exhibited in 1746, comprised wearing apparel, 11 pewter plates and dishes and £8 5s of ready money, the entirety of which was bequeathed to her uncle and cousin.[38] Similarly, Jane Gitton, a spinster of Bridgnorth, left a solitary 'chest with drawers' amongst an estate of wearing apparel and ready money in 1766.[39] This situation was also replicated in the case of another Margaret Jones who died in Bridgnorth in 1740 leaving only a chest of drawers and a box, wearing apparel and a comparatively extensive £62 in debts, promissory notes and money.[40] Of course, Jones may well have existed as a *rentier* on the accumulated capital and, like William Stout in his later years, boarded elsewhere. Another Bridgnorth singlewoman, Ann Lythall, possessed a minimal material estate consisting of some basic linen, a bed, a side saddle, a wheel, boxes and wearing apparel when appraised in 1684. However, amongst some small trifles of precious metals, Lythall bequeathed a silver watch and chain, a small jewel and over £228 in 'moneys at use, in purse and otherwise

---

[38]   LRO, Mary Lunn, spinster, Lichfield, 1697. Hereford Record Office (HRO), Margaret Jones, singlewoman, Ludlow, 1746.

[39]   LRO, Jane Gitton, spinster, Bridgnorth, 1766. The estate comprised solely wearing apparel (£4), the chest (£1) and money (£8 18s 6d).

[40]   LRO, Margaret Jones, spinster, Bridgnorth, 1740.

owing'.[41] Other examples from the Bridgnorth sample abound. Jane Sadler's estate, proved in 1748, would not have troubled probate without a £60 bond; Sarah Walker left over £102 in money and money at interest in 1742; Elizabeth Weal died in 1714 with £79 due in debts, an interest-bearing lease, wearing apparel and money; and Hannah Salt owned merely an interest in a leasehold tenement worth £6 when appraised in 1757.[42]

In all these inventories domestic goods were very limited, if, indeed, they were deemed worthy of record at all. By way of contrast, the probate record occasionally captured wealthy spinsters. Thus, Katherine Thacker of Lichfield – who died in 1664 with a movable estate of some £172 and an array of cash and lands disposed of in her will – appears not to have been a single householder, but to have occupied a suite of rooms in her brother's house. As such, Thacker was located in the 'flexible and permeable framework of the household-family', albeit in an elevated status.[43] The goods of her parlour were valued at £10 and she had clearly invested in linen, napery ware and wearing apparel. The rest of the schedule was comprised wholly of debts (£130).[44] Similarly, in 1816 Mary Walters, a spinster of Coleham near Shrewsbury, bequeathed an interest-bearing legacy of over £300 and other annuities that had been left to her by her former master, Mr Shuker, for whom Walters had acted as housekeeper. Whilst Walters' inventory and administration meticulously detailed debts, rent and funerary expenses incurred, like Thacker, the fact that no household goods were itemised may indicate that she resided in the household of others.[45]

These examples show an apparently marked separation between the individual testator and the ownership of household goods. In the Bridgnorth sample, where there is a high degree of internal consistency and conformity in the practice of appraisers, this suggests that the absence of the kinds of utilitarian and functional goods common in discrete households was compensated somewhat by the presence of more decorative or affective items such as silver ware and clothing. Indeed, as Berg has argued, the greater affinity shown by women towards the cultural

---

[41]   LRO, Ann Lythall, spinster, Bridgnorth, 1684.

[42]   LRO, Jane Sadler, spinster, Bridgnorth, 1748. Household goods and wearing apparel added only £2 12s to the bond. LRO, Sarah Walker, spinster, Bridgnorth, 1742. The estate was appraised at £114 1s 4d. LRO, Elizabeth Weal, spinster, Bridgnorth, 1714. LRO, Hannah Salt, spinster, Bridgnorth, 1757.

[43]   N. Tadmor, *Family and Friends in Eighteenth-Century England* (Cambridge: Cambridge University Press, 2001), p. 25.

[44]   LRO, Katharine Thacker, spinster, Lichfield, 1664. See also the commentary in D.G. Vaisey (ed.), *Probate Inventories of Lichfield and District, 1568–1680* (Collections for a History of Staffordshire, 4th Series, vol. 5, Staffordshire Record Office, 1969), p. 142.

[45]   LRO, Mary Walters, spinster, Coleham, 1816. The probate inventory and administration list foodstuffs (mostly cheese, wheat and potatoes) which had been supplied to Walters during her life, together with other expenses which amounted to £154 3s 7d. Walters owed £6 6s in rent, but it is not clear where she was living.

importance and affective resonance of material goods as located in the home and in the specific bequests to select kin and friends may have been amplified in the case of those singlewomen who were not intimately associated with heading separate households.[46] In short, women who did not enjoy the responsibility of directing household affairs and may have existed in some form of shared accommodation may have invested in movable wealth and inheritable financial devices as buttresses against potential economic uncertainty. This was, of course, not always the case. Singlewomen, as Froide has intimated, often maintained significant links with commercial society and, like the many widows who were able and willing to pursue trade, were important agents in the retail sector of many towns.[47] Thus, Mary Higgins, spinster of Chesterfield, ran a fully equipped mercer and haberdashery shop that carried just over £90 of stock and fittings when appraised in 1701.[48] However, she did not possess any household goods and appeared to be living with her father, the sole administrator and executor of the estate.

Whilst it is worth bearing in mind Overton et al.'s caveat that the simple omission of goods from probate schedules should not always be read as negative evidence – indeed such exclusions are common artefacts of the source – it is none the less clear that many singlewomen existed in the households of others, both near-kin and unrelated de facto employers.[49] As Catherine Hutton described during a tour of Wales in 1787, it was not uncommon for whole families and their servants to share rooms.[50] In such situations, the precarious position of many singlewomen was emphasised. For example, on moving to more appropriate accommodation in September 1817, the bachelor Benjamin Robert Haydon not only found that engaging servant help was a necessity, but also that it uncovered an especially fraught nexus of economic and physical power. Settling down on his first night under his own roof, he was disturbed by the proximity of his female house servant:

> The bed creaked. She was in and near me! Was it manly to let a nice girl sleep so near one and at least without making an attempt? I could hardly breathe! Was it manly, I thought, to take advantage of the helpless girl, whose father had expressed his great comfort in having his favourite daughter under my care!

---

[46]   M. Berg, 'Women's Consumption and the Industrial Classes of Eighteenth-Century England', *Journal of Social History*, 30/2 (1996), pp. 415–34.

[47]   A.M. Froide, *Never Married: Singlewomen in Early Modern England* (Oxford: Oxford University Press, 2007), pp. 87–116.

[48]   LRO, Mary Higgins, spinster, Chesterfield, 1701. See also the discussion in Chapter 4.

[49]   M. Overton, J. Whittle, D. Dean and A. Hann, *Production and Consumption in English Households, 1600–1750* (London and New York: Routledge, 2004), pp. 16–18.

[50]   Hutton also observed that the food was extremely simple and that there was an 'almost a complete lack of window glass': Catherine Hutton Beale, *Reminiscences of a Gentlewoman of the Last Century: Letters of Catherine Hutton* (Birmingham: Cornish Brothers, 1891), pp. 47–8.

Perturbed by this psychic assault on the accepted codes of respectable masculine behaviour, Haydon 'determined to conquer [his] temptation, and lay down'.[51] Whilst Haydon congratulated himself on his 'manly' resistance – manliness here plainly associated with self-denial and the fettering of base intentions – it is clear that the economic and cultural hegemony exerted by male masters over singlewomen servants often resulted in sexual assault.[52]

It is more difficult to tease out the possessions of single men who, although evidently captured in the probate record, are obscured by the emphasis on male occupation over considerations of status. However, occasionally probate suggests similar kinds of lodging or boarding arrangements implied in the estates of singlewomen. In 1695, Zachary Turnpenny, a barber-surgeon of Wolverhampton, divided his goods between two locations. Tools, implements, business goods, books and wearing apparel were located in his shop and adjoining chamber, whilst his bed, its furniture and some highly personalised items – a tortoiseshell tobacco box with the king's picture on it and a studded watch – were 'at John Turnepennys house'.[53] More explicitly, in 1705 the inventory of Francis Tompson, bachelor of Whateley in Warwickshire, listed a full schedule of due debts, ready money and cash lent at interest on which the deceased clearly existed. In terms of personalty, Tompson owned only a few sheep, a heifer leased out to his brother and a fairly meagre scattering of goods: a moderately expensive collection of wearing apparel, linens and woollens; a box, a pair of old boots and a hat; a comb and case; a knife and fork and an inkhorn.[54] Tompson's affairs were tied so intimately with that of his immediate kin – his brothers were principal debtors and severally acted as the executors and administrators of the estate – it appears that the scanty array of goods, redolent of a single existence, was offset by the shared use of familial house space. In contrast, the probate of Captain John Haughton of Ludlow in 1702 reveals a rather different but no less common domestic configuration. Haughton, a widower, had died nominally intestate with an estate that included the kind of goods regularly associated with a discrete household. Thus, he had extensive wearing apparel, bedding, curtains, linen, a range of pewter ware, some silver, books and £68 of money in debts. Yet Haughton was not the sole householder or head of a separate establishment; a nuncupative memorandum specified that he had died 'in the dwelling house of [his mother] Mrs Dorothy Kennett scituate in the towne of Ludlowe being then the place of his habitat~on, residence or abode'. Haughton's final quietus was met on a sickbed in the family home – a widowed son returning to the natal house, albeit a son surrounded by the material culture of a once-independent domestic existence.[55]

[51]   Pope (ed.), *Diary of Robert Haydon*, p. 132.
[52]   For manliness as denial, see Tosh 'Old Adam', pp. 233–4 and J. Gregory, '"Homo Religiosus": Masculinity and Religion in the Long Eighteenth Century' in T. Hitchcock and M. Cohen (eds), *English Masculinities, 1660–1800* (London: Longman, 1999), pp. 85–110.
[53]   LRO, Zachary Turnpenny, barber-surgeon, Wolverhampton, 1695.
[54]   LRO, Francis Tompson, bachelor, Whateley in Kingsbury, Warwickshire, 1705.
[55]   HRO, Capt. John Haughton, widower, Ludlow, 1702.

Lodging Space in Context: Residential Spaces, Criminal Opportunities and the Proceedings of the Old Bailey

The analysis of probate material has indicated an outline of the types of domestic situation available to single men and women in the period. In the main, these spaces were often shoehorned in and around the conjugal households of kin, friends and, in the case of servants, employers – or may have been expressed as simply rented rooms. This is not to say that single persons did not head up their own households and, indeed, this was commonplace for both widows left with an appreciable share of the marital inheritance and in particular those widowers who may have chosen to remain unmarried despite the social and economic pressures to do otherwise. None the less, probate provides a fairly bald account of possession: a schedule of goods with occasionally an inference of location within the domestic arena, but with little or no indication of the importance attached to each commodity. Whilst wills may flesh out this picture somewhat with the details of provenance or a scintilla of affective resonance applied to a particular good, there is very little here that can describe the point of articulation between occupier and domestic space. What did single men and women feel about their surroundings? Were the goods that surrounded them simply the material collateral of everyday life, the ballast to the understanding or display of comfort and decency, or charged with rather more significance?

These questions – relevant of all households, whether marital or single – were amplified in the case of those who were lodgers or shared domestic space through boarding arrangements where, by the very nature of the accommodation, they were faced with a more transient and impermanent existence. In order to address the rather arid association between testator and goods outlined in probate, this section attempts to animate the lived environment of middling sort and plebeian unmarried lodgers by examining the domestic interiors revealed through the Proceedings of the Central Criminal Court of London, the Old Bailey.[56] The Proceedings have been widely used to illuminate a variety of non-legal attitudes to cultural behaviour and social activity,[57] but it is largely the work of John Styles that has demonstrated how the depositions and examinations can be deployed to

---

[56]   The Old Bailey Proceedings (OBP) are available at http://www.oldbaileyonline. org. For a discussion of the source and its wider uses, see T. Hitchcock and R.B. Shoemaker, *Tales from the Hanging Court* (London: Hodder Arnold, 2006), pp. xxii–xxix, 162–7, 176– 9; and R.B. Shoemaker, 'The Old Bailey Proceedings and the Representation of Crime and Criminal Justice in Eighteenth-Century London', *Journal of British Studies*, 47/3 (2008), pp. 559–80.

[57]   See, for example, L. MacKay, 'Why They Stole: Women in the Old Bailey, 1779– 1789', *Journal of Social History*, 32 (1999), pp. 623–39; J. Hurl-Eamon, *Gender and Petty Violence in London, 1680–1720* (Columbus: Ohio State University Press, 2005), especially ch. 3; and J. Hurl-Eamon, 'Insights into Plebeian Marriage: Soldiers, Sailors, and their Wives in the Old Bailey Proceedings', *London Journal*, 30/1 (2005), pp. 22–38.

illuminate the intersection between lodgings, lodgers and their affinity with an array of goods that they clearly regarded as their own, even if they did not strictly own them.[58] In this context, it is worth emphasising that London represented a unique urban environment in pre- and early industrial England; and the light the Proceedings cast on the lives of the metropolitan criminal classes and their victims, bystanders, witnesses and assorted deponents has a similarly exceptional aspect that translates imperfectly to the national picture. For example, by the late seventeenth century London was already a vast, sprawling city in comparison to the more perambulatory extents and cultural mentalities of other contemporary towns such as Norwich and Bristol; and, although the industrialisation and subsequent urbanisation of the Midlands and the North in the later eighteenth and nineteenth centuries eased this imbalance, London remained a demographic giant and arguably both the major generative force in the wider national economy and a barometer of cultural change.[59]

The sense of otherness was a marked feature of metropolitan life. As Hitchcock, Shoemaker and Earle have intimated, London was a city where identities were made, broken and refashioned often by simply relocating to another part of the urban setting.[60] This was reflected in the sheer multiplicity of the lodging accommodation available to an increasingly mobile and flexible population. For example, on arriving in England in 1782 the German traveller Carl Philip Moritz was able to procure comfortable lodgings through the good offices of two men who had shared the voyage to London. Moritz paid a rather inflated 16s per week for a two-room apartment off the Strand in George Street located within the home of a tailor's widow, the house being shared with the landlady, her two young sons and a single maidservant. None the less, Moritz was happy with the arrangement, contrasting his situation favourably with his experience of Berlin:

> I now occupy a large front room on the ground floor, with carpets, mats, and very good furniture: the chairs are upholstered in leather and the tables are of mahogany. Adjoining this I have another large chamber. I can do just as I like, and I keep my own tea, coffee, and butter and bread in a glass-fronted cupboard with a lock, which my landlady has provided for me.

58 Styles, 'Lodging at the Old Bailey', pp. 61–80.
59 For descriptions of London and its physical and cultural difference, see P. Earle, *A City Full of People: Men and Women of London, 1650–1750* (London: Methuen, 1994); L.D. Schwarz, *London in the Age of Industrialisation: Entrepreneurs, Labour Force and Living Conditions, 1700–1850* (Cambridge: Cambridge University Press, 1992).
60 Hitchcock, *Down and Out*, pp. 1–22; R.B. Shoemaker, *The London Mob: Violence and Disorder in Eighteenth-Century England* (London, Hambledon, 2004), pp. 1–26; and P. Earle, *The Making of the English Middle Class: Business, Society and Family Life in London, 1660–1730* (London: Methuen, 1989), pp. 327–37.

Curiously, Moritz was not invited to dine with the family and obtaining sustenance was not straightforward. In particular, he was not happy with the solution suggested by his two travelling companions, who took him to a local eating-house – clearly a chop house of dubious reputation – where he was scandalised to pay 'a shilling for a little salad and roast meat'. Moritz decided in future to source his own meals and eat them alone in his rooms. Pickled salmon eaten with oil and vinegar was 'a very refreshing and satisfying food', although hardly the stuff of polite dining. Even so, Moritz delighted in his snug lodgings and appreciated both sleeping between sheets and wool blankets rather than a 'feather-filled bedcover' and having an open fire rather than the closed stoves he was used to in Germany. What Moritz gained in material comfort, however, was lost in terms of quietude: a visit to a German Lutheran pastor who had rooms in the New Inn with access to a well-stocked library threw his temporary lodgings into sharp and unflattering contrast.[61]

Moritz's encounter with London indicates how straightforward it was to locate suitable accommodation, even for someone who was clearly an outsider. This availability was apparent in the case of the convicted bigamist William Bury, alias Henry Parminter, who was able to perpetuate his deception by moving his infatuated victim, Sarah Proctor, around a series of lodging rooms of variable quality and extent in Chelsea and Covent Garden in 1739. Bury had first maintained an attachment to Proctor by seducing her with fine words and ostensibly respectable intentions in the parlour of her lodgings at Mrs Davidge's, a milliner in Covent Garden. Thereafter Proctor, who seems to have consented to sexual relations in a proximate bagnio, was readily accepted by the various landlords and landladies with whom Bury procured rooms without demur, passing her status off as either a genteel spinster just up from Somerset or a young wife awaiting the arrival of her betrothed.[62]

Part of Proctor's case was that Bury had 'wrote a great many Letters full of Love' which although secured in a locked box, were subsequently forcibly removed by the defendant and only partially retrieved. The letters and the attempt to destroy the evidence effectively damned Bury as it confirmed that Proctor's intimate integrity in both material and bodily aspects had been duplicitously compromised. Indeed, as Vickery has emphasised, the locked chest, trunk or box was perhaps the only mechanism through which lodgers and servants could attempt to preserve personal items of economic and affective worth from the casual depredations of landlords, inquisitive fellow boarders and any number of light-fingered transient visitors.[63] For example, in 1741 Peter Wilkinson found that his fellow servant Robert Parkinson had helped himself to a fair chunk of his savings, breaking into

---

[61]   C.P. Moritz, *Journeys of a German in England in 1782*, translated and edited by Reginald Nettel (London: Jonathan Cape, 1965), pp. 27–37.

[62]   OBP, trial of William Bury, June 1742 (t17420603-18).

[63]   A. Vickery, *Behind Closed Doors: At Home in Georgian England* (New Haven and London: Yale University Press, 2009), pp. 38–48.

his box in the room they shared in the London residence of the Earl of Albermarle.[64] Parkinson's case indicates how the necessary portability of goods owned by the vast majority of lodgers and servants combined with the ease of access to their accommodation encouraged opportunistic theft. Such insecurity none the less permits an oblique snapshot of the goods of single lodgers and, indeed, their often single landlords and landladies. Moreover, the cases brought before the Old Bailey indicate the significance that individuals ascribed to both their immediate domestic surroundings and goods through which these locations were given depth and meaning. For example, when in 1742 Ann Thomas of St Martin-in-the-Fields was acquitted of stealing a dressing glass and a pair of silver buckles from Jane Coates, it transpired that Coates – who lived with another woman, Elizabeth Carter – was renting out rooms in a fairly genteel establishment. Carter affirmed that 'the Looking-Glass was in the Back-Room', presumably Coates' private space, and the defendant was last seen in the fore-parlour, after which she and the items went missing. The fact that Coates' maid had access to the goods and was also by extension partially if not wholly suspect of the theft probably saved Thomas from the charge of grand larceny, and the gallows.[65]

The example indicates that opportunities for theft were rife, particularly where goods were on semi-public display in the parlours and shared spaces of the communal lodging houses and boarding establishments frequented by single men and women. In 1832, for example, Charlotte Davis was indicted for receiving two necklaces, worth £6, stolen from Clementina Caines. Caines deposed that this was a simple case of burglary: she was a 'parlour boarder', a position that elevated her from that of an ordinary lodger,[66] in a well-to-do house in Hendon and had placed 'some necklaces and trinkets, and money in a small box ... safe on the drawers in the parlour' of the house. On returning, some two and a quarter hours later, Caines found the box missing. The drawers, Caines explained, were located in the ground floor parlour within a few yards of an open window with the blinds pulled down, enough to attract passing interest but 'not near enough for anyone to put his arm in and reach the box'; a low railing separated the window from the street.[67] In this instance, Caines clearly regarded the parlour as both a secure and proper place to leave her goods and that it was entirely appropriate to place jewellery of such worth – she describes a pearl necklace and cornelian amongst the missing items – in such a semi-public space and not presumably in her private sleeping quarters.

Whilst Caines and, to a lesser extent, Thomas inhabited respectable and even, as in the case of Caines, well-appointed rooms, the bulk of the lodging accommodation available to single Londoners was of a far more variable quality. Certainly, at the extreme base of this lodging hierarchy there existed a multitude

---

[64]   Parkinson had left 'two Bits of Iron' as a makeweight for the money stolen: OBP, Ordinary of Newgate's Account, 18 March 1741 (OA17410318).

[65]   OBP, trial of Ann Thomas, September 1742 (t17420909-22).

[66]   For the status of parlour boarder, see Quennell (ed.), *Hickey*, p. 27.

[67]   OBP, trial of Charlotte Davis, September 1832 (t18320906-80).

of barely furnished rooms in dilapidated, poorly partitioned and semi-derelict buildings. Such rooms were available for short-term use and, if the clientele arraigned before the Old Bailey were representative of the general pattern, were more than likely let out as the specific and transitory requirements of an overnight stay, temporary furlough or more nefarious trades demanded. For example, in 1791 Susannah Blakeway deposed that whilst asleep she had most of her clothes, valued at £1 14s, spirited away from her temporary lodgings by Elizabeth Gulliver. Blakeway, it transpired, had just come up to London from Shropshire to get a place and was inveigled by Gulliver – a 'girl of the town' – to share her room, for which Blakeway paid the landlady threepence.[68] In a similar fashion, Israel Myers – a paid-off sailor with almost £7 of wages burning a hole in his pocket – was robbed of all but one penny at a sailors' common boarding house in Wapping in 1842. The fact that Myers, a cripple, was shown to an upstairs room in the ill-lit house and had no means whatsoever of securing his money from casual pilfering suggests that the rudimentary nature of the accommodation, if not the complicity of the proprietress, actively contributed to his loss.[69] Indeed, many of these low-quality flophouses and scruffy lodging rooms, famously described as 'a calamitous medley of extemporal divisions and subdivisions', appear as favoured loci for petty felonies and were frequently arenas where unsuspecting men looking for a sexual encounter were divested of rather more than the few shillings with which they had initially bargained.[70] This was exactly the case with Jane Harland, who relieved the suitably inebriated Richard Bentley of his silver watch, classically the collateral required to seal prospective business, at her lodging room in Marigold Court off the Strand in 1760.[71] As the young William Hickey recalled, the site of his youthful sexual education took place in a similar 'den of wretchedness', an 'indifferent-looking apartment up three pairs of stairs in a dark, narrow court out of Drury Lane'. Subsequent liaisons with a variety of street whores, women of the town and assorted 'hard goers' – dissipated male libertines – led Hickey to the inevitable denouement: robbed and abandoned in a 'strange, dismal-looking room' at the Cross Keys bagnio in Little Russell Street.[72] However, one should not read too much into Hickey's fond recollections: these rooms also sufficed for a large

---

[68]   OBP, trial of Elizabeth Gulliver, September 1791 (t17910914-21).

[69]   OBP, trial of Jacob Small, October 1842 (t18421024-2858).

[70]   'Buildings – Mansions – Flats – Residences – Dwellings', *The Builder*, 36/1823 (January 1878), p. 31 quoted in Marcus, *Apartment Stories*, p. 105. See also T. Henderson, *Disorderly Women in Eighteenth-Century London: Prostitution and Control in the Metropolis, 1730–1830* (London: Longman, 1999), pp. 33–5, 61, 101, 147; and J. Black, 'Illegitimacy, Sexual Relations and Location in Metropolitan London' in T. Hitchcock and H. Shore, *The Streets of London from the Great Fire to the Great Stink* (London: Rivers Oram Press, 2003), pp. 101–18 for similar types of lodging accommodation.

[71]   OBP, trial of Jane Harland, February 1760 (t17600227-36).

[72]   Quennell (ed.), *Hickey*, pp. 64–5.

tranche of the poor, the dispossessed; the servant between places or without an adequately remunerative situation; and a host of others who shaded in and out of a plebeian economy of makeshift wherein precarious formal employment – seamstressing, charring, millinery, general labouring and the like – was often necessarily combined with less licit activities.[73]

On a slightly more decent if none the less equally temporary level were the many ready-furnished rooms that could be had in virtually any part of town. One such room, let to Susanna Addis, a widow, illustrates the expectancies of landlord and lessee and the sense of mutual distrust that could arise over both the use of goods located in such rooms and the status of the tenant. In 1759, Addis contracted for a room in a lodging house owned by Michael and Elizabeth Hawkins for 2s 3d per week and lodged there unmolested for three or four months. However, the owners – who were non-resident and thus could not extend the kind of direct surveillance commonly applied to most live-in lodgers – claimed that a number of articles, including a linen sheet, a copper tea kettle and a pewter pot, were surreptitiously lifted from the property on a number of nebulous pretexts. When Elizabeth Hawkins demanded restitution, Addis barred entry to the room, saying that the goods were 'very safe' and that Hawkins had no right to go into the room. Furthermore, Addis had claimed that she was a single woman, arguing that 'she could better pay ... than if she had a husband'. However, it transpired that she was married, albeit in practice deserted by a soldier since dead who had taken the goods and 'put them into another woman's lap'. With culpability flimsily placed on the deceased, Addis was acquitted.[74] Although Addis was able to argue her innocence convincingly, it is interesting that she was able to maintain some right of privacy over the owner from forcibly entering the threshold of the room. Other cases indicate that single people were occasionally able to exploit this situation by simply stripping ready-furnished rooms and making off with the proceeds and the key, which partially delayed any prompt appraisal of goods on the part of the landlord.[75] Such cases which make great play of the criminal agency of unattached single women are none the less dwarfed by the general sense of insecurity that pervaded most lodging accommodation. In 1699, for instance, Mary Pemberton and Jane Chatterton of St Giles-in-the-Fields were sentenced to be summarily whipped for stealing the goods of Ann Malsfret, spinster. Malsfret deposed that 'she did Lodge in the Room with them, and when she was gone out they took her Trunk and Goods, and went away with them; which were afterwards found upon them'.[76] In this type of shared space – where the multiple use of goods confused

---

[73] T. Hitchcock, *English Sexualities, 1700–1800* (London: Macmillan, 1997), pp. 94–8.

[74] OBP, trial of Susanna Addis, September 1760 (t17600910-10).

[75] See, for example, OBP, trial of Eleanor Bird, April 1760 (t17600416-36). Bird, a widow, had made off with 5s worth of linen and bedclothes from a lodging room in 1757, taking 'the key away with her'. She was only apprehended some two and a half years later.

[76] OBP, trial of Mary Pemberton and Jane Chatterton, October 1699 (t16991011-34).

the divisions between common and private property – pilfering, deception and sporadic violence were rife.[77]

Obviously, the apprehension of social status and, indeed, cultural capital were at play when landlords rented out accommodation. Thus, the appearance of gentility or even the vague whiff of respectability and independent means were often enough to permit access to superior lodging situations. In 1738, whilst shopping at a cane chairmaker's establishment in the Minories, Mary Williams overheard Lucy Brooks, nominally a gentlewoman, casually enquiring after suitable board and lodgings. Williams, clearly impressed that Brooks had intimated that 'she had something coming in yearly', offered space in her own house, subsequently showing her 'a Room above Stairs, where there was a corner Cupboard, in which we kept our Plate'. With Williams forced to depart, Brooks was left with the maid, Ann Griffiths, in the garret. Griffiths deposed that:

> When my Mistress (Williams) was gone out, the Prisoner went up Stairs with me into the Garret, to help me tie up some Lines, while we were there, she ask'd me for a Chamber-pot; I told her there was one in my Room, and she went down again by herself; after this she wanted Snuff: I said, if she would go down and sit by the Kitchen-Fire 'till I had done, I would fetch her some, but when I came down she was gone, I stepp'd to the Chandlers Shop at next Door, and there I found her; she told me she was only going to see her Mother at the Tower, and would come again, but she never did. She did not stay long in the Garret with me, but went down a Quarter of an Hour before me.

With the distraction complete, Brooks helped herself to over £8 worth of gold, silver and jewellery – which was rapidly pawned.[78] Notwithstanding the effrontery of the crime, Brooks' position as a potential lodger of the better sort clearly permitted her access to the wider facilities of the building and the command of the staff. Single lodgers of quality could expect some latitude in the use of the wider household infrastructure and domestic goods, and could thus experience a level of material comfort normally associated with the marital home. This, however, came at a price, both monetarily and in the additional and occasionally fractious problem of negotiating unfamiliar or shared spaces with strangers.

The tensions inherent in this type of arrangement are ably illustrated through two cases of sexual assault in the later eighteenth century.[79] In 1773, John Lennard, Thomas Graves and James Guy were prosecuted for raping Ann Boss, a

---

[77]   See OBP, trial of Johanna Baker, July 1740 (t17400709-41). Baker lived with Mary Low in a room in Allhallows Lane. She stripped it of goods when Low was out buying bread, leaving the key under the door.

[78]   OBP, trial of Lucy Brooks, October 1738 (t17381011-9).

[79]   For a useful discussion of rape and sexual assault, see R. Trumbach, *Sex and the Gender Revolution. Volume 1: Heterosexuality and the Third Gender in Enlightenment London* (Chicago and London: University of Chicago Press, 1998), pp. 276–322.

spinster who was a lodger and boarder at a Mr Brailsford's house in Petty France. Brailsford had temporarily vacated the premises, leaving it in the care of Boss, her maidservant and a trusted gentleman, Henry Houseman – Boss being persuaded to stay because 'there were some things of my brother's and mine there'. The defendants were bailiffs instructed to occupy the house in distraint of an unpaid debt, Lennard committing the violent assault whilst Boss was alone in her bedchamber. In the course of the cross-examination, Boss revealed the nature of her domestic situation. It appears that she had been resident in the house for two and a half years and occupied a back chamber 'up two pairs of stairs', next to the sleeping quarters of Brailsford and his wife. She had no other room solely for her own use and her maid held lodgings elsewhere. However, on the ground floor there were two well-appointed parlours in which Boss could dine and entertain both friends and respectable mixed company with a measure of gentility and decorum. There was also a kitchen on this floor that sufficed for receiving guests and taking tea less formally, below which was a fully stocked wine cellar. The house was furnished with a large garden that backed onto St James's Park. In the course of the trial, a series of neighbours, servants and acquaintances deposed that after Houseman was unceremoniously turfed out of the house by the defendants, Boss and the maidservant were placed in an uncomfortable predicament, compounded by the inadequate provision of security to the internal rooms of the dwelling. Boss occupied a room fastened only by a latch (whereas the wine cellar was tellingly secured by a lock) which she was unaccustomed to applying during the day. With the bailiffs in possession of the house, Boss was not able to ward off the attack.[80]

Boss clearly regarded her lodgings as home, and such was the affinity with domestic space and personal property, she resisted quitting what was clearly an uncertain and potentially dangerous situation despite ample opportunity to do so.[81] In contrast, the case of Daniel Lackey, acquitted of raping Christian Streeter, spinster, in 1757 reveals a rather different but still extensive form of single person's lodging accommodation.[82] The bare outline of the trial hinged on the credibility and probity of the alleged victim and assailant. Streeter asserted that she was a lodger in Berkeley Street near Piccadilly and only recently up from the country. She was approached by Lackey whilst walking in St James's Park and, convinced of his character and swayed by his blandishments regarding her home county, Sussex, accompanied him to a glove shop, an inn and thence via a decidedly circuitous coach ride to his lodgings in Rider Street, Westminster. Lackey then invited her into his two-roomed apartment on the pretext that his footman, William Ellis, also a man

---

[80]   OBP, trial of John Lennard, Thomas Graves and James Guy, July 1773 (t17730707-2).

[81]   Houseman deposed that despite spending the night alone with the maidservant, Boss delayed leaving because 'she was washing some little things … [and] … as soon as she had got them dried she would go away': OBP, trial of John Lennard, Thomas Graves and James Guy, July 1773 (t17730707-2).

[82]   OBP, trial of Daniel Lackey, April 1757 (t17570420-42).

of Sussex, would duly escort her home. It was in his bedroom, with the connivance of the servant, that the assault took place. Fearing for her life, Streeter was not able to escape until the following morning – and then only after consenting to taking tea and muffins, a guinea, having her hair cut and dressed in the French style and making further promises to her assailant. She raised the alarm on returning to her lodgings. Lackey's version of events struck a predictably contrary tone. He had simply picked up a girl whilst casually strolling along Birdcage Walk, a notorious site for sexual cruising, and had assumed that she was a woman of the town on account of her appearing without gloves. Streeter had subsequently acquiesced to being bought gloves, waited with Lackey whilst he dined at an inn and freely accompanied him back to his lodgings. She had consented to sex, evidenced by the palpable lack of commotion and the testimonies to that effect from the landlady, maidservant and Lackey's own, heavily implicated, manservant.

It is, however, the testimony of these ancillary witnesses that throws light on the lodging accommodation. Intent that the house was regarded as reputable, sober and only let out to a 'good sort [of] gentlemen, creditable', the landlady, Mrs Cox, and her maidservant, Mary Head, deposed that Lackey had inhabited the Rider Street premises for a year and three quarters and prior to that the rooms were let to a genteel family. None the less, Head described the dwelling as but 'a very small shell of a house', the entire first floor of which was occupied by Lackey. This consisted of a dining room which contained seating and serving furniture, a fire and at least three looking or pier glasses. It was here that Lackey both received meals prepared in the ground-floor kitchen and entertained company. Indeed, Lackey was keen to impress upon the court that whilst gentleman friends were commonly invited to dine with him, and he would take tea in his dining room, it was highly irregular that a single woman was permitted access.[83] This was why he had attempted to deceive the landlady by feigning Streeter's departure. The dining room abutted onto a chamber that housed the bed and associated furniture, including a mahogany waiter. There was no passageway between the adjoining rooms and both the landlady, who occupied the second floor, and the servants, Head and Ellis, who were housed in the garrets, had to snake past Lackey's apartment to access their own quarters. Flimsy partitioning made even conversation, let alone a violent struggle, eminently audible. Whilst Lackey was clearly a more socially elevated lodger than, for example, Boss or Malsfret, it was this – the permeability of his lodgings to surveillance and to the incrimination of sound – along with some inconsistencies in Streeter's account and the marshalling of 11 character witnesses of commendable status and importance that ensured his eventual acquittal.[84]

---

[83]   See Chapter 4 for the problems associated with entertaining.

[84]   Lackey was able to call on the former Lord Mayor, Sir Crispin Gascoyne; his son and MP Bamber Gascoyne; Alderman Blakiston; Anthony Langley Swimmer; Colonel Forster; Sir Charles Kemys; the Hon. Robert Lee; Sir John Hind Coton; Sir John Phillips; Lord Ward and the Earl of Lichfield.

Privacy, Property and the Single Homemaker

Perhaps the most striking aspects of the lodging and boarding accommodation described in the Old Bailey Proceedings are how concerns for security and privacy were paramount. As we have seen, the goods of lodgers – and especially those of single men and women – were fair game to the depredations of a host of light-fingered felons; and whilst landlords may have occasionally seen their paltry furnishings spirited away, the lodging world remained an exceptionally insecure place for those forced by circumstance or lifecycle to endure it. Home was subject not merely to the subtle intrusions of living within and around the space of others, but also to the direct invasion of areas such as sleeping quarters and closets increasingly regarded in the familial household as private. Door locks, where these were even present at all, could be broken and boxes, trunks and chests – often the sole secure repositories of personal importance and objects of material and affective worth – were easily jemmied open.[85] This was not solely confined to lower-order boarding houses and metropolitan apartments. For example, only a matter of months after Thomas Giordani Wright had bombastically praised his newly acquired cultural status within the practice of his master, James McIntyre, he was forced into a more cold-eyed appraisal of his situation and, by extension, his standing within McIntyre's household. His lovingly described 'sanctum' was subject to the casual and regular thievery of the ever-changing domestic staff.[86] Wright's splutteringly affronted diatribe against the theft – a breastpin given by his mother, left 'sticking in the corner' of his dressing glass – reveals not only the concerns of slighted bourgeois masculinity but also the impermanence of his domestic condition. 'If any excuse for my not putting the brooch into a more safe place be wanted or allowed', Wright opined:

> I may state that I have in this large, new, *in*convenient house, neither closet, drawers, or wardrobe of any kind to keep an article in. My trunks are occupied by my linen and other vestments, so that two open wash stand drawers are all I have upstairs to put anything of that kind into, and my writing box downstairs (four stories from my dressing glass) is an inconvenient receptacle for such ornaments.

It is also clear that in the close-built, ad hoc dwellings of many major towns and cities, the poorly subdivided and cramped rooms offered little in the way of privacy. For example, in 1704 Mary Price was accused of committing unnatural

---

[85]   See, for example, OBP, trial of William Phillips for rape, May 1771 (t17710515-6). Here a witness, nominally apprenticed to learn tambour-work, complained about 'lying in the rooms, without locks to the door, when they had so many men in the house; as sometimes they had five or six'. See also Vickery, *Behind Closed Doors*, pp. 31–46 for the importance of domestic security.

[86]   Johnson (ed.), *Diary of Thomas Giordani Wright*, pp. 303–4.

sexual acts on her dog by a malicious fellow-lodger who had spied the offence through 'a Hole in the Floor, [which] broke through the Ceiling, whereby she could see into the Prisoners Room'.[87] Ann Boss's testimony held so much weight because the servant of the next door property could clearly hear her protests, there being 'but a thin partition' between the discrete dwellings. Similarly, the occupants of Daniel Lackey's lodgings in Rider Street, Westminster, could hear each other talking and moving about, so much so that Lackey habitually employed a 'low tone' when at home. The hawkish landlady, Mrs Cox, affirmed the absence of vociferous objection on the part of the prosecutrix by tartly remarking: 'if any body snores in his [Lackey's] room I can hear them in mine'.

The spaces between separate households, the landings, passageways and shared facilities, were also fraught with potential moral and physical danger. These liminal interzones, where no one household had sole proprietary claim, were therefore often sites of conflict. Landings – favoured spots for communal drying, airing and storage – were unguarded bran tubs for casual sneak thieves; and corridors, stairs and entrances were habitual sites of altercation and violence. William Stout, for example, recounted how in the hastily cut-about guts of the once-large mansion he occupied with two other tenants in 1691, shared spaces became areas of contestation. The house in question was refashioned into three distinct zones: the 'street part, tenanted by a master of a ship in the Virginia trade, who had only a wife, one child and maid servant'; the kitchen part and the rooms over it, let to Stout's colleague, John Bryer; and 'the great parlor, seller under it and three bed rooms above', taken by Stout and his ersatz family. All three households shared the brewhouse. However, the main problem for Stout lay in the set of stairs to the upper chambers used in common with his street-side neighbours. Here, Stout was brazenly importuned, his neighbour taking 'all opertunetys in conversation and other insinuations to alure me to her bed or to introduce her selfe to myne'. Stout, characteristically, threw himself into a long excursus on temptation, inconstancy and lewd behaviour; but his misgivings concerning the permeability of his accommodation to both external and internal disruption were only fully assuaged when more agreeable (and more private) neighbours moved in some three years later.[88]

For the middling sort, however, privacy was an important consideration in shaping domestic space. From chambers and closets to libraries, studies and dens, interiority and the opportunities that it facilitated clearly engaged men and women homemakers.[89] Undoubtedly, the intrusion of work and the everyday management

---

[87]   OBP, trial of Mary Price, April 1704 (t17040426-42).

[88]   Marshall (ed.), *Stout*, pp. 102–5, 109–10.

[89]   For interiority, see Retford, 'From the Interior', pp. 291–3; Vickery, *Behind Closed Doors*, pp. 196–7, 204–5; I. Bryden and J. Floyd, 'Introduction' in I. Bryden and J. Floyd (eds), *Domestic Space: Reading the Nineteenth-Century Interior* (Manchester: Manchester University Press, 1999), pp. 1–17; M. Wigley, 'Untitled: The Housing of Gender' in B. Colomina (ed.), *Sexuality and Space* (Princeton: Princeton Architectural Press, 1992), pp.

of household affairs often severely impinged upon private or reflective time, or indeed plain solitude in the case of the occasionally curmudgeonly Stout. Stout was not alone and the self-obsessed singleton was not simply a caricaturised figure of fiction. When in 1772 Caroline Herschel came from Germany to keep house for her brother, the astronomer William Herschel, she was effectively isolated within the home. Having no friends in England and with her brother's time, thoughts and indeed social acquaintances wholly concerned with his work, Caroline bemoaned the fact that after the day's work, when a married couple might ordinarily be expected to spend time together in the parlour, William took himself off to the privacy of his bedroom. His put-upon and forgiving sister recorded in her diary that:

> I seldom saw my brother in the evening, for it may easily be supposed that after faging for 12 hours together he would be glad to retire to his own room and favourite authors (with a bason of Milk, Sago or a glass of water) where he spent [the] best part of the night with reading.[90]

Hershel is an extreme example of the singleton actively shunning company, the standard by which respectability and politeness – the watchwords of middling sort cultural performance – were measured. Yet even such a connected and sociable contemporary as the literary inclined Catherine Hutton could bemoan the invasion of personal space. Whilst visiting the resort of Barmouth, Hutton bridled at the domestic strictures imposed on her as a visitor: 'I have made my room so nice', she confided, 'having obtained a hearth-brush to myself, that it was not easy to prevent it from becoming a drawing-room for the ladies,'[91] For many of the middling sorts, however, a writing desk or bureau, a few books and a bookcase kept in a chamber or closet could provide an individual with both the reason and means to withdraw from the melee of the busy household required for writing, account-keeping, reading or simply quiet reflection. Thus, for example, for the widow Jane Browne – continuing her husband's trade as a plumber and glazier – the presence of a bureau in the best bedroom of her large house in Bridgnorth appears to have offered a sanctuary from the bustle of the shop and workshop and the demands of a growing family.[92] Indeed, writing desks, bureaux and especially books and bookcases were all objects associated with the recreation of the self and as such fed into identifiably middling sort forms of consumption and material

---

350–51. See also L.C. Orlin, *Locating Privacy in Tudor London* (Oxford: Oxford University Press, 2007) for a study of the earlier period.

[90] M. Hoskin (ed.), *Caroline Herschel's Autobiographies* (Cambridge: Science History Publications, 2003), p. 51.

[91] Beale, *Reminiscences of a Gentlewoman*, pp. 118.

[92] LRO, Jane Browne, widow, Bridgnorth, 1797.

culture.[93] Despite this, whereas books appear not infrequently in the inventory sample to 1750, significant as the ownership of books often followed marked gender lines, there is an almost complete absence of writing desks and bureaux.[94] This is not surprising since furniture of this sort, made in more varied types of wood by a cabinetmaker, was only beginning to become widely available from the mid-eighteenth century.[95] Consonant with this, the later years of the sample (1750–1850) reveal that households in both urban and rural locations increasingly possessed a writing desk or bureau. These were mostly situated (or rather described) in bedrooms, emphasising the practice demonstrated by Browne that privacy required for work was commonly positioned in chambers within middling sort or petit bourgeois households.

Thus, the significance of a writing desk, bureau or escritoire as both a piece of furniture to be shaped to personal requirements and as an object for conveying concepts of pride and ownership was key. In a similar fashion, Catherine Hutton recalled that, as a studious 10-year-old deprived of the educational sanctuary of a boarding school, she was given by her father 'in compensation … a handsome chest of drawers; one drawer, by my especial order, being fitted up as a writing desk'. When the chest was destroyed in the Birmingham riots, the sense of loss – in a material, affective and representational sense – was palpable: 'This chest *was my own* till July, 1791', writes Hutton, 'when, with its contents, which consisted of many clothes, many papers, and a good sum of money, it was destroyed by the rioters.'[96]

Similarly, James Woodforde's diary indicates the importance attached to such forms of solid, yet culturally positional consumption. Whilst a writing desk and bookcases sufficed for the study of his rooms at New College Oxford, on graduating in 1763 Woodforde progressed to acquiring more substantial furniture. Returning to the family seat in Castle Cary, Woodforde went to Sherbourne 'to get me a Beaurou of one Hoddinett a cabinet-Maker … looked upon several Beaurou's and fixed upon a Norway Oak Beaurou which he is to send me to Morrow, and for which he asks, he sending it Home 3.3.0.' The object of Woodforde's desire was intended as an investment piece that sufficed as a physical cipher of his status as a prospective clergyman and, more prosaically, constituted the tools of his trade for the serious and, for Woodforde, tedious business of writing sermons. However, Woodforde's career did not progress smoothly and after both his parents died he remained in Somerset whilst attempting to procure a suitably remunerative living. Here his patience was tried by his often drunk, impecunious and rakish younger brother, Jack. On 19 June 1769 he wrote:

[93]   L. Weatherill, *Consumer Behaviour and Material Culture in Britain, 1660–1760* (2nd edn, London and New York: Routledge, 1996), pp. 177, 180–81.

[94]   Only five instances are recorded between 1700 and 1750.

[95]   C. Edwards, *Eighteenth-Century Furniture* (Manchester: Manchester University Press, 1996), pp. 74–80, 94–9.

[96]   Beale, *Reminiscences of a Gentlewoman*, pp. 4–5.

> He [Jack] spent the evening at Parsonage & made a Riot there being in want of money. Jack had a new Mohogany Beaurou brought him this Afternoon to the L. House [Lower House where James lived some of the time] from one Smart of Glastonbury and a very neat one it is, but dearish, he asking for it 5.0.0. Whenever Jack wants money he disturbs both Houses.[97]

Apart from the drunkenness and extravagance, Woodforde was clearly piqued that the profligate younger sibling had acquired an expensive mahogany bureau in comparison to his functional oak piece, especially when Woodforde had a more serious claim to the use of an appropriate writing desk and bookcase. Indeed, the labour of writing was a distinctly middling sort and bourgeois endeavour that more than often spilled into the domestic realm of single men. Woollcombe, for instance, divided his day between formal hours at his legal practice and informal hours at home wherein business affairs – talking to clients, reading up on case law, processing the accounts – habitually intruded.[98] Similarly, in 1848 the Reverend Robert Norgrave Pemberton occupied an eight-bedroom rectory in Church Stretton which had writing tables in all the good bedrooms, including Pemberton's own – a cosy room with a chintz-covered easy chair and a carpet and hearth rug before the fire, along with the usual bedroom furniture. More serious sermon writing could also be undertaken in the downstairs library.[99]

Arguably, the need for privacy was greater for the single individual sharing domestic space than for an independent person with a home of their own. In Jane Austen's *Mansfield Park*, the much put upon Fanny Price is relegated to a poor room furnished with hand-me-down cast-offs better suited to a servant than a family member. However, for Fanny it is a haven of tranquillity, a retreat wherein her key possessions – a writing desk, books and house plants – are located and nurtured.[100] In a similar fashion, the brother and sister, Thomas and Ann Heeley, shared their home in Birmingham, subdividing it into distinct areas of individual operation. Part of the premises was given over to Ann's grocery shop and part to Thomas's metalwares workshop, leaving no room for a parlour.[101] They each used their bedchamber as a sitting room, one of which contained a bureau bookcase. The presence of mirrors, pictures and better storage facilities for clothing points to the other bedroom being used by Ann. If this gendered reading of the inventory is correct then Thomas used the bedroom with the bureau for private correspondence as well as keeping his business accounts. Likewise James Watt when living at The Rookery made use of his bedroom for writing letters before he moved to Thornhill

---

[97] David Hughes (ed.), *The Diary of a Country Parson: The Revd James Woodforde* (London: Folio Society, 1992), 19 June 1769.

[98] Woollcombe, *Diary*, 31 July–2 August 1818.

[99] Shropshire Archives (SA), D3651/B/9/6/2/5 Inventory of Rev. R.N. Pemberton, rectory, Church Stretton, 1848.

[100] Jane Austen, *Mansfield Park* (Harmondsworth: Penguin, 1985 [1814]), p. 173.

[101] LRO Thomas Heeley, 1764.

House and could create a library.[102] None the less, in a reduced household when a single person was effectively limited to just one room the idea of a bedroom as a sanctuary was difficult to maintain. For example, in 1800 Elizabeth Joyce – a spinster of Whitchurch, Shropshire – died a lodger. She had few items of furniture beyond the standard table and a few chairs, a chest to keep her clothes in and, significantly, a bureau. Although the schedule contained numerous smaller items, such as silver and silk clothing, that suggested that Joyce had once had a reasonable residual income (and quite possibly her own home), it is clear that such artefacts of a former life were now compressed into the confines of a single space.[103]

Unencumbered by Spouse: Single Life and Institutional Space

Thus far we have encountered single men and women who had at least some degree of latitude in defining and to a certain extent ordering their domestic arrangements. Even the lowly lodger or servant could – and in many instances did – leave a distinctive mark on the perfunctory arrangements that may have described their often transitory in-house existence. However, single life was often circumscribed by the discipline of institutional space. In particular, for the young and the old – the stations of a person's lifecycle most likely to confer single status – homemaking was constrained by conformity to the kind of normative behaviour often imposed as the direct result of scholarly or vocational training, military service or charitable care. In these situations an element of communal living intruded upon conceptions of both the self and home. Whilst some forms of institutional life were clearly antithetical to the routines of normative domesticity – explicitly so in the case of the regimented, liveried existence endured by soldiery, naval ratings, the workhouse poor and the incarcerated dissolute – others imposed a more flexible but none the less distinctive way of life on those subjected to them.

For many middling sort men, apprenticeship formed the route to occupational independence and thence adulthood. However, for the growing professional classes extended periods of training either at formal establishments of learning or through practice was required. Most comfortably off men acquired an education, although this was often ad hoc in nature. William Hickey, for want of aptitude and application in a suitably appropriate trade or calling, was packed off to a boarding school in Streatham. Here, the young Hickey's superior command of the triangulation of economic, social and cultural capital enabled him to circumvent the homogenising communal environment of the dormitory and secure a room of his own. This petty kingdom permitted some of the creature comforts befitting his elevated status as well as the privacy to conduct some primary forays into his sexual initiation.[104] In contrast, Thomas Giordani Wright of Newcastle

---

[102] BCA, MS 3219/6/35 James Watt 'Household Memorandum'.

[103] LRO, Elizabeth Joyce, spinster, Whitchurch, 1800.

[104] Quennell (ed.), *Hickey*, pp. 27–30.

supplemented his practical apprenticeship with a limited and somewhat diffuse semi-formal medical education, spending six months at Edinburgh. For Wright, his peripatetic engagement with the university did not include college rooms, and for him studying represented a freedom from the surveillance and strictures of his medical indenture. Wright took lodgings – 'a large, handsomely furnished sitting room, with a closet bed adjoining, and a small bedroom, with a large four-post bed in it' – a situation that permitted him 'to be … in my own house (as it were) and for the first time in my life completely and independently my own master'.[105]

Naturally, university life and the ambivalent comforts of college rooms constituted a rather different experience from the feelings of levity and autonomy expressed by Wright. To an extent, the regimen of college existence imposed a fairly rigid structure on the domestic arrangements of its members. The traveller Carl Philip Moritz captures something of the monastic austerity that must have pervaded many Oxford and Cambridge courts and quadrangles in the eighteenth century when he described meeting the clergyman Mr Modd in Oxford in 1782. Modd's tour of the town and the university precincts included his rooms at Corpus Christi College. Moritz, however, was singularly unimpressed, remarking that they 'seemed very like a cell, being on the ground floor and very low and gloomy'.[106] Thomas Gray's protégé, the young Swiss nobleman Charles Victor de Bonstetten, was equally bemused by the suffocating, cloistered environment of Cambridge.[107] Gray's own accommodation at both Peterhouse and Pembroke colleges was at best frugal, although as his fame, private income, library and personal requirements expanded he migrated from a simple, single, large chamber ('a hugeous one that little i is quite lost in it') to a suite of rooms that facilitated his scholarly interests and also housed his servant in separate quarters.[108] Scholarly pursuits, literary affectations, simple reticence and a host of other influences – the desire for solitude, the ability to live as a gentleman relatively cheaply or latent sexual proclivity – often commended a university career to many single men or, conversely, conferred lifelong singleness on men of such inclinations.[109]

---

[105]   Johnson (ed.), *Diary of Thomas Giordani Wright*, p. 65.

[106]   Moritz, *Journeys of a German in England*, p. 135.

[107]   See P. Toynbee and L. Whibley (eds), *Correspondence of Thomas Gray*, 3 vols (Oxford: Clarendon, 1971), vol. 2, p. 512; *Oxford Dictionary of National Biography* (*ODNB*) online, http://www.oxforddnb.com/view/article/11356?docPos=2 (accessed 6 June 2010); J.A. Venn (ed.), *Alumni Cantabrigiensis* (Cambridge: Cambridge University Press, 1922).

[108]   Toynbee and Whibley (eds), *Correspondence of Thomas Gray*, Appendix K, pp. 1221–3. Gray's 'plate, watches, rings, china-ware, bed-linnen & table-linnen, & the furniture' of his chambers in Cambridge were bequeathed to his two cousins; and a pair of 'large blue & white old Japan-China Jarrs' was left to Lady Goring. The estate was valued at over £7,000: Appendix X, pp. 1283–6.

[109]   In the case of Gray, these factors were especially prominent: see R.L. Mack, *Thomas Gray: A Life* (New Haven and London: Yale University Press, 2000).

Men such as Thomas Hearne, the English antiquary, who lived his entire adult life in university chambers and halls, were effectively institutionalised singletons.[110] However, for every Gray or Hearne there existed many far more prosaic men – men like the Rev. William Jones, curate of Broxbourne, for whom the 'dismal college-walls' of Oxford were simply the temporary stepping stone to careers of both clerical and secular preferment and, of course, marriage.[111]

A more vibrant and certainly less austere account of college life can be glimpsed in the diary of James Woodforde. Woodforde sailed through his time studying theology at New College Oxford in the early 1760s, wherein his bon vivant passion for company and good living were fully indulged. Woodforde's rooms were elegantly furnished, despite the regularly boorish and drunken interventions of his friends. He had his rooms papered 'by Ward the Upholsterer' and a 'bookcase put up in my Study by Bozwell'. When he left in 1763 he sold all his furniture to a Mr Collins who was in attendance when Ward the Upholsterer came to value everything. The items so valued were:

7 Matted Chairs 1.9.0.
One two flapped Oak Table 0.16.0
One Piller Cherry tree table 0.8.6
One Mohogany writing Table 1.1.0
A Feather Bed, Bolster, Pillow Quilt, and three Blankets 3.3.0
Two pr of Sheets & two Pillow cases 0.11.0
Shovel, Tongs, Poker, Bellows & Brush 0.5.0
A Pr of brass candlesticks 0.3.6

The sum total of Ward's appraisal realised £7 17s, from which was deducted £1 4s for the hire of 'an an Old Fashioned Glass for three Years at 2s 0d Per Quarter'; 12d for a bedstead and curtains and a 'small broken glass'; and additional moneys for papering the room and other sundries expended in 1759. A further 2d was expended on porter in the Bachelors' Common Room.[112] As well as dining within the college, it is clear that Woodforde and a number of his colleagues utilised their rooms as social and dining spaces wherein work was completed and social alliances brokered. Food, perhaps the one coherent theme of Woodforde's diary, clearly acted as a key social bond, albeit one that within college remained something of a mixed pleasure. For example, on 17 February 1763 Woodforde recorded: 'I dined at the chaplains Table with Pickering and Waring, upon a roasted Tongue and Udder, and we went on each of us for it 0.1.9. N.B. I shall not dine on a roasted

---

[110]   For the career of Hearne, who resided in St Edmund Hall, Oxford, from 1695 to his death in 1735, see *ODNB*, http://www.oxforddnb.com/view/article/12827?docPos=1 (accessed 6 June 2010).

[111]   O.F. Christie (ed.), *The Diary of the Revd. William Jones, 1777–1821* (London: Brentano's, 1921), pp. 1–8.

[112]   Hughes (ed.), *Diary of a Country Parson*, entries for 1759–63.

Tongue and Udder again very soon.' A number of references in the diary suggest that he and an assortment of friends took it in turns, a week at a time, to provide breakfast for each other in their rooms.[113]

Almshouses: Institutional Living for Singles?

Although almshouses survive in great numbers in English towns and villages there are few period descriptions of their interiors. One writer presents a charming and homely scene as they approached one example:

> up the flagged-side path of a shaven lawn, and into a lengthened cloister; and such a cloister as few except more ambitious collegiate buildings can at this day show. Here were some attendants with lanterns, but the richest and warmest light fell far and wide upon the cloistered pavement and through an open door. To this I was taken; and a little scene was before my delighted eyes that, for its air of comfort – I might almost say opulence – its excessive quaintness, its sense of holy, nay, as it impressed me, its religious peace, will never fade from me whilst life remains.[114]

This idyllic view is not taken from a Victorian novel but a piece of journalism describing the writer's visit to a female relative who lived in the hospital or almshouses at Preston on the Wealdmoors near Wellington in Shropshire. The reference to the cloister-like ambience is a commonly applied metaphor when almshouses are described, mainly due to the architectural forms that they adopted. Additional elements made almshouses appear monastic. Many of them employed sexual segregation, cell-like apartments and habit-like uniforms. While a huge variation existed in almshouses, and only a very small proportion of the population lived in them, they still provided homes predominantly for singletons. Looking in detail at this type of accommodation highlights a number of themes already identified in this book. These were the problems faced by people due to lifecycle singleness, the tendency for society in general to marginalise single people; and for single women in particular there was the problem of controlling space that they might call home. How this provision changed over time provides an insight into how single men and women were perceived as needy and deserving of charity by society.

The tradition of providing accommodation and care for the sick and elderly goes back to the hospitals in religious houses that also provided overnight accommodation to travellers. The accommodation was in a single hall with a

---

[113]   On college rooms in the later nineteenth century, see Hamlett, *Material Relations*, pp. 154–63.

[114]   Anon, 'An Almshouse in Shropshire', *Chambers Journal*, 23 September 1856, pp. 104–5.

chapel at one end. Over time the space was divided into 'cells' – a rare survival of this form is in Chichester at St Mary's Hospital. Built before 1300, the church-like structure was divided into separate rooms in the late seventeenth century.[115] After the Dissolution of the Monasteries, independent hospitals or almshouses were set up by a variety of bodies such as cathedrals, individual charities and by towns using funds bequeathed for the purpose.[116] At this period accommodation was basic, with just the barest of necessities provided. Thomas Aliston, an almsman at St Leonard's Hospital near Boston in Lincolnshire, owned just some clothing, bedding, 2 chests valued at 20d and 'other husselments' valued at 6d when he died in 1594.[117] A mattress and his meals were probably provided by the almshouse.

Almshouses built in the sixteenth and seventeenth centuries onwards were already divided into separate units. Most comprised single-storey dwellings with one or sometimes two rooms each. The units were set around a courtyard, or a half-H plan or a row. Later examples, built in the eighteenth and nineteenth centuries, might be on two floors. Most were self-contained units and only occasionally were they built with connecting internal corridors. Therefore, by the mid-seventeenth century almshouses were built as individual dwellings that were physically related to one another and architecturally different from other buildings in the towns and villages in which they were situated, leading to the comparisons with cloisters and courts of monasteries and the Oxford and Cambridge colleges.[118] As well as the physical similarities, the almshouses also formed a community – at least in the centuries immediately following the Dissolution. In addition, there was an emphasis on single people rather than married couples, and many almshouses had a chaplain, matron or warden who lived in one of the dwellings (usually larger than the others) and this person was allowed to be married, again a similarity with Oxbridge colleges.

In the early modern period, the numbers of men housed in almshouses was greater than the number of women. This was in large part due to the terms of the individual charities stipulating who was to benefit from them. Approximately 34 per cent were only for men, 24 per cent were only for women and the remaining

---

[115]   Alec Clifton-Taylor, *Chichester* (London: BBC, 1978), p. 14.

[116]   Most were purpose-built structures, but sometimes in larger towns the accommodation was in lodgings paid for by the charity. See Ian Atherton, E. McGrath and A. Tompkins, '"Pressed Down by Want and Afflicted with Poverty, Wounded and Maimed in War or Worn Down with Age?" Cathedral Almsmen in England 1538–1914' in Anne Borsay and Peter Shapely (eds), *Medicine Charity and Mutual Aid: The Consumption of Health in Britain, c. 1550–1950* (Aldershot: Ashgate, 2007). See also Nigel Goose and Leanne Moden, *A History of Doughty's Hospital Norwich, 1687–2009* (Hatfield: University of Hertfordshire Press, 2010).

[117]   Lincolnshire Archives, INV 85/97 Inventory of Thomas Aliston, marital status unknown, St Leonard's, 1594.

[118]   Mark Girouard, *The English Town* (New Haven and London: Yale University Press, 1990), p. 62.

42 per cent were for both. This produces figures of about 55 per cent men and 45 per cent women being housed.[119] Quite why there was this disparity is not known. It might have been linked to their early monastic heritage. Some almshouses were founded by trade guilds or aimed specifically at old soldiers and sailors, and therefore naturally favoured men over women as recipients of the charity. To some extent, men were also seen as more needy because they were less able to take care of themselves. However, some charities were specifically set up to help women: for example Sir John Trevor, Speaker of the House of Commons in the early eighteenth century, founded St Martin's Almshouses near Chirk to house six poor widows.[120] Similarly, the Parminter cousins, Jane and Mary, in Exmouth, Devon, founded almshouses for six women in 1811. They wished to favour the never married over the widowed and stipulated that a Jewess who had converted to Christianity should be given preference over other candidates. The idiosyncrasies of the bequests concerning almshouses defy their being easily categorised.

By the early to mid-nineteenth century the trend had shifted in favour of more places being occupied by women. Using the census between 1841 and 1901, Nigel Goose's research suggests that there was a shift to 75 per cent women and 25 per cent men being accommodated.[121] This trend has been particularly noted by research carried out at the former Geffrye Almshouses in London, now a museum. The 14 houses – divided into four apartments, each with a single room with a closet – were founded for members of the Ironmongers' Guild. Originally, couples inhabited the Geffrye Almshouses; however by the early nineteenth century most were no longer connected with this trade, and most occupants were single individuals. By the 1891 census, all but one of the inmates were female and they had formerly been employed as governesses, companions and teachers.[122]

Only the privileged few were able to take advantage of almshouse accommodation, and these were the respectable poor rather than the neediest in society.[123] Although provision increased in the nineteenth century so also did the population. In addition, the centres of most population growth due to industrialisation also provided the lowest number of almshouses. With these qualifications noted, almshouses still provided valuable housing to single people and when looked at on a local level their importance can be better appreciated.

[119] Nigel Goose, 'The English Almshouse and the Mixed Economy of Welfare c. 1500–1900', Social Science History Conference, Ghent, 13–16 April 2010.

[120] Sylvia Watts, *Shropshire Almshouses* (Little Logaston: Logaston Press, 2010), p. 98.

[121] Goose, 'English Almshouse'.

[122] Kathy Haslam, *A History of the Geffrye Almshouses* (London: The Geffrye Museum, 2005), p. 39.

[123] Nigel Goose has given an estimate of 1.5 per cent of the population over 60 years of age living in almshouses in this period: 'Variations in the Demographic Profile of Almshouse Residents over Time and Space', unpublished conference paper, The Local Population Studies Society Autumn Conference, Cambridge, 21 November 2009.

Residents of Almshouses in the West Midlands: Evidence from the 1851 Census

Sir Francis Russell and his wife Anne created almshouses in the early eighteenth century in the village of Strensham, Worcestershire. The family lived at Strensham Court and the almshouses were built immediately outside the gates to their park so they were able to observe the recipients of their charity and their conduct. Some degree of surveillance of one kind or another is a common theme in almshouse living. Built in brick, each tenement consisted of a sitting room and a bedroom, arranged over two storeys and in a half-H plan, with a plaque dedicated to Sir Francis Russell over the central bay.

The Russell Almshouses were for six poor widows of the parish of Strensham aged 60 and over. If there were not sufficient women to take up the places then they would be offered to poor men and their wives.[124] The six people would receive 6d a week to buy bread, they were given a ton of coals or 'so many coals as might be bought ... for 10s' and a gown of the value of 20s. Every other year they were to receive new linen. Religious observation was encouraged by giving a further 3s a year on Christmas Day if they received the sacrament at least three times a year. The six tenements were increased to nine by Russell's daughter, Lady Anne Guise, who stipulated that the accommodation was to provide homes for six single women and three men, one with his wife – so continuing the preference for women in this example.

The 1851 census records eight of the nine tenements with residents and shows that they did not all conform to the terms of the charity – with four widows, one single man and three men with their wives. In two instances a daughter was also in residence, which would have made these small homes rather crowded. In most almshouses the Trustees could use their discretion as to who should benefit from the accommodation provided by the terms of the charity. In Strensham the parish had a total of 93 households in 1851 and of these eight were in the Russell Almshouses – therefore making a significant contribution to housing in the parish and providing homes, in this farming community, for agricultural labourers and their widows who could no longer manage to sustain their own homes (Table 5.2).

The city of Worcester had a long history of providing almshouse accommodation and some nine or 10 were founded. The earliest was probably Queen Elizabeth or Trinity Hospital, founded in 1561 and endowed by the queen for 29 poor women. Their allowance was just 1s 3d per month. Inglethorp, Nash and Berkeley almshouses were all founded in the seventeenth century and Wyatt, Shewring, Gouldings, Geary and Hackett were founded in the eighteenth and nineteenth centuries. Most seem to have been founded to cater for both men and women and some included married couples, although Shewring's was founded in 1702 for six 'poor widows or ancient maidens' and stipulated that preference should be given

---

[124]   Worcester Record Office (WRO), 850 Strensham BA 8716, parcel 10, rules of the almshouse and two account books.

Table 5.2   Strensham Almshouse in the 1851 census

1	Elizabeth Clifford widow 60 Agricultural labourer
2	Margaret Pusey widow 72 pauper
3	James Rivers married 68 Agricultural labourer Elizabeth Rivers wife 50 Agricultural labourer
4	William Martin married 58 Agricultural labourer Mary Martin wife 58 Agricultural labourer's wife Emma Martin daughter 12 Agricultural labourer's daughter
5	Elizabeth Findon widow 73 pauper Agricultural labourer
6	Mary Lippett widow 70 Agricultural labourer
7	John Rees married pauper miller Mary wife 62 pauper miller's wife Ann Rees daughter spinster 26
8	Thomas Chamberlain bachelor 70 pauper former Agricultural labourer

to women who had formerly been housekeepers.[125] This suggests that the founder was aware that women with a live-in position might be in need of a home when age or ill health meant they had to cease working.

By the 1840s new rules and regulations were introduced to tidy up the situation of numerous charities providing accommodation in the city.[126] These stipulated that inmates could not be in receipt of parochial relief and could not have lodgers; they must keep themselves and their rooms clean; and if they married they must vacate the almshouse in which they lived. The introduction of rules was meant to tighten up the running of charities in the city and was in response to nationwide criticisms of badly run almshouses and other church-related positions later explored in Anthony Trollope's novel *The Warden* (1855). In Worcester there had been something of a scandal in the 1820s concerning the mismanagement of the endowment of St Oswald's Hospital.[127]

Berkeley's Hospital in Worcester was built around a courtyard with a painted statue of its founder set in a niche (Figure 5.2).[128] The building included its own

[125]   Valentine Green, *A Survey of the City of Worcester* (Worcester: Butler and Gamidge, 1764), pp. 239–46 lists the charitable institutions in Worcester.

[126]   WRO, 899:800 BA9564 printed 'Rules and Regulations for the Good Government of the Inmates of Almshouses', 1836. The rules governing individual endowed charities were also affected at this period especially, after the Charitable Trusts Act was passed in 1853. See Goose and Moden, *Doughty's Hospital*.

[127]   Claire and Terry Wardle, *The History of Barbourne: The Early Development of North Worcester* (Worcester: MTC Ltd, 2007), p. 27.

[128]   Photographed by the authors.

Figure 5.2   Berkeley Hospital, Worcester, was built in a typical style for almshouses. The rooms are single storey and arranged around a quadrangle, with the sponsor's statue above the chapel. *Source*: Photograph by the authors.

Table 5.3   Inglethorpe Almshouses, Worcester, in the 1851 census

1	James Kelly widower 68 [no occupation] Ann Kelly sister spinster 46
2	Susannah Webley widow 61 formerly gloveress Mary Webley daughter spinster 39 laundress William Webley son bachelor 32 glover
3	Joseph Perry widower 77 trunkmaker
4	Ann Bedford widow 79 formerly nurse
5	John Wanklin bachelor 73 tailor
6	George Jenkins widower 76 fisherman George Jenkins grandson bachelor 20 fisherman
7	Thomas Hope widower 88 formerly porter
8	Edward Wills widower 77 formerly leather grinder
9	Joseph Bond widower 69 [no occupation]
10	Richard Darke widower 78 bookbinder Agnes Darke daughter spinster 33 gloveress Elvia Pierce lodger spinster 35 gloveress
11	James Williams widow 76 glover
12	Elizabeth Wickett widow 82 formerly gloveress

Table 5.4   Wyatt's Almshouses, Worcester, in the 1851 census

1	George Gardner widower 63 late tailor
2	Jonathan Oseman widower 70 shoemaker
3	James Kingett widower 65 glover
4	William Darke widower late glover
5	Charles Clarke widower 68 late glover
6	John Shingleton widower 73 formerly schoolmaster Joseph Marsh lodger unmarried 55 glover
7	Mary Aldridge widow 68 plain sewer
8	Sarah Woodward widow 89 nurse William Woodward son unmarried 54 hawker of cakes

chapel and the chaplain also acted as the warden of the almshouse, with a much larger house by the entrance gate. In 1851 the chaplain was a bachelor – Edwyn Bultner, aged 53 – who was also chaplain of the City Gaol. He lived with his unmarried sister Jane, aged 45, and an unmarried female servant aged 49. The former occupations of the inmates reflected the city's situation rather than the agricultural nature of Strensham. Here there were former servants, a bookbinder, a china painter, a butcher and a soldier.

The priority given to single people and the status of inmates can be gauged from the residents in 1851 in Inglethorpe and Wyatt's Almshouses (both now demolished). Inglethorpe had 12 dwellings listed, eight with a male head of household and four with a female head. However, four of them had other family members living with them and one even had a lodger, although by now this was against the rules (Tables 5.3 and 5.4).

John Shingleton at Wyatt's is unusual for almshouse residents in Worcester for having been in a profession. He was designated blind in the census, which perhaps accounts for his inability to provide for his old age and his need for a lodger.

Shrewsbury had a number of almshouses and the history of several of them illustrates that they did not always continue the original benefactor's good intentions. Lack of funding and poor management could lead to some almshouses being described as 'wretched hovels' by the eighteenth and nineteenth centuries. Such was the case with St Chad's and St Mary's Almshouses, endowed by the Mercers' and Drapers' Guild respectively. St Chad's had been insufficiently endowed and therefore poorly maintained for many years when in 1790 and then again in 1808 one of the houses fell down. Due to their poor condition and because they were in the way of improvements to the street, they were finally demolished in 1858 (Figure 5.3).[129] Despite the buildings' condition, the inhabitants of St Chad's were keen to remain and claimed that they found their homes very comfortable.[130]

St Mary's Almshouses had been well maintained in the seventeenth century and individual fireplaces and chimneys were installed. However, by 1808 they were described as 'wretched, filthy, and dangerously unwholesome', and they were demolished in about 1824 when the road was widened and new almshouses were built nearby.[131] St Mary's had been endowed for 12 poor people from the parish of St Mary's. Candidates for places were to be over 50 years of age and should be single – except for a married couple who would live in a central hall and who would nurse the sick. A further requirement was that anyone admitted to the hospital should come with a winding sheet with 4d wrapped up in it for their burial. The original houses, according to a report made in 1808, contained 'only a single apartment, 11 feet by 8, without any outlet. It is also to be feared that some of these houses are not very favourable to the morality of the lower

---

[129]   SA 6001/5326/50, Watercolour of Mercers' or St Chad's Almshouses, Shrewsbury.

[130]   Watts, *Shropshire Almshouses*, p. 108.

[131]   Anon, *Some Account of the Ancient and Present State of Shrewsbury* (Shrewsbury, 1808), p. 327.

Figure 5.3   Mercers' or St Chad's Almshouses, Shrewsbury. Painted in the early nineteenth century, this watercolour shows the dilapidation of the building and the patching up on the gable end after rooms had fallen down in 1790 and 1808. The residents, however, found their rooms comfortable and were reluctant to give up their homes when they were demolished in 1858. *Source:* Shrophire Archives.

classes.'[132] It is unclear what this refers to but apart from the risk to health of poor sanitation, it seems to suggest that the apartments were being used inappropriately. By 1851, in the newly built dwellings the inhabitants were predominantly single women: seven were spinsters, four were widows and one dwelling was inhabited by a married couple (Table 5.5).

Table 5.5   St Mary's Almshouse, Shrewsbury, in the 1851 census

1	Hannah Phipps spinster 56 almswoman Martha Phipps sister, visitor spinster 59 retired housekeeper
2	Ann Price widow 69 almswoman
3	Ann Mills spinster 72 almswoman
4	Mary Owen spinster 39 almswoman
5	Ann Vickers spinster 64 almswoman
6	Mary Jones widow 57 almswoman, late Grocer Harriet Jones daughter spinster 19 dressmaker
7	Elizabeth Powell spinster 26 dressmaker
8	Elizabeth Henley widow 79 almswoman Rebecca Jackson visitor spinster 25
9	Richard Jackson 75 almsman, formerly tailor Sophia Jackson wife 73 almswoman
10	Sarah Spenlow spinster 78 almswoman
11	Elizabeth Davies widow 63 almswoman

Making a Home in an Almshouse

Quite what the experience was like for people making the transition from their own home to living in an almshouse is impossible to gauge and probably depended on the circumstances at each almshouse as well as on an individual's character and how flexible they were to change. Whether almshouses should be viewed as providing individual homes for their occupants or as an institutional life depends on a number of factors that changed over time. Amanda Vickery ends the 'Introduction' to *Behind Closed Doors* with the comment that a 'house where an inmate has nil autonomy is a prison'.[133] Living in an almshouse was certainly preferable to a prison but all institutions have a certain amount in common. In the early modern period, the Bridewell prisons were usually filthy, unsanitary and dreadful places. However, the lack of organisation in the prison

---

[132]   Anon, *Some Account*, pp. 326–7.
[133]   Vickery, *Behind Closed Doors*, p. 24.

system did allow anomalies to exist, especially for non-criminal prisoners or if the prisoner was able to pay the gaoler for better provisions. For example, Leigh Hunt, editor of the *Examiner*, was sent to prison for libel in 1814 and served his time in a cell in Horsemonger Lane Gaol in London. Although incarcerated, this was not in a cell as they came to be fashioned. Hunt had two rooms 'where he was allowed to install his family and which he decorated as a bower of beauty, containing a piano, pictures, bookcases and busts. Venetian blinds concealed the window bars and there was even a little garden.'[134] From the later eighteenth century onwards, however, prisons began to be built along rather different lines. These were purpose-built and fortress-like, with an emphasis on surveillance and strict discipline. It was these new correctional prisons that the nineteenth century workhouses, after the Poor Law Amendment Act of 1834, were modelled on and were often referred to as 'Bastilles'. The design of Ludlow's workhouse closely resembled the example used in Pugin's *Contrasts*, which was meant to convey the inhumane treatment of its residents and which he contrasts with a medieval monastery with hospital.[135]

In the early to mid-nineteenth century there were clear moves to make workhouses better regulated and at the same time as forbidding and unpleasant as possible to deter dependency. One aspect of these changes was to strip away inmates' individuality and expression of personality through material artefacts. When John Castle entered the Union Workhouse in Chipping Hill, Essex, in 1838 he described the first day, when he and his brother 'were ordered to strip and put on the regimentals of the Union, which were composed of a pair of thick leather breeches, leather coat, low shoes, ribbed stocking, and a hairy cap with peak'. They worked hard all day making flock for filling mattresses, and they were always hungry. The evenings were spent with 30–40 other men and boys in 'a large room with a good fire ... wondering where this poverty would take us'.[136] For many people, gaining a place in an almshouse saved them from the workhouse; but some inmates who became too infirm to care for themselves ended their lives in the local 'Bastille'.[137]

---

[134] Penelope Hughes-Hallett, *The Immortal Dinner* (Chicago: New Amsterdam Books, 2002), pp. 62–3.

[135] A.W.N. Pugin, *Contrasts* (New York: Humanities Press, Leicester University Press, 1973 [1836]); D. Williams, 'The Ludlow Union Workhouse 1839–1900' in D.J. Lloyd, R. Payne, C.J. Train and D. Williams (eds), *Victorian Ludlow* (Ludlow Historical Research Group, Bucknell: Scenesetters, 2004). Interiors of prisons and workhouses are reproduced in Christopher Gilbert, *English Vernacular Furniture 1750–1900* (New Haven and London: Yale University Press, 1991).

[136] Extracts from the memoirs of John Castle reproduced in A.F.J. Brown, *Essex People 1750–1900: From Their Diaries, Memoirs and Letters* (Chelmsford: Essex Record Office Publications No. 59, 1972), pp. 116–32. There are many descriptions of the experience of being in a workhouse in working-class autobiographies but few if any of almshouses.

[137] Watts, *Shropshire Almshouses*, p. 24.

The feeling of an institution was created in almshouses at the outset by stipulating a great many rules and regulations governing the life of inmates. Although these might vary from one to another, a similarity of concerns governed the rules set out; and after 1836; when an Act of Parliament transferred responsibility for the old corporation charities to independent trustees, these became even more uniform.[138] The level of cleanliness required inmates to clean their rooms and launder bed linen and clothing on a regular basis. Attempts to regulate hours were enforced by stipulating a time, usually 9pm, for all inmates to be within the almshouse complex – and in some cases doors or gates were then locked. Generally, good behaviour was expected, with punishments for drunkenness or bad language and the ultimate penalty of being removed from the accommodation, although this seems to have rarely been carried out. Inmates were expected to reside in their rooms every night and any period away had to be sanctioned in advance. The ultimate regulation was that inmates who had been accepted as single people could not subsequently marry without permission; the same restriction was imposed on married couples who had been admitted. When one of them died, they could not remarry. Some almshouses forbade married couples and subsequent marriages altogether.[139] To enforce the rules, many almshouses had a resident warden or chaplain to observe and report misdemeanours; and the rules usually stipulated that the Trustees would inspect the premises yearly. This level of surveillance to some extent prevented the residents circumventing the rules with regard to their behaviour but also in making changes to the fabric of their apartments.[140]

However, many of the rules were broken and some almshouses were not efficient in imposing them. One resident that forced the hand of the Trustees was Hannah Hall at Millington's Hospital in Shrewsbury. Not only did she fail to attend prayers, she was also 'dirty and annoyed the other residents by her behaviour, for instance her habit of emptying her chamber pot from her window'.[141] Less extreme misdemeanours were recorded in George Gitton's diary concerning an almshouse resident in Bridgnorth. He often arrived home late to find Ann Evans in the kitchen with his servant, Susan. The late evenings that Gitton recorded demonstrate that Evans was not worried about a curfew at the almshouse in Church Street, or abstemious in her habits. A typical entry was for 3 March 1866: 'Ann Evans down here this night from 8 till near 12 at night & had rum & water (gave her 3d

[138]   As in the case of Worcester referred to above in printed 'Rules and Regulations for the Good Government of the Inmates of Almshouses', WRO 899:800, BA 9564.

[139]   Girouard, *The English Town*, p. 63 reproduces the rules for the Great Yarmouth Fisherman's Hospital that forbade marriage.

[140]   Unlike twentieth-century tenants of state housing. See Judith Attfield, 'Inside Pram Town: A Case Study of Harlow House Interiors, 1951–1961' in Judith Attfield and Pat Kirkham (eds), *A View from the Interior* (London: The Women's Press, 1995).

[141]   Watts, *Shropshire Almshouses*, p. 17.

to pay her coal ticket).'[142] Although Gitton was irritated at the regularity of Ann Evans coming to his home – stressed by underlining words and the liberal use of exclamation marks in his diary – it did not stop him giving her ale and rum and the occasional meals or small sums of money, no doubt recognising her comparative poverty.

The physical appearance and the material qualities of almshouses imposed an institutional setting to some extent and therefore any potential for making the interior of an almshouse into an individualised space was important, particularly after 1834, to emphasise their differences from Victorian institutions with a correctional purpose. The architecture always marked them out as different from other domestic dwellings in the built environment. This was as much true of newly built or rebuilt almshouses in the nineteenth century. For example the rebuilt St Mary's Almshouses in Shrewsbury and the Laslett Almshouses in Worcester were designed in Tudor style and built around a quadrangle. The decoration of almshouses was almost certainly also of an institutional nature, with all units decorated periodically in a uniform manner and done as cheaply as possible.[143]

Although the regulations of almshouses commonly reference the provision of clothing, bread and coal, they hardly ever mention furniture. The Geffrye Almshouses stipulated that the inhabitants must bring their own furniture to provide objects to sell if the person ran up debts and to pay for their funeral. A rare survival of an inventory for an inmate of the St Peter's or Merchants' Almshouses in Bristol lists a surprising amount of furniture for a two-room dwelling, one of which seems to have been little more than a closet.[144] Mary Brown, a widow, died in 1728 and her belongings included a bedstead complete with curtains and valance, a chest of drawers, a coffer, a cupboard, a writing desk, stools and chairs. In addition, her home contained earthenware, two brass kettles and a frying pan, a looking glass, three prints, linen and window curtains. Most items, however, included the comment that they were old or small, and she had just one pewter plate and one candlestick. This was clearly a pared down and poor habitation: the total value of Brown's goods was only £4 16s 9d; however, this was a complete home with something of everything.

It seems probable that most almshouses provided the main elements of furniture. Items that survive in situ are usually of a regional type and some are

---

[142]   M.D.G. Wanklyn (ed.), *The Diary of George Gitton of Bridgnorth for 1866* (Keele: University of Keele, Shropshire Record series, volume 2, 1998), pp. xviii and 23.

[143]   For example the Mannings Charity in Hartlebury, Worcestershire, provided almshouse accommodation for poor widows; in 1890 the houses were redecorated with whitewash and 'suitable papers about 6d per piece'. The exterior colours were to be the same as before. WRO BA10459/7/iii/10.

[144]   Edwin and Stella George (eds), *Bristol Probate Inventories, Part III: 1690–1804* (Bristol: The Bristol Record Society, 60, 2008). Inventory of Mary Brown, widow, Bristol, 1728.

built into the fabric of the interiors.[145] At the Berkeley Almshouses in Worcester, for example, the small dwellings had a bed that hinged to the wall to give more space in the daytime.[146] Other almshouses had built-in box or recess beds as was common in Scottish domestic interiors. This was the case at Preston: the reporter described them as 'raised above the floor, and across it … drawn a curtain – the only thing that rather grated on my sight, and gave an alms-house air to the otherwise handsome room'.[147] In Ludlow and Shrewsbury several almshouses followed the Welsh tradition, with a sleeping platform (known as a crogloft), accessed by a ladder.[148] All of these arrangements were unlike the usual domestic arrangements in the nineteenth century of a freestanding bed.

Built-in furniture was space saving in small single-room dwellings and the extra-narrow doors in many almshouses made the accommodation of normal furniture difficult. For example, at Coningsby Hospital in Hereford the door frames to individual almshouses are only about 52 cm wide, which is far less than the usual width of external doors for domestic dwellings. While such design features added to the quaintness of these homes, they made furnishing them difficult. The regional style of furniture found in almshouses also gave them a particular appearance and character. While regional furniture had been common in less wealthy middling sort homes in the seventeenth and eighteenth centuries, it became less desirable for middle-class homes in the nineteenth century. This simple regional or vernacular style made the material culture of the rooms different from rented lodging rooms, where a mixture of furniture would be encountered – some of it regional but other items fashionable if second-hand and in poor condition. This consideration would have increased the anachronistic ambience of almshouses around the mid-nineteenth century, when fashionable furniture was more readily available than previously – hence the interiors at Preston being described as 'quaint'. At Coningsby Hospital the country-style chairs that were in use and the narrow doors of individual rooms can be seen in a photograph dated to 1854,[149] The photograph shows a resident being treated by the visiting 'village corn doctor'. It was perhaps the quaintness of the scene that prompted the early photographer to capture the incident (Figure 5.4).[150]

---

[145]   See Gilbert, *Vernacular Furniture* for examples.

[146]   Annual Report for 2009, Worcester Municipal Charities, p. 25.

[147]   Anon, 'An Almshouse in Shropshire', p. 104.

[148]   Shrewsbury Drapers Company, http://www.shrewsburydrapers.org.uk/almshouses (accessed 30 July 2010).

[149]   A number of photographs in Coningsby Museum show residents using a variety of regional chairs to sit outside their homes. The armchair on the left of this photograph appears to be a 'fancy chair' based on a regional style and fashionable in the Regency period. See David Knell, *English Country Furniture: The National and Regional Vernacular 1500–1900* (London: Barrie & Jenkins, 1992), p. 187.

[150]   Photograph of the 'Village Corn Doctor' dated 1854, in the collection at Coningsby Hospital Museum.

Figure 5.4   Coningsby Hospital, Hereford. A photograph dated to 1854 showing a resident being treated by the visiting 'village corn doctor'. Different types of regional chair are in use and the narrow doors show that bulky furniture could not be accommodated. *Source:* Coningsby Hospital Museum.

By the end of the period the interiors of almshouses were filled with more objects. This to some extent made up for the lack of fashionable goods; but the emphasis on regional items continued well beyond the mid-nineteenth century, as illustrated by two house sales after the death of occupants of Powell's Almshouses in Ludlow in the early twentieth century.[151] The lists only ran to oak and elm chairs, oak chests, settles, dresser and shelves, corner cupboards and, in one sale, a clock with an inlaid case made by Griffiths of Ludlow. This last item was probably old since Griffiths were in the Ludlow directories in the 1860s.[152] The many items made in oak reflected the availability of this timber in the Welsh borderlands. The Preston on the Wealdmoors almshouses were furnished by the inmates themselves and perhaps this added to their general air of attractiveness that was noted in the description. The writer drew attention to the doors standing open and 'affording pretty glimpses of interiors; deep casement ledges filled with plants; snow caps and bright silk gowns; and if the belfry clock struck four, tea-tables and pleasant occupants'. Therefore, residents were participating in teatime rituals and visiting each other's homes. The privacy and cosiness is further emphasised by the stock use of the hearth to signify home: 'Then going in, there was her glowing hearth, her small round table near it, her spotless handkerchief, her books, her light, her room all nicety and neatness with pretty landscapes round its wall, the work of daughter-like accomplished nieces, and herself-the brightest picture in the room.'[153] In short, here was everything that was needed for a home – and inhabited by a deserving occupant.

The institutional aspects of almshouses were countered by the privacy provided by the separate dwellings. For most middling and labouring sort people, having one room to themselves was a luxury and some almshouses provided a sitting room as well as a bedroom. Some almshouses did provide uniforms – or at least clothing that was chosen by the Trustees – and sometimes particular pews in the local church were set aside for them, all requirements that would have made almshouse inhabitants stand out from the crowd. However, for some there was pride in wearing the uniform – as in the case of the Coningsby Almshouses in Hereford that were founded for 'eleven poore ould servitors that have been souldiers, mariners, or serving men'.[154] These 'servitors' were issued with a distinctive red uniform, pre-dating the similar ones worn at the Chelsea Royal Hospital, in which they were

---

[151]   SA 4924/2/38/3 auction notice, 1911; 4924/1/27/22/1 notebook with auctioneer's list, 1901.

[152]   William Griffiths, watch and clockmaker, 60 Broad Street, Ludlow: *Harrod's Directory of Shropshire* (1861).

[153]   The 'daughter-like nieces' suggest she was a spinster. Anon, 'An Almshouse in Shropshire', p. 104.

[154]   A.K. Beese, *Coningsby Hospital* (Hereford: The Coningsby Trust, 1971), p. 6. These almshouses took over from an earlier hostelry and chapel of the Knights Hospitallers of St John of Jerusalem. A chapel and hall date from this earlier period.

marched to the cathedral every Sunday.[155] The stigma of living in a workhouse, where the inmates suffered the additional misery of being segregated by sex from other members of a family, was far more pronounced than receiving the charity of almshouse accommodation.[156]

In the majority of almshouses, the inmates were expected to cook their own meals, usually on an open fire in the sitting room, rather than being provided with meals that were eaten communally. At St Mary's in Shrewsbury, for example – founded in the fifteenth century – meals had originally been taken in a communal hall, and this was the only room that was heated. By the seventeenth century, however, individual fireplaces were installed for heating and cooking. Although meals would inevitably have been simple and basic, still individual preferences could be observed and it was better than being given gruel as the inmates in a workhouse were by the nineteenth century, a measure calculated to further strip away individuality from workhouse inmates.

While the main ingredients of furnishing the almshouse were provided by the Trustees there was still room for personalising individual space using bedding, curtains, rugs, cooking equipment and eating utensils retained from earlier times, which were therefore potentially invested with memories. These smaller items could then express individual choice and were important for creating a home. The inmates of workhouses would have lost all possessions before being admitted. Perhaps the most important aspect in making an inmate of an almshouse feel at home was the security it offered. Before the welfare state provided pensions, most elderly people who were unable to work and provide an income to keep themselves were extremely vulnerable and dependent on extended family. Unmarried people were least able to call on kin in this way since they lacked children to provide them with a home.

The almshouses in the Midlands looked at here corresponded with the general trend found in Goose's research, with the shift in provision towards places for women rather than men by the early to mid-nineteenth century. The trend noted at the Geffrye Almshouses towards educated middle-class women who had been teachers and governesses was probably a symptom of London attracting single women in search of careers, the opportunities for which were beginning to open up by the late nineteenth century. These women would be particularly vulnerable in old age since they had moved away from other family members to pursue their careers; and in any case the extended family were less likely to offer support by

---

[155]   The provision of meals in the Hall at Coningsby seems to have continued long after the building of separate dwellings. Information supplied by Coningsby Museum.

[156]   For a comparison of almshouses and workhouses, see Alannah Tomkins, 'Almshouse Versus Workhouse: Residential Welfare in Eighteenth-Century Oxford', *Family and Community History*, 7/1 (2004), pp. 45–58. See also Sarah Lloyd, '"Agents in Their Own Concerns"? Charity and the Economy of Makeshifts in Eighteenth-Century Britain' in Steven King and Alannah Tomkins (eds), *The Poor in England, 1700–1850* (Manchester: Manchester University Press, 2003), pp. 100–136.

this time than they had been in the early modern period. In provincial locations, a mixed background and reflecting local trades and forms of employment probably continued to hold sway, although more research using late nineteenth-century census data is required to verify this. A similar trend, however, was noted at Preston. A reporter commented that:

> the class of recipients [in the almshouse] seems to have been raised, till it now embraces the widows and orphans of clergymen, surgeons, landed proprietors, and others of the educated middle classes. The further this proceeds the better: educated poverty is peculiarly deserving of compassion.[157]

The educated wives and daughters of professional men were peculiarly situated. They had been used to a respectable if somewhat impoverished lifestyle that often could not be maintained into old age.[158]

The greater preponderance towards almshouses being populated by women does have a curious parallel with a phenomenon noted by Styles when analysing representations of cottages in late eighteenth-century genre paintings.[159] He contrasts two paintings by William Redmore Bigg as typifying a trend. In one picture, called *Poor Old Woman's Comfort* (see Figure 3.4), a sad old woman is depicted in a simply furnished cottage, her situation enhanced however by the presence of material comforts in the form of tea wares, a clock, the cottage hearth and a cat for company. In the companion picture, *The Husbandman's Enjoyment* (1793), a smiling young man is shown with beer to drink, a pipe and tobacco, a pig fattening up eating scraps and, most importantly, the man sits *outside* the cottage door. Styles concludes that at this period 'the cottage acquires a distinct identity. It emerges as the territory, indeed the sanctuary, of the old, the vulnerable and, above all, the female.' Almshouses – with their often tiny, one-room apartments arranged around a quadrangle, either in an ancient building or newly built in Tudor style – produced a similar effect but did indeed offer a physical sanctuary for a few vulnerable women.

While *Poor Old Woman's Comfort* suggests something of the sanctuary enjoyed by elderly, single, female residents of almshouses, it is also a reminder of the marginalisation of single women throughout the period. For Anna Lepine, spinsters were 'socially invisible' and had to inhabit the margins of society both metaphorically and physically.[160] The idyllic image conveyed by the description of

---

[157]   Anon, 'An Almshouse in Shropshire', p. 104.

[158]   On the impoverishment of widows of lawyers and clergymen, see Cynthia Curran, *When I First Began My Life Anew: Middle-Class Widows in Nineteenth-Century Britain* (Bristol, IN: Wyndham Hall Press, 2000), pp. 5–6.

[159]   John Styles 'Picturing Domesticity: The Cottage Genre in Late Eighteenth-Century Britain' in Jeremy Aynsley and Charlotte Grant (eds), *Imagined Interiors: Representing the Domestic Interior since the Renaissance* (London: V&A Publications, 2006), pp. 154–5.

[160]   Anna Lepine, '"Strange and Rare Visitants": Spinsters and Domestic Space in Elizabeth Gaskell's *Cranford*', *Nineteenth-Century Contexts*, 32/2 (2010), pp. 121–37.

the almshouses at Preston on the Wealdmoors was in part inspired by the attractive setting and the grand style of architecture.[161] These dwellings were meant to reflect well on the Earls of Bradford who had endowed them and who took an active interest in their management.[162] The classical façade in a plain baroque style with large hall and arcades around a central court and with ornate wrought-iron gates gave them a distinctly country house look. This was augmented by the beautiful open countryside 4 miles outside Wellington. However, for the inhabitants the location was hardly convenient. The women lived here in a grand style but they were extremely isolated.

Conclusion

The homemaking of most of the singletons dealt with in this chapter was limited due to lack of financial freedom, which in turn caused them to live in circumstances where physical space was at a premium. Migration to towns for work meant that many young unmarried people needed to live in lodgings rather than in their parental home or that of other kin. While offering more freedom in their life choices, homemaking was mostly confined to accepting what was offered rather than choosing and fashioning their own homes. A similar situation was the fate of people who returned to singleness in old age, although for a lucky few the comparative freedom offered by almshouses gave a reduced household but at least the semblance of a home.

---

[161]   John Cornforth, 'Charity on a Noble Scale', *Country Life*, 16 April 1964, pp. 902–5.

[162]   Preston almshouses were originally set up by Catherine, Lady Herbert, the sister of the 2nd Earl of Bradford. Watt, *Shropshire Almshouses*, p. 90.

Conclusion

The title of this book combines the two central threads of our research concerns, the single state and the material culture of the home. While women's history has focused on the position in society and the economic constraints on unmarried and widowed women there has been little work published on their homemaking strategies. Even less research has been conducted on the position of bachelors and widowers. The central aim of this book has been to highlight these neglected areas of early modern cultural and gender history. Of course, unlike today, many single people remained closely involved in the network of family; and indeed many remained throughout their lives within the homes of near kin if not the parental home. However, even when economically dependent on kin the single person was a separate unit of consumption and taste if this was only realised through minor forms of expression. More freedom in homemaking practices was afforded to a minority of men and, to a lesser extent, women due to economic independence. It is this individual and gendered viewpoint that we wished to retrieve from the evidence, to produce, if only as a first tentative contribution, a dual analysis of gender and the unmarried state as expressed through the material culture of the home.

Between 1650 and 1850 single people experienced practical problems in their homemaking that were exacerbated by a number of key social and cultural disadvantages in the way that their homes functioned and were perceived. This book has highlighted that, although a significant number of people remained single throughout their lives – and many more experienced lifecycle singleness where a form of semi-independent homemaking was required – single men and women were positioned on the margins of acceptable social practice. This was especially the case for women. From the late seventeenth and early eighteenth centuries, social mores had become increasingly antagonistic towards the never-married woman. For many unmarried women, and certainly those not insulated by private wealth, controlling domestic space was often impossible; and a home is not worthy of the name if an individual lacks the freedom to use the space as they wish.

Perceptions of singleness took on fresh meanings in the nineteenth century with the increased currency of the notion of the 'surplus woman': in the eyes of social commentators, far from being liminal beings, women who were and would remain unmarried automatically imposed an economic and, by extension, moral drain on (re)productive society. The 1851 census gave numerical expression to this tendency, solidifying what had been long suspected as a significant demographic trend. For a variety of reasons – chiefly male emigration, desertion and early death in war – singleness became an issue in the female population of Britain:

a quantifiable phenomenon to be addressed. At the same time, attitudes to homemaking in the nineteenth century positioned the family at its heart: de facto, a household without a family was lacking perhaps the most essential ingredient necessary to participate fully in society. However, whilst such attitudes celebrated the home and conjugality, from the mid-nineteenth century the first wave of feminism suggested that a career and an independent life were viable alternatives to marriage to a growing number of middle-class women.

Yet, despite the practical, social and cultural difficulties faced by single homemakers, it is clear that home remained a focal point and the diversity of ways to which single men and women resorted indicates the primacy of domestic life. However, there is insufficient evidence of a discrete culture of consumption in these homes: we are at pains to stress that a 'subculture of singleness', even if this could be isolated, was not directly observable in the homemaking strategies and material possessions of the middling sort. Without doubt, the drive for conformity, the simple absorption into wider norms and practices that gave structure, meaning and identity to the home, was strong across society and largely independent of marital status. Thus, throughout the period most single people strove to configure their homes in much the same ways as the normative example of the nuptial household – either by recreating an ad hoc household family, like William Stout, or by simply replicating the standards of homemaking apparent amongst social and cultural contemporaries.

None the less, some differences, albeit slight and understated, are observable in the homemaking practices of men and women singletons. Single men were more likely to adopt a 'monastic' style of life whether or not they remained attached to their Oxbridge colleges, and such men often indulged their research interests with libraries and allied collections. This gender bias was due in part to the lack of professional openings for women during the period. Women like Caroline Herschel, with her astronomical apparatus on the roof of the outbuildings in which she lived, were few and far between. Her scientific pursuits would almost certainly not have been possible if she had been a wife and mother. Single men were also generally more likely to create individualised interiors that reflected their particular interests and were influenced by their occupations. This included allowing work-related items and practices to encroach on their domesticity. Thus, Henry Woollcombe's house was open to the regular intrusions of his legal practice, whilst his later residence was refashioned to accommodate his extensive literary interests. It is certainly probable that the reworking of domestic space was in part permitted by Woollcombe's unmarried estate: although Woollcombe desired marriage, he contended that any alliance would invoke considerable compromise with his academic endeavours. In many ways, Woollcombe was far more able to suit himself with regard to his domestic arrangements than his contemporaries. Through such strategies he negotiated the psychic pain of singleness.

In contrast, women were arguably better placed than men to manage their homemaking through the skills and competencies taught them by their mothers. Whereas many men were barely competent at even basic forms of household organisation – the first-time homemaker Julius Hardy is a case in point here – lone women were, by and large, more able to construct amenable and culturally acceptable domestic spaces. In many cases, this translated into the material improvement of the domestic interior: the widows and spinsters described in the sample of probate material, for instance, often possessed minor items of household use and decoration which directly contributed to comfort-enhancing domestic practices. In addition, most women's interests ran along domestic lines such as plain and fancy sewing and embroidery, which would have enabled them to enhance their homes, although items related to these activities would often not be revealed in an inventory. To an extent, these enhancements were not necessarily 'strategies for showing' per se but devices that smoothed the edges of a single existence, although the many minor items in female households connected with serving food and drink perhaps indicate more participation in entertaining guests than their male counterparts. The homes of single women also reveal subtle differences in how domestic space was viewed and constructed. It is perhaps significant that in these contexts, even financially constrained single men, like George Gitton of Bridgnorth, sought out female housekeepers to bring order, direction and perhaps agreeable company to their otherwise single lives.

The research for this book has brought together a large amount of previously unpublished material concerning individuals where little is known and of whom little will ever be known beyond a scant probate document. Alongside these, more substantial evidence has been used of individual lives in the form of letters and diaries. Some of these latter sources have been previously published and are well known; others are less so and most have not been used for evidence of homemaking. The diary of Henry Nussey, for example, has often been quoted due to his connection with the Brontës; but the inventory of his home has never been used in conjunction with his diary recording his early professional life in Sussex. These documents are of interest not only in illustrating the life of this failed suitor of Charlotte but also simply as an example of a young clergyman surviving his bachelor days and creating a temporary home with the help of his sisters.

We have followed a well-trodden path in constructing a dataset of probate inventories and associated testamentary material across the period. The differences in the emphasis of our work – its focus on singleness and the material culture of the home – have begun to uncover the nuances collapsed within the homemaking practices of single people. This is distinct from the indices of ownership constructed from wider regional and national examples. Yet clearly, more intensive work needs to be extended to those households omitted from our survey. In particular, sifting out the widowers and bachelors from the amorphous collection of male trades is a task that has only just begun. Similarly, there are many more spinster and widow homes not captured in this research process that require further analysis. None the less, we are aware that probate, by its very nature, can only offer a brief, post-mortem snapshot of the 'bald facts' of possession, often stripped of the affective, cultural and personal resonances that translate the simple act of 'having' into the dynamic process of 'consuming'. We have used our sample as a base line, a jumping-off point through which the life experiences of single people, both lifecycle singletons and the never married, can be examined through a sharper lens. In consequence, we have constructed a series of detailed case studies that have utilised a range of discursive qualitative sources to cast light on the single condition. This approach is not without problems – it tends to valorise the outstanding individual over the ordinary and the extraordinary incident over the mundane. Yet, through such means, the kinds of arrangements and adjustments to which single people resorted in order to counter the challenges of singleness in an often hostile social environment have been described. More work is required, but this book has in some small way re-oriented our attention to single homemakers.

Singleness was the result of a complexity of factors. Age, opportunity, ability, dependency, class, status and personal inclination affected or debarred entry into marriage and these factors either jointly or severally were subtly combined in the most central area of personal expression, the singleton's home. This was often merely a simple room in a lodging house or a cell in an almshouse. However, other singletons were able to establish themselves in substantial and well-furnished homes – such as Anne Boulton at Thornhill House in Birmingham or the sweeping grandeur of Henry Woollcombe's newly built Plymouth residence. Whatever the size and status, home intimately reflected the self. For singletons like Julius Hardy, energetically constructing his Methodist prayer meetings and fretting about the opprobrium of his pregnant servant, or George Gitton happily clipping his toenails in his Bridgnorth parlour, home remained a site of anxiety and triumph, of competition and relaxation. Without a spouse to consider, the single person inevitably made gendered decisions concerning taste, organisation, arrangement and consumption. Shorn of the restraining hand of partnership, for at least a short while, these middle-ranking singletons could, within measure, construct a home of their own.

Bibliography

Manuscript Sources

Birmingham Central Archives

669002, MS 218 Diary of Julius Hardy, Button-Maker of Birmingham
Matthew Boulton Archive MBP MS 3782
MS 319/1–14 Family Papers, will and auction pamphlet for J. Bissell
MS 805 Diary of Thomas Jordan
MS 1081/1–8 Eld and Chamberlain catalogue and receipts for Wace
James Watt Archive MS 3219

British Library

Egerton MSS 3268A Henry Nussey journal

Hereford Record Office

H/D/3/3–6 Wills, Probate Inventories and Administrations

Lincolnshire Archives

INV 85/97 Inventory of Thomas Aliston, St Leonard's, 1594

Lichfield Record Office

B/C/5 Cause Papers: Wills, Probate Inventories and Administrations
B/C/10 Wills, Probate Inventories and Administrations

Plymouth and West Devon Record Office

710/391–7 Diaries of Henry Woollcombe II, 1796–1828
710/398 Henry Woollcombe, inventory of wine, silver, plate, glass ware and china, December 1841
2395 An Account of the Antiquarian and Archaeological Manuscripts of Henry Woollcombe, FSA, c.1839

Shropshire Archives

1045/522 Will of Pemberton dated 1834
4924/1/27/22/1 Notebook with auctioneer's list, 1901
4924/2/38/3 Auction notice, 1911
6000/12167 Auctioneer's notebook: James Mullock, bachelor, Whitchurch, 1804
6000/15309 Auctioneer catalogue: Ann Fox, spinster, Cleobury Mortimer, 1813
6001/4/4645–4647 Auction notice, 7 February 1810
D3651/B/9/6/2/5 Auctioneer's inventory of Rev. Robert Norgrave Pemberton, Church Stretton, 1848
Watton Cuttings, volume 8

Walsall Local History Centre

920GEE 'The Life and Times of James Gee of Walsall 1746–1827' Transcription

West Sussex Record Office, Chichester

Add. Mss. 2239 Samuel Peat day book
Add. Mss. 2245 Henry and William Peat notebook
Add. Mss. 19026 Diary of John Lush
Wills, Probate Inventories and Administrations

Worcester Record Office and History Centre

1851 Census for Worcester, Strensham and Shrewsbury
850 Strensham BA 8716, parcel 10, rules of the almshouse and two account books
899:800 BA9564 printed 'Rules and Regulations for the Good Government of the Inmates of Almshouses', 1836
BA10459/7/iii/10 Mannings Charity, Hartlebury, Worcestershire
Wills, Probate Inventories and Administrations

Printed Primary Sources

Anon, *The Accomplish'd Housewife: or the Gentlewoman's Companion* (London, 1745)
Anon, *Some Account of the Ancient and Present State of Shrewsbury* (Shrewsbury, 1808)
Anon, *Practical Economy* (London, 1822)
Anon, *The Footman's Directory and Butler's Remembrancer* (London: Hatchard and Son, 1823)
Anon, *The Servants' Guide and Family Manual* (London, 1830)

Anon, *The Family Economist: A Penny Monthly Magazine for the Industrious Classes* (London: Groombridge and Sons, volume 6, 1853)

Anon, 'An Almshouse in Shropshire', *Chambers Journal*, 23 September 1856, pp. 104–5

Aris's Birmingham Gazette

Austen, J., *Mansfield Park* (Harmondsworth: Penguin, 1985 [1814])

Beale, C.H., *Reminiscences of a Gentlewoman of the Last Century: Letters of Catherine Hutton* (Birmingham: Cornish Brothers, 1891)

Beeton, I., *Beeton's Book of Household Management* (London: Chancellor Press, 1997 facsimile of 1859–61 edition)

Beresford, J. (ed.), *The Diary of a Country Parson, 1758–1802: James Woodforde* (London: Oxford University Press, 1967)

Beresford, J. (ed.), *Woodforde: Passages from the Five Volumes of the Diary of a Country Parson, 1758–1802: The Reverend James Woodforde* (London: Oxford University Press, 6th edn, 1967 [1935])

Boyle, P., *The Ladies Complete Visiting Guide* (London, 1800)

Brontë, C., *Shirley* (Harmondsworth: Penguin, 1985 [1849])

Brown, A.F.J., *Essex People 1750–1900: From Their Diaries, Memoirs and Letters* (Chelmsford: Essex Record Office Publications No. 59, 1972)

Christie, O.F. (ed.), *The Diary of the Revd. William Jones, 1777–1821* (London: Brentano's, 1921)

Dickens, C., *Dombey and Son* (Harmondsworth: Penguin, 1985 [1848])

Directory of Shropshire (Manchester: Slater, 1844)

Directory of Shropshire (London: Bagshaw, 1851)

Directory of Shropshire and Staffordshire (London: Post Office, 1870)

Disraeli, B., *Sybil or The Two Nations* (Oxford: Oxford University Press, 1981 [1845])

Djabri, S.C. (ed.), *The Diaries of Sarah Hurst 1759–1762: Life and Love in Eighteenth-Century Horsham* (Stroud: Amberley, 2009)

Dresser, M. (ed.), *The Diary of Sarah Fox, née Champion, Bristol, 1745–1802* (Bristol: Bristol Record Society, 55, 2003)

Eighteenth Century Collections Online (ECCO), Catalogue of all the Household Goods of Miss Lamprey, Canterbury, 1764 (Gale document number CW107372180); available at http://gale.cengage.co.uk/product-highlights/history/eighteenth-century-collections-online.aspx.

Eland, G. (ed.), *Purefoy Letters 1735–1753* (London: Sidgwick & Jackson, 1931)

Ellis, W., *The Country Housewife's Family Companion* (London: James Hodges, 1750)

Gaskell, E., *Cranford* (Harmondsworth: Penguin, 1976, [1851])

George, E. and S. (eds), *Bristol Probate Inventories, Part III: 1690–1804* (Bristol: Bristol Record Society, 60, 2008)

Green, V., *A Survey of the City of Worcester* (Worcester: Butler and Gamidge, 1764)

Harrod's Directory of Shropshire (1861)

Hay, D.R., *The Laws of Harmonious Colouring* (Edinburgh and London: William Blackwood and Sons, 1847 [1836])

Horner, C. (ed.), *The Diary of Edmund Harrold, Wigmaker of Manchester, 1712–15* (Aldershot: Ashgate, 2008)

Hoskin, M. (ed.), *Caroline Herschel's Autobiographies* (Cambridge: Science History Publications, 2003)

Hughes, D. (ed.), *The Diary of a Country Parson: The Revd James Woodforde* (London: Folio Society, 1992)

Johnson, A. (ed.), *The Diary of Thomas Giordani Wright, Newcastle Doctor, 1826–1829* (Surtees Society, 206, 2001)

Kerr, R., *The Gentleman's House or How to Plan English Residences from the Parsonage to the Palace* (London: John Murray, 1864)

Lady, A, *The Home Book: or Young Housekeeper's Assistant* (London: Smith, Elder and Co, 1829)

Loudon, J.C., *The Suburban Gardener and Villa Companion* (London: Longman, Orme, Brown, Green and Longmans, 1838)

Marshall, J.D. (ed.), *The Autobiography of William Stout, 1665–1752* (Manchester: Manchester University Press for the Chetham Society, 1967)

Moritz, C.P., *Journeys of a German in England in 1782*, translated and edited by Reginald Nettel (London: Jonathan Cape, 1965)

Parkes, Mrs W., *Domestic Duties* (London, 1828)

Pope, W.B. (ed.), *The Diary of Robert Haydon* (Cambridge, MA: Harvard University Press, 1960)

Proceedings of the Old Bailey Online, http://www.oldbaileyonline.org

Quennell, P. (ed.), *Memoirs of William Hickey* (London: Routledge & Kegan Paul, 1975)

Ralph, E. and M.E. Williams (eds), *The Inhabitants of Bristol in 1696: Assessments under the 1694 Marriage Act* (Bristol: Bristol Record Society, 25, 1968)

Salopian Journal

Schopenhauer, J., *A Lady's Travels: Journeys in England and Scotland from the Diaries of Johanna Schopenhauer*, translated and edited by R. Michaelis-Jena and W. Merson (London: Routledge, 1988)

Scott, W., *The Antiquary* (Edinburgh: Adam & Charles Black, 1886 [1816])

Sussex Agricultural Express

Taylor, Mrs, *Practical Hints to Young Females: On the Duties of a Wife, a Mother, and a Mistress* (London, 1822).

Toynbee, P. and L. Whibley (eds), *Correspondence of Thomas Gray*, 3 vols (Oxford: Clarendon, 1971)

Trinder, B. and J. Cox (eds), *Yeomen and Colliers in Telford: Probate Inventories for Dawley, Lilleshall, Wellington and Wrockwardine, 1660–1750* (Chichester: Phillimore, 1980)

Trinder, B. and N. Cox (eds), *Miners and Mariners of the Severn Gorge: Probate Inventories for Benthall, Broseley, Little Wenlock and Madeley, 1660–1764* (Chichester: Phillimore, 2000)

Vaisey, D.G. (ed.), *Probate Inventories of Lichfield and District, 1568–1680*, Collections for a History of Staffordshire, 4th Series, vol. 5 (Stafford: Staffordshire Record Office, 1969)

Wace, H.T. *Palm Leaves from the Nile: Being a Portion of the Diary of a Wanderer in Egypt* (Shrewsbury: Leake and Evans, Printers, 1865)

Walsh, J.H., *A Manual of Domestic Economy* (London: Routledge, 1857)

Wanklyn, M.D.G. (ed.), *Inventories of Worcestershire Landed Gentry 1537–1786*, Worcestershire Historical Society New Series, vol. 16 (Worcester: Worcestershire Historical Society, 1998)

Wanklyn, M.D.G. (ed.), *The Diary of George Gitton of Bridgnorth for 1866*. Shropshire Record Series, vol. 2 (Keele: University of Keele, 1998)

Woolf, V., *A Room of One's Own* (Harmondsworth: Penguin, 1995 [1929])

Yorke, P.C. (ed.), *The Diary of John Baker, Barrister of the Middle Temple, Solicitor-General of the Leeward Islands* (London: Hutchinson, 1931)

Secondary Sources

Alcock, N., *People at Home: Living in a Warwickshire Village, 1500–1800* (Chichester: Phillimore, 1993)

Alexander, C. and M. Smith, *The Oxford Companion to the Brontës* (Oxford: Oxford University Press, 2003)

Anderson, M., *Family Structure in Nineteenth-Century Lancashire* (Cambridge: Cambridge University Press, 1971)

Anderson, M., 'The Social Position of Spinsters in Mid-Victorian Britain', *Journal of Family History*, 9 (1984), pp. 377–93

Andrews, J., 'The Churches of Shobdon' in *A History of Shobdon Church* (booklet, n.d.)

Ardener, S., *Women and Space: Ground Rules and Social Maps* (Oxford: Berg, 1993)

Arkell, T., 'Interpreting Probate Inventories' in T. Arkell, N. Evans and N. Goose (eds), *When Death Do Us Part: Understanding and Interpreting the Probate Records of Early Modern England* (Oxford: Leopard's Head Press, 2000)

Arkell, T., N. Evans and N. Goose (eds), *When Death Do us Part: Understanding and Interpreting the Probate Records of Early Modern England* (Oxford: Leopard's Head Press, 2000)

Ashton, H. and K. Davies, *I Had a Sister* (London: Lovat Dickson Limited, 1937)

Atherton, I., E. McGrath and A. Tompkins, '"Pressed Down by Want and Afflicted with Poverty, Wounded and Maimed in War or Worn Down with Age?" Cathedral Almsmen in England 1538–1914' in A. Borsay and P. Shapely (eds), *Medicine Charity and Mutual Aid: The Consumption of Health in Britain, c. 1550–1950* (Aldershot: Ashgate, 2007)

Attfield, J., 'Inside Pram Town: A Case Study of Harlow House Interiors, 1951–
1961' in J. Attfield and P. Kirkham (eds), *A View from the Interior* (London:
The Women's Press, 1995)

Bailey, J., 'Favoured or Oppressed? Married Women, Property and "Coverture" in
England, 1660–1800', *Continuity and Change*, 17/3 (2002), pp. 351–72

Bailey, J., *Unquiet Lives: Marriage and Marriage Breakdown in England, 1660–
1800* (Cambridge: Cambridge University Press, 2003)

Barker, H., The *Business of Women: Female Enterprise and Urban Development
in Northern England 1760–1830* (Oxford: Oxford University Press, 2006)

Barker, H., 'Soul, Purse and Family: Middling and Lower-Class Masculinity in
Eighteenth-Century Manchester', *Social History*, 33/1 (2008), pp. 12–35.

Barker, H. and K. Harvey, 'Women Entrepreneurs and Urban Expansion:
Manchester, 1760–1820' in R. Sweet and P. Lane (eds), *Women and Urban Life
in Eighteenth-Century England: 'On the Town'* (Aldershot: Ashgate, 2003)

Barry, J., and C. Brooks (eds), *The Middling Sort of People: Culture, Society and
Politics in England, 1550–1800* (Basingstoke: Macmillan, 1994)

Baugh, G.C., *Victoria County History of Shropshire. Vol. 10: Wenlock, Upper
Corve Dale, and the Stretton Hills* (Oxford: Oxford University Press for the
Institute of Historical Research, 1998)

Beese, A.K., *Coningsby Hospital* (Hereford: The Coningsby Trust, 1971)

Benjamin, M. (ed.), *Science and Sensibility: Gender and Scientific Enquiry, 1780–
1945* (Oxford: Basil Blackwell, 1991)

Bennett, J.M. and A.M. Froide (eds), *Singlewomen in the European Past 1250–
1800* (Philadelphia: University of Pennsylvania Press, 1999)

Berg, M., 'Women's Consumption and the Industrial Classes of Eighteenth-
Century England', *Journal of Social History*, 30/2 (1996), pp. 415–34

Berg, M., *Luxury and Pleasure in Eighteenth-Century Britain* (Oxford: Oxford
University Press, 2005)

Berg, M. and E. Eger, 'The Rise and Fall of the Luxury Debates' in M. Berg
and E. Eger (eds), *Luxury in the Eighteenth Century: Debates, Desires and
Delectable Goods* (Basingstoke: Palgrave Macmillan, 2003), pp. 7–21

Berry, H., 'Rethinking Politeness in Eighteenth-Century England: Moll King's
Coffee House and the significance of "Flash Talk"', *Transactions of the Royal
Historical Society*, 6th Series, 11 (2001), pp. 65–81

Birrell, T.A., 'Reading as Pastime: The Place of Light Literature in Some
Gentlemen's Libraries in the 17th Century' in R. Myers and M. Harris (eds),
*Property of a Gentleman: The Formation, Organisation and Dispersal of the
Private Library, 1620–1920* (Winchester: St Paul's Bibliographies, 1991), pp.
113–31

Black, B.J., 'The Pleasure of Your Company in Late-Victorian Clubland',
Nineteenth-Century Contexts, 32/4 (2010), pp. 281–304

Black, J., 'Illegitimacy, Sexual Relations and Location in Metropolitan London'
in T. Hitchcock and H. Shore, *The Streets of London from the Great Fire to the
Great Stink* (London: Rivers Oram Press, 2003), pp. 101–18

Borsay, P., 'Health and Leisure Resorts' in P. Clark (ed.), *The Cambridge Urban History of Britain: Volume 2, 1540–1840* (Cambridge: Cambridge University Press, 2000), pp. 775–804

Borsay, P. (ed.), *The Eighteenth-Century Town, 1688–1820* (London: Longman, 1990)

Bothelo, L., *Old Age and the English Poor Law, 1500–1700* (Woodbridge: The Boydell Press, 2004)

Boulton, J., 'London Widowhood Revisited: The Decline of Female Remarriage in the Seventeenth and Early Eighteenth Centuries', *Continuity and Change*, 5/3 (1990), pp. 323–55

Branca, P., *Silent Sisterhood: Middle-Class Women in the Victorian Home* (London: Croom Helm, 1975)

Breward, C., *The Hidden Consumer: Masculinities, Fashion and City Life, 1860–1914* (Manchester: Manchester University Press, 1999)

Brock, C., *The Comet Sweeper: Caroline Herschel's Astronomical Ambition* (Cambridge: Icon Books, 2007)

Bryden, I. and J. Floyd, 'Introduction' in I. Bryden and J. Floyd (eds), *Domestic Space: Reading the Nineteenth-Century Interior* (Manchester: Manchester University Press, 1999), pp. 1–17

Burnett, J., *A Social History of Housing 1815–1970* (Newton Abbott: David & Charles, 1978)

Burnett, J., D. Vincent and D. Mayall (eds), *The Autobiography of the Working Class: An Annotated Critical Bibliography, Vol. 1, 1790–1900* (Brighton: Harvester, 1984)

Campbell, C., 'Understanding Traditional and Modern Practices of Consumption in Eighteenth-Century England: A Character-Action Approach' in J. Brewer and R. Porter (eds), *Consumption and the World of Goods* (London: Routledge, 1993), pp. 40–57

Campbell Orr, C. (ed.), *Women in the Victorian Art World* (Manchester and New York: Manchester University Press, 1996)

Capern, A.L. and J.M. Spicksley, 'Introduction', *Women's History Review*, 16/3 (2007), pp. 289–96

Carter, P., *Men and the Emergence of Polite Society, Britain, 1660–1800* (Harlow: Longman, 2001)

Cavallo, S. and L. Warner (eds), *Widowhood in Medieval and Early Modern Europe* (London: Longman, 1999)

Chudacoff, H.P., *The Age of the Bachelor: Creating an American Subculture* (Princeton: Princeton University Press, 1999)

Clark, P., 'Migrants in the City: The Process of Social Adaptation in English Towns, 1500–1800' in P. Clark and D. Souden (eds), *Migration and Society in Early Modern England* (London: Hutchinson, 1987)

Clark, P. (ed.), *The Transformation of English Towns, 1600–1800* (London: Hutchinson, 1984)

Clark, P. and R.A. Houston, 'Culture and Leisure, 1700–1840' in P. Clark (ed.), *The Cambridge Urban History of Britain: Volume 2, 1540–1840* (Cambridge: Cambridge University Press, 2000), pp. 575–614

Clifton-Taylor, A., *Chichester* (London: BBC, 1978)

Cockayne, E., *Hubbub: Filth, Noise and Stench in England* (New Haven and London: Yale University Press, 2007)

Cocks, H.G., *Nameless Offences: Homosexual Desire in the Nineteenth Century* (London: I.B. Taurus, 2003)

Cocks, H.G., 'Making the Sodomite Speak: Voices of the Accused in English Sodomy Trials, c.1800–98', *Gender and History*, 18/1 (2006), pp. 87–107

Cohen, D., *Household Gods: The British and their Possessions* (New Haven and London: Yale University Press, 2006)

Cohen, M., *Fashioning Masculinity: National Identity and Language in the Eighteenth Century* (London: Routledge, 1996)

Collins, S., '"A Kind of Lawful Adultery": English Attitudes to the Remarriage of Widows, 1550–1800' in P.C. Jupp and G. Howarth (eds), *The Changing Face of Death: Historical Accounts of Death and Disposal* (Basingstoke: Macmillan, 1997), pp. 34–47

Connell, R.W., *Masculinities* (2nd edn, Cambridge: Polity Press, 2005)

Connors, R., 'Poor Women, the Parish and the Politics of Poverty' in H. Barker and E. Chalus (eds), *Gender in Eighteenth-Century England: Roles, Representations and Responsibilities* (London: Longman, 1997)

Cornforth, J., 'Charity on a Noble Scale', *Country Life*, 16 April 1964, pp. 902–5

Cowan, B., 'What was Masculine about the Public Sphere? Gender and the Coffee House Milieu in Post-Restoration England', *History Workshop Journal*, 51 (2001), pp. 127–57

Cowan, B., The *Social Life of Coffee: The Emergence of the British Coffeehouse* (New Haven and London: Yale University Press, 2005)

Cox, N.C., *The Complete Tradesman: A Study of Retailing 1550–1820* (Aldershot: Ashgate, 2000)

Cox, N.C. and K. Dannehl, *Perceptions of Retailing in Early Modern England* (Aldershot: Ashgate, 2007)

Cox, N.C. and K. Dannehl (eds), 'The Dictionary of Traded Goods', *British History Online* (http://www.british-history.ac.uk/source.aspx?pubid=739 2008)

Curran, C., 'Private Women, Public Needs: Middle-Class Widows in Victorian England', *Albion*, 25/2 (1993), pp. 217–36

Curran, C., *When I First Began My Life Anew: Middle-Class Widows in Nineteenth-Century Britain* (Bristol, IN: Wyndham Hall Press, 2000)

Dannehl, K., '"To Families Furnishing Kitchens": Domestic Utensils and their Use in the Eighteenth-Century Home', in D.P. Hussey and M. Ponsonby (eds), *Buying for the Home: Shopping for the Domestic from the Seventeenth Century to the Present* (Aldershot: Ashgate, 2008), pp. 27–46

Davidoff, L., *The Best Circles* (London: Croom Helm, 1973)

Davidoff, L. and C. Hall, *Family Fortunes: Men and Women of the English Middle Class 1780–1850* (London: Hutchinson, 1987)

Davidoff, L., M. Doolittle, J. Fink and K. Holden, *The Family Story: Blood, Contract and Intimacy, 1830–1960* (London and New York: Longman, 1999)

de Bellaigue, C., *Educating Women: Schooling and Identity in England and France, 1800–1867* (Oxford: Oxford University Press, 2007)

de Vries, J., 'Between Purchasing Power and the World of Goods: Understanding the Household Economy in Early Modern Europe' in J. Brewer and R. Porter (eds), *Consumption and the World of Goods* (London: Routledge, 1993)

de Vries, J., *The Industrious Revolution: Consumer Behaviour and the Household Economy, 1650 to the Present* (Cambridge: Cambridge University Press, 2008)

Dellamora, R., *Masculine Desire: The Sexual Politics of Victorian Aestheticism* (Chapel Hill and London: University of North Carolina Press, 1990)

Douglas, M., *Purity and Danger: An Analysis of Concepts of Pollution and Taboo* (Harmondsworth: Penguin, 1996)

Downs, C., 'The Business Letters of Daniel Eccleston of Lancaster (1745–1821): Trade, Commerce, and Marine Insurance in Late-Eighteenth-Century Liverpool, Lancaster, and Whitehaven', *Northern History*, 41/1 (2004), pp. 129–48

Durant, D.N., *Living in the Past: An Insider's Social History of Historic Houses* (London: Aurum Press, 1988)

Earle, P., 'The Female Labour Market in London in the Late Seventeenth and Early Eighteenth Century', *Economic History Review*, 42 (1989), pp. 328–53

Earle, P., *The Making of the English Middle Class: Business, Society and Family Life in London, 1660–1730* (London: Methuen, 1989)

Earle, P., *A City Full of People: Men and Women of London, 1650–1750* (London: Methuen, 1994)

Edwards, C., *Eighteenth-Century Furniture* (Manchester: Manchester University Press, 1996)

Edwards, C., *Turning Houses into Homes: A History of the Retailing and Consumption of Domestic Furnishings* (Aldershot: Ashgate, 2005)

Edwards, C. and M. Ponsonby, 'Desirable Commodity or Practical Necessity? The Sale and Consumption of Second-Hand Furniture' in D. Hussey and M. Ponsonby (eds), *Buying for the Home: Shopping for the Domestic from the Seventeenth Century to the Present* (Aldershot: Ashgate, 2008), pp. 117–38

Elias, N., *The Civilising Process* (Oxford: Blackwell, 1978)

Emerson, J., 'The Lodging Market in a Victorian City: Exeter', *Southern History*, 9 (1987), pp. 103–13

Erickson, A.L., *Women and Property in Early Modern England* (London: Routledge, 1993)

Erickson, A.L., 'Property and Widowhood in England, 1600–1840' in S. Cavallo and L. Walker (eds), *Widowhood in Medieval and Early Modern Europe* (Harlow: Pearson, 1999), pp. 145–63

Erickson, A.L., 'Coverture and Capitalism', *History Workshop Journal*, 59 (2005), pp. 1–16

Erickson, A.L., 'Possession – and the Other One-Tenth of the Law: Assessing Women's Ownership and Economic Roles in Early Modern England', *Women's History Review*, 16/3 (2007), pp. 369–85

Estabrook, C., *Urbane and Rustic England: Cultural Ties and Social Spheres in the Provinces, 1660–1780* (Manchester: Manchester University Press, 1998)

Evans, S., 'Houses of Character: Eccentric Personalities in National Trust Houses', *The Royal Oak Newsletter* (Fall 2006)

Evans, T., *Unfortunate Objects: Lone Mothers in Eighteenth-Century London* (London: Palgrave Macmillan, 2007)

Fellows, W., *A Passion to Preserve: Gay Men as Keepers of Culture* (Madison: University of Wisconsin Press, 2004)

Finn, M., 'Men's Things: Masculine Possession in the Consumer Revolution', *Social History*, 25/2 (2000), pp. 133–55

Flather, A., *Gender and Space in Early Modern England* (London: The Royal Historical Society, The Boydell Press, 2007)

Fletcher, A., *Gender, Sex and Subordination in England, 1500–1800* (New Haven and London: Yale University Press, 1995)

Ford, D.N., 'Royal Berkshire History' (http://www.berkshirehistory.com/castles/priory)

Forty, A., *Objects of Desire: Design and Society 1750–1980* (London: Thames & Hudson, 1987)

Foyster, E.A., *Manhood in Early Modern England: Honour, Sex and Marriage* (London and New York: Longman, 1999)

Foyster, E.A., *Marital Violence: An English Family History, 1600–1857* (Cambridge: Cambridge University Press, 2005)

French, H.R., 'The Search for the "Middle Sort of People" in England, 1600–1800', *Historical Journal*, 43/1 (2000), pp. 277–93

French, H.R., *The Middle Sort of People in Provincial England, 1600–1750* (Oxford: Oxford University Press, 2007)

Froide, A.M., 'Marital Status as a Category of Difference: Singlewomen and Widows in Early Modern England' in J.M. Bennett and A.M. Froide (eds), *Singlewomen in the European Past 1250–1800* (Philadelphia: University of Pennsylvania Press, 1999), pp. 236–69

Froide, A.M., 'Old Maids: The Lifecycle of Single Women in Early Modern England' in L. Botelho and P. Thane (eds), *Women and Aging in British Society since 1500* (London: Pearson, 2001), pp. 89–110

Froide, A.M., *Never Married: Singlewomen in Early Modern England* (Oxford: Oxford University Press, 2007)

Frost, G., *Promises Broken: Courtship, Class and Gender in Victorian England* (Charlottesville: University of Virginia Press, 1995)

Frost, G., *Living in Sin: Cohabiting as Husband and Wife in Nineteenth-Century England* (Manchester: Manchester University Press, 2008)

Gérin, W., *Charlotte Brontë: The Evolution of Genius* (Oxford: Clarendon Press, 1967)

Gilbert, C., *English Vernacular Furniture 1750–1900* (New Haven and London: Yale University Press, 1991)

Girouard, M., *The English Town* (New Haven and London: Yale University Press, 1990)

Glanville, P. and H. Young, *Elegant Eating: Four Hundred Years of Dining in Style* (London: V&A Publications, 2002)

Glazier, M., 'Common Lodging Houses in Chester, 1841–71' in R. Swift (ed.), *Victorian Chester: Essays in Social History, 1830–1900* (Liverpool: Liverpool University Press, 1996), pp. 53–83

Gleadale, K., *British Women in the Nineteenth Century* (London: Palgrave Macmillan, 2001)

Glenn, V., 'George Bullock, Richard Bridgens and James Watt's Regency Furnishing Schemes', *Furniture History*, 15 (1979), pp. 54–67

Goffman, E., *The Presentation of the Self in Everyday Life* (Woodstock, NY: Overlook Press, 1959)

Goose, N. and L. Moden, *A History of Doughty's Hospital Norwich, 1687–2009* (Hatfield: University of Hertfordshire Press, 2010)

Green, D.R. and A. Owens, 'Gentlewomanly Capitalism? Spinster, Widows, and Wealth Holding in England and Wales, c. 1800–1860', *Economic History Review*, 46 (2003), pp. 510–36

Gregory, J., '"Homo Religiosus": Masculinity and Religion in the Long Eighteenth Century' in T. Hitchcock and M. Cohen (eds), *English Masculinities, 1660–1800* (London: Longman, 1999), pp. 85–110

Grieg, H., and G. Riello, 'Eighteenth-Century Interiors – Redesigning the Georgian: Introduction', *Journal of Design History*, 20/4 (2007), pp. 273–89

Guillery, P., *The Small House in Eighteenth-Century London: A Social and Architectural History* (New Haven and London: Yale University Press, 2004)

Hall, L., *Period House Fixtures and Fittings 1300–1900* (Newbury: Countryside Books, 2005)

Hamlett, J., 'Managing and Making the Home: Domestic Advice Books' in J. Aynsley and C. Grant (eds), *Imagined Interiors: Representing the Domestic Interior Since the Renaissance* (London: V&A Publications, 2006)

Hamlett, J., *Material Relations: Domestic Interiors and Middle-Class Families in England, 1850–1910* (Manchester: Manchester University Press, 2010).

Harvey, K., 'Men Making Home: Masculinity and Domesticity in Eighteenth-Century Britain', *Gender and History*, 21/3 (2009), pp. 520–40

Haslam, K., *A History of the Geffrye Almshouses* (London: The Geffrye Museum, 2005)

Henderson, T., *Disorderly Women in Eighteenth-Century London: Prostitution and Control in the Metropolis, 1730–1830* (London: Longman, 1999)

Hetherington, K., 'Secondhandness: Consumption, Disposal and Absent Presence', *Environment and Planning D: Society and Space*, 22 (2004), pp. 157–73.

Hey, D., 'The North-West Midlands: Derbyshire, Staffordshire, Cheshire, and Shropshire' in J. Thirsk (ed.), *The Agrarian History of England and Wales: Volume 5, 1640–1750* (Cambridge: Cambridge University Press, 1984)

Hill, B., *Eighteenth-Century Women: An Anthology* (London: Allen & Unwin, 1984)

Hill, B., Women, *Work and Sexual Politics in Eighteenth-Century England* (London: UCL Press, 1994)

Hill, B., *Servants: English Domestics in the Eighteenth Century* (Oxford: Oxford University Press, 1996)

Hill, B., *Women Alone: Spinsters in England, 1660–1850* (New Haven and London: Yale University Press, 2001)

Hindle, S., *On the Parish? The Micro-Politics of Poor Relief in Rural England c.1550–1750* (Oxford: Clarendon, 2004)

Hindson, J., 'The Marriage Duty Acts and the Social Topography of the Early Modern Town – Shrewsbury, 1695–8', *Local Population Studies*, 31 (1983), pp. 21–8

Hitchcock, T., *English Sexualities, 1700–1800* (London: Macmillan, 1997)

Hitchcock, T., 'Redefining Sex in Eighteenth-Century England' in K.M. Phillips and B. Reay (eds), *Sexualities in History: A Reader* (London: Routledge, 2002), pp. 185–202

Hitchcock, T., *Down and Out in Eighteenth-Century London* (London: Hambledon, 2004)

Hitchcock, T. and M. Cohen (eds), *English Masculinities, 1660–1800* (London: Longman, 1999)

Hitchcock, T. and R. Shoemaker, *Tales from the Hanging Court* (London: Hodder Arnold, 2006)

Holloway, G., *Women and Work in Britain since 1840* (London: Routledge, 2005)

Holmes, R., *The Age of Wonder: How the Romantic Generation Discovered the Beauty and Terror of Science* (New York: Pantheon Books, 2008)

Houlbrooke, R., *The English Family, 1450–1700* (London: Longman, 1984)

Houlbrooke, R., *Death, Religion and the Family in England, 1480–1750* (Oxford: Oxford University Press, 1998)

Hufton, O., 'Women without Men: Widows and Spinsters in Britain and France in the Eighteenth Century', *Journal of Family Studies*, 9 (1984), pp. 355–76

Hughes-Hallett, P., *The Immortal Dinner* (Chicago: New Amsterdam Books, 2002)

Hunt, M.R., *The Middling Sort: Commerce, Gender, and the Family in England, 1680–1780* (Berkeley and Los Angeles: University of California Press, 1996)

Hunt, M.R., 'The Sapphic Strain: English Lesbians in the Long Eighteenth Century' in J.M. Bennett and A.M. Froide (eds), *Singlewomen in the European Past 1250–1800* (Philadelphia: University of Pennsylvania Press, 1999)

Hurl-Eamon, J., 'Insights into Plebeian Marriage: Soldiers, Sailors, and their Wives in the Old Bailey Proceedings', *London Journal*, 30/1 (2005), pp. 22–38

Hurl-Eamon, J., *Gender and Petty Violence in London, 1680–1720* (Columbus: Ohio State University Press, 2005)

Hussey, D.P., *Coastal and River Trade in Pre-Industrial England: Bristol and Its Region, 1680–1730* (Exeter: Exeter University Press, 2000)

Hussey, D.P., 'Guns, Horses and Stylish Waistcoats? Male Consumer Activity and Domestic Shopping in Late Eighteenth- and Nineteenth-Century England' in D.P. Hussey and M. Ponsonby (eds), *Buying for the Home: Shopping for the Domestic from the Seventeenth Century to the Present* (Aldershot: Ashgate, 2008), pp. 47–69

Hutchinson, M., *Number 57: The History of a House* (London: Headline, 2003)

Irving, W., *Bracebridge Hall* (London: Macmillan, 1882 [1822])

Jackson-Stops, G. and James Pipkin, *The English Country House: A Grand Tour* (London: Phoenix Illustrated and National Trust, 1993)

John, E., 'At Home with the London Middling Sort – The Inventory Evidence for Furnishings and Room Use, 1570–1720', *Regional Furniture*, 22 (2008), pp. 27–52

Jones, V., 'The Seductions of Conduct: Pleasure and Conduct Literature' in R. Porter and M.M. Mulvey (eds), *Pleasure in the Eighteenth Century* (London: Macmillan, 1996), pp. 108–32

Kennedy, R., 'Taking Tea' in M. Snodin and J. Styles (eds), *Design and the Decorative Arts: Britain 1500–1900* (London: V&A Publications, 2001)

Kent, D.A., 'Ubiquitous but Invisible: Female Domestic Servants in Mid-Eighteenth Century London', *History Workshop Journal*, 28/1 (1989), pp. 111–28

Kinchin, J., 'Interiors: Nineteenth-Century Essays on the "Masculine" and the "Feminine" Room in P. Kirkham (ed.), *The Gendered Object* (Manchester: Manchester University Press, 1996), pp. 12–29

King, S. and A. Tomkins (eds), *The Poor in England, 1700–1850: An Economy of Makeshifts* (Manchester: Manchester University Press, 2003)

Klein, L.E., 'Politeness for Plebes: Consumption and Social Identity in Early Eighteenth-Century England' in A. Bermingham and J. Brewer (eds), *The Consumption of Culture, 1600–1800: Image, Object, Text* (London: Routledge, 1995), pp. 362–82

Klein, L.E., 'Gender and the Public/Private Distinction in the Eighteenth Century: Some Questions about Evidence and Analytic Procedure', *Eighteenth-Century Studies*, 29/1 (1995), pp. 97–109

Knell, D., *English Country Furniture: The National and Regional Vernacular 1500–1900* (London: Barrie & Jenkins, 1992)

Kowaleski, M., 'Singlewomen in Medieval and Early Modern Europe: The Demographic Perspective' in J.M. Bennett and A.M. Froide (eds), *Singlewomen in the European Past 1250–1800* (Philadelphia: University of Pennsylvania Press, 1999), pp. 38–81

Kowalski-Wallace, E., *Consuming Subjects: Women, Shopping and Business in the Eighteenth Century* (New York: Columbia University Press, 1997)

Kuchta, D., *The Three-Piece Suit and Modern Masculinity: England, 1550–1850* (Berkeley and Los Angeles: University of California Press, 2002)

Langford, P., 'The Uses of Eighteenth-Century Politeness', *Transactions of the Royal Historical Society*, 12 (2002), pp. 311–31

Larsen, R., 'For Want of a Good Fortune: Elite Single Women's Experiences in Yorkshire, 1730–1860', *Women's History Review*, 16/3 (2007), pp. 387–401

Laslett, P., *The World We Have Lost* (2nd edn, London: Methuen, 1971)

Laslett, P., 'Mean Household Size in England since the Sixteenth Century' in P. Laslett (ed.), *Household and Family in Past Time* (Cambridge: Cambridge University Press, 1972), pp. 145–7

Laslett, P., *Family Life and Illicit Love in Earlier Generations* (Cambridge: Cambridge University Press, 1977)

Laslett, P., 'The Institution of Service', *Local Population Studies*, 40 (1988)

Lemire, B., *The Business of Everyday Life: Gender, Practice and Social Politics in England, c. 1600–1900* (Manchester: Manchester University Press, 2005)

Lepine, A., '"Strange and Rare Visitants": Spinsters and Domestic Space in Elizabeth Gaskell's *Cranford*', *Nineteenth-Century Contexts*, 32/2 (2010), pp. 121–37

Levine, P., *Victorian Feminism 1850–1900* (Gainesville: University Press of Florida, 1994)

Levitan, K., 'Redundancy, the "Surplus Woman" Problem, and the British Census, 1851–1861', *Women's History Review*, 17/3 (2008), pp. 359–76

Lipsedge, K., '"Enter into Thy Closet": Women, Closet Culture, and the Eighteenth-Century English Novel' in J. Styles and A. Vickery (eds), *Gender, Taste and Material Culture in Britain and North America, 1700–1830* (New Haven: Yale University Press, 2006), pp. 107–22

Lloyd, D., *Broad Street: Its Houses and Residents through Eight Centuries* (Birmingham: Ludlow Research Papers, 3, 1979)

Lloyd, S., '"Agents in Their Own Concerns"? Charity and the Economy of Makeshifts in Eighteenth-Century Britain' in S. King and A. Tomkins (eds), *The Poor in England, 1700–1850* (Manchester: Manchester University Press, 2003), pp. 100–136

Logan, T., *The Victorian Parlour* (London: Cambridge University Press, 2001)

Mack, R.L., *Thomas Gray: A Life* (New Haven and London: Yale University Press, 2000)

MacKay, L., 'Why They Stole: Women in the Old Bailey, 1779–1789', *Journal of Social History*, 32/3 (1999), pp. 623–39

Marcus, S., *Apartment Stories: City and Home in Nineteenth-Century Paris and London* (Berkeley: University of California Press, 1999)

Marcus, S., *Between Women: Friendship, Desire, and Marriage in Victorian England* (Princeton: Princeton University Press, 2007), pp. 270–96

Mason, S., *The Hardware Man's Daughter: Matthew Boulton and his 'Dear Girl'* (Chichester: Phillimore, 2005)

Mavor, E., *The Ladies of Llangollen* (London: Penguin, 1971)

McCants, A.E.C., 'The Not-So-Merry Widows of Amsterdam, 1740–1782', *Journal of Family History*, 24/4 (1999), pp. 441–67

McDonald, M., 'Tranquil Havens: Critiquing the Idea of Home as the Middle Class Sanctuary' in I. Bryden and J. Floyd (eds), *Domestic Space: Reading the Nineteenth-Century Interior* (Manchester: Manchester University Press, 1999), pp. 103–20

McIntyre, I., *Joshua Reynolds: The Life and Times of the First President of the Royal Academy* (London: Penguin, 2004)

Meldrum, T., *Domestic Service and Gender, 1660–1750: Life and Work in the London Household* (Harlow: Pearson, 2000)

Midgley, C., *Women Against Slavery* (London: Routledge, 1992)

Miller, D. (ed.), *Home Possessions: Material Culture Behind Closed Doors* (Oxford: Berg, 2001)

Milne-Smith, A., 'A Flight to Domesticity? Making a Home in the Gentleman's Clubs of London, 1880–1914', *Journal of British Studies*, 25/4 (2006) pp. 796–818

Moore, J.S., 'Probate Inventories: Problems and Products' in P. Riden (ed.), *Probate Records and the Local Community* (Gloucester: Sutton Press, 1985)

Morgan, F.C., 'Woolhope Naturalists' Field Club: An Outline of Its History 1851–1951' in *Herefordshire: Its Natural History, Archaeology, and History* (Gloucester: The British Publishing Company, 1954)

Myers, J.E., 'A Case of Murderous Sensibility: James Hackman, Interiority and Masculine Agency in Late Eighteenth-Century England', *Gender and History*, 20/2 (2008), pp. 312–31.

Neale, R.S., *Bath 1680–1850: A Social History, or, a Valley of Pleasure, yet a Sink of Iniquity* (London: Routledge & Kegan Paul, 1981)

Newman-Brown, W., 'The Receipt of Poor Relief and Family Situation: Aldenham, Hertfordshire 1630–90' in R.M. Smith (ed.), *Land, Kinship and Life-Cycle* (Cambridge: Cambridge University Press, 1984), pp. 405–22

Norton, R., *Mother Clap's Molly House: The Gay Subculture in England, 1700–1830* (Stroud: Chalford, 2006)

Orlin, L.C., *Locating Privacy in Tudor London* (Oxford: Oxford University Press, 2007)

Overton, M., J. Whittle, D. Dean and A. Hann, *Production and Consumption in English Households, 1600–1750* (London and New York: Routledge, 2004)

Oxford Dictionary of National Biography (http://www.oxforddnb.com)

Page, W. and J.W. Willis Bund, *Victoria County History: Worcestershire, vol. 2* (London: James Street, 1906)

Pearce, B.L., 'Horace Walpole: The Creation of a Persona' in *A Tribute to Horace Walpole and Strawberry Hill House: On the Occasion of the Bicentenary of his Death on 2 March 1797* (London: Borough of Twickenham Local History Society, paper Number 74, 1997)

Pelling, M., 'Finding Widowers: Men without Women in English Towns before 1700' in S. Cavallo and L. Walker (eds), *Widowhood in Medieval and Early Modern Europe* (Harlow: Pearson, 1999), pp. 37–54

Pennell, S., 'Consumption and Consumerism in Early Modern England', *Historical Journal*, 42/2 (1999), pp. 549–64

Perkin, J., *Women and Marriage in Nineteenth-Century England* (London: Routledge, 1989)

Peters, C., 'Single Women in Early Modern England: Attitudes and Expectations', *Continuity and Change*, 12/3 (1997), pp. 325–45

Pevsner, N., *The Buildings of England: Herefordshire* (Harmondsworth: Penguin, 1963)

Phillips, R., *Putting Asunder: A History of Divorce in Western Society* (Cambridge: Cambridge University Press, 1988)

Pinches, S., 'Women as Objects and Agents of Charity in Eighteenth-Century Birmingham' in R. Sweet and P. Lane (eds), *Women and Urban Life in Eighteenth-Century England: 'On the Town'* (Aldershot: Ashgate, 2003), pp. 65–86

Ponsonby, M., 'Towards an Interpretation of Textiles in the Provincial Domestic Interior: Three Homes in the West Midlands, 1780–1848', *Textile History*, 38/2 (2007), pp. 165–78

Ponsonby, M., *Stories from Home: English Domestic Interiors, 1750–1850* (Aldershot: Ashgate, 2007)

Priestley, U. and P.J. Corfield, 'Rooms and Room Use in Norwich Housing, 1580–1730', *Post-Medieval Archaeology*, 16 (1982), pp. 93–123

Pugin, A.W.N., *Contrasts* (New York: Humanities Press, Leicester University Press, 1973 [1836])

Raistrick, A., *Quakers in Science and Industry: Being an Account of the Quaker Contribution to Science and Industry during the 17th and 18th Centuries* (Newton Abbott: David & Charles, 1968)

Retford, K., 'From the Interior to Interiority: The Conversation Piece in Georgian England', *Journal of Design History*, 20/4 (2007), pp. 291–307

Richards, S., *Eighteenth-Century Ceramics: Products for a Civilised Society* (Manchester: Manchester University Press, 1999)

Riden, P. (ed.), *Probate Records and the Local Community* (Gloucester: Sutton Press, 1985)

Robson, J.M., *Marriage or Celibacy? The Daily Telegraph on a Victorian Dilemma* (Toronto: University of Toronto Press, 1995)

Rogers, M., *Master Drawings from the National Portrait Gallery* (London: National Portrait Gallery, 1993)

Sarin, S., 'The Floorcloth and other Floor Coverings in the London Domestic Interior 1700–1800', *Journal of Design History*, 18/2 (2005), pp. 133–46

Schmidt, A., 'Survival Strategies of Widows and their Families in Early Modern Holland, c.1580–1750', *The History of the Family*, 12/4 (2007), pp. 268–81

Schofield, R.S., 'English Marriage Patterns Revisited', *Journal of Family History*, 10 (1985), pp. 2–10

Schofield, R.S., 'Did the Mothers Really Die? Three Centuries of Maternal Mortality in "The World We have Lost"' in L. Bonfield, R.M. Smith and K.

Wrightson (eds), *The World We Have Gained* (Oxford: Oxford University Press, 1986)

Schurer, K., 'Variations in Household Structure in the Late Seventeenth Century: Towards a Regional Analysis' in K. Schurer and T. Arkell (eds), *Surveying the People: The Interpretation and Use of Document Sources for the Study of Population in the Later Seventeenth Century* (Oxford: Leopard's Head Press, 1992)

Schwarz, L.D., *London in the Age of Industrialisation: Entrepreneurs, Labour Force and Living Conditions, 1700–1850* (Cambridge: Cambridge University Press, 1992)

Shammas, C., 'The Domestic Environment in Early Modern England and America', *Journal of Social History*, 14 (1980), pp. 1–24

Shammas, C., *The Pre-Industrial Consumer in England and America* (Oxford: Oxford University Press, 1990)

Shammas, C., 'Changes in English and Anglo-American Consumption from 1550 to 1800' in J. Brewer and R. Porter (eds), *Consumption and the World of Goods* (London: Routledge, 1993), pp. 177–205

Shannon, B., 'Re-fashioning Men: Fashion, Masculinity and the Cultivation of the Male Consumer in Britain, 1860–1914', *Victorian Studies*, 46 (2004), pp. 597–630

Sharp, K., 'Women's Creativity and Display in the Eighteenth-Century British Domestic Interior' in S. McKellar and P. Sparke (eds), *Interior Design and Identity* (Manchester and New York: Manchester University Press, 2004)

Sharpe, P., 'Literally Spinsters: A New Interpretation of Local Economy and Demography in Colyton in the Seventeenth and Eighteenth Centuries', *Economic History Review*, 44/1 (1991), pp. 46–65

Sharpe, P., 'Dealing with Love: the Ambiguous Independence of the Single Woman in Early Modern England', *Gender and History*, 11/2 (1999), pp. 202–32

Sharpe, P., 'Survival Strategies and Stories: Poor Widows and Widowers in Early Industrial England' in S. Cavallo and L. Walker (eds), *Widowhood in Medieval and Early Modern Europe* (Harlow: Pearson, 1999), pp. 220–39

Sharpe, P., 'Population and Society, 1700–1840' in P. Clark (ed.), *The Cambridge Urban History of Britain: Volume 2, 1540–1840* (Cambridge: Cambridge University Press, 2000)

Shepard, A., *Meanings of Manhood in Early Modern England* (Oxford: Oxford University Press, 2003)

Shepard, A. and K. Harvey, 'What Have Historians Done with Masculinity? Reflections on Five Centuries of British History, circa 1500–1950', *Journal of British Studies*, 44 (2005), pp. 274–80

Shoemaker, R.B., *Gender in English Society, 1650–1850: The Emergence of Separate Spheres?* (London: Longman, 1998)

Shoemaker, R.B., *The London Mob: Violence and Disorder in Eighteenth-Century England* (London: Hambledon, 2004)

Shoemaker, R.B., 'The Old Bailey Proceedings and the Representation of Crime and Criminal Justice in Eighteenth-Century London', *Journal of British Studies*, 47/3 (2008), pp. 559–80

Shore, H., 'Crime, Criminal Networks and the Survival Strategies of the Poor in Eighteenth-Century London' in S. King and A. Tomkins (eds), *The Poor in England, 1700–1850: An Economy of Makeshifts* (Manchester: Manchester University Press, 2003), pp. 137–65

Short, B.M., 'The South-East: Kent, Surrey, and Sussex' in J. Thirsk (ed.), *The Agrarian History of England and Wales: Volume 5, 1640–1750* (Cambridge: Cambridge University Press, 1984)

Shrewsbury Drapers' Guild, 'Shrewsbury Almshouses' (http://www.shrewsburydrapers.org.uk/almshouses)

Smith, W.D., *Consumption and the Making of Respectability, 1600–1800* (London: Routledge, 2002)

Spicksley, J.M., 'To Be or Not to Be Married: Single Women, Money-Lending and the Question of Choice in Late Tudor and Stuart England' in D.M. Kehler and L. Amtower (eds), *The Single Woman in Medieval and Early Modern England: Her Life and Representation* (Tempe: Arizona Center for Medieval and Renaissance Studies, 2003), pp. 65–96

Spicksley, J.M., 'A Dynamic Model of Social Relations: Celibacy, Credit and the Identity of the 'Spinster' in Seventeenth-Century England', in H.R. French and J. Barry (eds), *Identity and Agency in English Society, 1500–1800* (Basingstoke: Palgrave Macmillan, 2004), pp. 106–46

Spicksley, J.M., '"Fly with a Duck in thy Mouth": Single Women as Sources of Credit in Seventeenth Century England', *Social History*, 32/2 (2007), pp. 187–207

Spicksley, J.M., 'Usury Legislation, Cash, and Credit: The Development of the Female Investor in the Late Tudor and Stuart Periods', *Economic History Review*, 61/2 (2008), pp. 277–301

Spufford, M., 'The Limitations of the Probate Inventory' in J. Chartres and D. Hey (eds), *English Rural Society: Essays in Honour of Joan Thirsk* (Cambridge: Cambridge University Press, 1990), pp. 139–74

Staves, S., *Married Women's Separate Property in England, 1660–1833* (Cambridge, MA: Harvard University Press, 1990)

Steedman, C., 'What a Rag Rug Means' in I. Bryden and J. Floyd (eds), *Domestic Space: Reading the Nineteenth-Century Interior* (Manchester: Manchester University Press, 1999), pp. 18–39

Steedman, C., 'The Servant's Labour: the Business of Life, England, 1760–1820', *Social History* 29/1 (2004), pp. 1–29

Stobart, J., A. Hann and V. Morgan, *Spaces of Consumption: Leisure and Shopping in the English Town, c.1680–1830* (London: Routledge, 2007)

Stone, L., *The Family, Sex and Marriage in England, 1500–1800* (London: Weidenfeld & Nicolson, 1977)

Stone, L., *The Road to Divorce: England, 1530–1987* (Oxford: Oxford University Press, 1995)

Stretton, T., 'Marriage, Separation and the Common Law in England, 1540–1660' in H. Berry and E. Foyster (eds), *The Family in Early Modern England* (Cambridge: Cambridge University Press, 2007), pp. 18–39

Styles, J., 'Lodging at the Old Bailey: Lodgings and their Furnishing in Eighteenth-Century London' in J. Styles and A. Vickery (eds), *Gender, Taste and Material Culture in Britain and North America, 1700–1830* (New Haven and London: Yale University Press, 2006), pp. 61–80

Styles, J., 'Picturing Domesticity: The Cottage Genre in Late Eighteenth-Century Britain' in J. Aynsley and C. Grant (eds), *Imagined Interiors: Representing the Domestic Interior since the Renaissance* (London: V&A Publications, 2006).

Styles, J. and A. Vickery, 'Introduction' in J. Styles and A. Vickery (eds), *Gender, Taste and Material Culture in Britain and North America, 1700–1830* (New Haven and London: Yale University Press, 2006), pp. 1–36

Sykes, C.S., *The Country House Camera* (London: Weidenfeld & Nicolson, 1980)

Tadmor, N., *Family and Friends in Eighteenth-Century England* (Cambridge: Cambridge University Press, 2001)

Thane, P., 'Old People and their Families in the Past' in M. Daunton (ed.), *Charity, Self-Interest and Welfare in the English Past* (London: UCL Press, 1996)

Thirsk, J., 'The South-West Midlands: Warwickshire, Worcestershire, Gloucestershire, and Herefordshire' in J. Thirsk (ed.), *The Agrarian History of England and Wales: Volume 5, 1640–1750* (Cambridge: Cambridge University Press, 1984)

Thirsk, J. (ed.), *The Agrarian History of England and Wales: Volume 5, 1640–1750* (Cambridge: Cambridge University Press, 1984).

Todd, B.J., 'The Remarrying Widow: A Stereotype Reconsidered' in M. Prior (ed.), *Women in English Society, 1500–1800* (London: Methuen, 1985), pp. 54–92

Todd, B.J., 'Demographic Determinism and Female Agency: The Remarrying Widow Reconsidered … Again', *Continuity and Change*, 9 (1994), pp. 421–50

Tomkins, A., 'Almshouse Versus Workhouse: Residential Welfare in Eighteenth-Century Oxford', *Family and Community History*, 7/1 (2004), pp. 45–58

Tosh, J., 'Domesticity and Manliness in the Victorian Middle Class: The Family of Edward White Benson' in M. Roper and J. Tosh (eds), *Manful Assertions: Masculinities in Britain since 1800* (London: Routledge, 1991)

Tosh, J., 'What Should Historians Do with Masculinity? Reflections on Nineteenth-Century Britain', *History Workshop Journal*, 38 (1994), pp. 179–202

Tosh, J., *A Man's Place: Masculinity and the Middle-Class Home in Victorian England* (New Haven and London: Yale University Press, 1999)

Tosh, J., 'The Old Adam and the New Man: Emerging Themes in the History of English Masculinities' in T. Hitchcock and M. Cohen (eds), *English Masculinities, 1660–1800* (London: Longman, 1999), pp. 217–38

Tosh, J., *Manliness and Masculinities in Nineteenth-Century Britain* (Harlow: Pearson, 2005)

Tosh, J., 'Gentlemanly Politeness and Manly Simplicity in Victorian England' in J. Tosh, *Manliness and Masculinities in Nineteenth-Century Britain* (Harlow: Pearson, 2005), pp. 83–102

Tosh, J., 'Middle-Class Masculinities in the Era of the Women's Suffrage Movement, 1860–1914' in J. Tosh, *Manliness and Masculinity in Nineteenth-Century Britain* (Harlow: Pearson, 2005), pp. 103–25

Trinder, B., *The Market Town Lodging House in Victorian England* (Leicester: Friends of the Centre for English Local History, 2001)

Tristram, P., *Living Space in Fact and Fiction* (London: Routledge, 1989)

Trumbach, R., *Sex and the Gender Revolution, Volume 1: Heterosexuality and the Third Gender in Enlightenment London* (Chicago and London: University of Chicago Press, 1998)

Turner, D.M., *Fashioning Adultery: Gender, Sex and Civility in England 1660–1740* (Cambridge: Cambridge University Press, 2002)

Uglow, J., *The Lunar Men* (London: Faber & Faber, 2003).

Venn, J.A. (ed.), *Alumni Cantabrigiensis* (Cambridge: Cambridge University Press, 1922)

Vickery, A., 'Golden Age to Separate Spheres: A Review of the Categories and Chronology of English Women's History', *Historical Journal*, 36/2 (1993), pp. 383–414

Vickery, A., 'Women and the World of Goods: A Lancashire Consumer and her Possessions, 1751–81' in J. Brewer and R. Porter (eds), *Consumption and the World of Goods* (London: Routledge, 1993), pp. 274–304

Vickery, A., *The Gentleman's Daughter: Women's Lives in Georgian England* (New Haven and London: Yale University Press, 1998)

Vickery, A., '"Neat and Not Too Showey": Words and Wallpaper in Regency England' in J. Styles and A. Vickery (eds), *Gender, Taste and Material Culture in Britain and North America, 1700–1830* (New Haven and London: Yale University Press, 2006), pp. 201–22

Vickery, A., *Behind Closed Doors: At Home in Georgian England* (New Haven and London: Yale University Press, 2009)

Vincent, D., 'Love and Death and the Nineteenth-Century Working Class', *Social History*, 5/2 (1980), pp. 223–47

Vincent, D., *Bread, Knowledge and Freedom: A Study of Nineteenth-Century Working Class Autobiography* (London: Europa, 1981)

Wainwright, C., *The Romantic Interior* (New Haven and London: Yale University Press, 1989)

Wainwright, C., 'The Library as Living Room' in R. Myers and M. Harris (eds), *Property of a Gentleman: The Formation, Organisation and Dispersal of the Private Library, 1620–1920* (Winchester: St Paul's Bibliographies, 1991), pp. 15–24

Wales, T., 'Poverty, Poor Relief and the Life-Cycle: Some Evidence from Seventeenth-Century Norfolk' in R.M. Smith (ed.), *Land, Kinship and Life-Cycle* (Cambridge: Cambridge University Press, 1984), pp. 351–404

Wall, R., 'Regional and Temporal Variations in English Household Structure from 1650', in J. Hobcraft and P. Rees (eds), *Regional Demographic Development* (London: Croom Helm, 1977), pp. 89–113

Wall, R., 'Woman Alone in English Society', *Annales de Demographie Historique*, 17 (1981), pp. 303–17

Wall, R., 'Leaving Home and the Process of Household Formation in Pre-Industrial England', *Continuity and Change*, 2 (1987), pp. 77–101

Walsh, C., 'Shop Design and the Display of Goods in Eighteenth-Century London', *Journal of Design History*, 8/3 (1995), pp. 157–76

Walsh, C., 'Shopping at First Hand? Mistresses, Servants and Shopping for the Household In Early-Modern England' in D. Hussey and M. Ponsonby (eds), *Buying for the Home: Shopping for the Domestic from the Seventeenth Century to the Present* (Aldershot: Ashgate, 2008), pp. 13–27

Walvin, J., *The Quakers: Money and Morals* (London: John Murray, 1997)

Wanklyn, M.D.G., 'Urban Revival in Early Modern England: Bridgnorth and the River Trade', *Midland History*, 18 (1993), pp. 37–64

Wanklyn, M.D.G., 'The Impact of Water Transport Facilities on the Economies of English River Ports, c.1660–c.1760', *Economic History Review*, 49/1 (1996), pp. 20–34

Ward, W.R., 'Mirror of the Soul: the Diary of an Early Methodist Preacher, John Bennet, 1714–1754', *English Historical Review*, 118 (2003), pp. 476–521

Wardle, C. and T., *The History of Barbourne: The Early Development of North Worcester* (Worcester: MTC Ltd, 2007)

Watts, S., *Shropshire Almshouses* (Little Logaston: Logaston Press, 2010)

Weatherill, L., 'A Possession of One's Own: Women and Consumer Behaviour in England, 1660–1740', *Journal of British Studies*, 25 (1986), pp. 131–56

Weatherill, L., 'The Meaning of Consumer Behaviour in Late Seventeenth- and Early Eighteenth-Century England' in J. Brewer and R. Porter (eds), *Consumption and the World of Goods* (London: Routledge, 1993), pp. 206–27

Weatherill, L., *Consumer Behaviour and Material Culture in Britain, 1660–1760* (2nd edn, London and New York: Routledge, 1996)

Weir, D.R., 'Rather Never than Late: Celibacy and Age at Marriage in English Cohort Fertility', *Journal of Family History*, 9 (1984), pp. 340–54

White, J., 'A World of Goods? The "Consumption Turn" and Eighteenth-Century British History', *Cultural and Social History*, 3/1 (2006), pp. 93–104

Wigley, M., 'Untitled: The Housing of Gender' in B. Colomina (ed.), *Sexuality and Space* (Princeton: Princeton Architectural Press, 1992), pp. 327–89

Williams, D., 'The Ludlow Union Workhouse 1839–1900' in D.J. Lloyd, R. Payne, C.J. Train and D. Williams (eds), *Victorian Ludlow* (Ludlow Historical Research Group, Bucknell: Scenesetters, 2004)

Wilson, R., 'The British Brewing Industry Since 1750', in L. Richmond and A. Turton (eds), *The Brewing Industry: A Guide to Historical Records* (Manchester and New York: Manchester University Press, 1990)

Woolley, L., '"Disreputable Housing in a Disreputable Parish"? Common Lodging-Houses in St. Thomas', Oxford, 1841–1901', *Midland History*, 35/2 (2010), pp. 215–36

Wright, S.J., '"Holding up Half the Sky": Women and their Occupations in Eighteenth-Century Ludlow', *Midland History*, 14 (1989), pp. 53–74

Wright, S.J., 'Sojourners and Lodgers in a Provincial Town: The Evidence from Eighteenth-Century Ludlow', *Urban History*, 17 (1990), pp. 14–35

Wrightson, K., *English Society, 1580–1680* (London: Hutchinson, 1981)

Wrightson, K., 'The Family in Early Modern England: Continuity and Change' in S. Taylor, R. Connors and C. Jones (eds), *Hanoverian Britain and Empire: Essays in Memory of Philip Lawson* (Woodbridge: The Boydell Press, 1998), pp. 1–22

Wrightson, K. and D. Levine, *Poverty and Piety in an English Village: Terling 1525–1700* (2nd edn, Oxford: Oxford University Press, 1995)

Wrigley, E.A. and R.S. Schofield, *The Population History of England, 1541–1871: A Reconstruction* (London: Edward Arnold, 1981)

Young, H., *English Porcelain, 1745–95: Its Makers, Design, Marketing and Consumption* (London: V&A Publications, 1999)

Young, L., *Middle-Class Culture in the Nineteenth Century: America, Australia and Britain* (Basingstoke: Palgrave Macmillan, 2003)

Unpublished Theses and Papers

Caddick, B., 'The Material Culture of the Household: Consumption and Domestic Economy in the Eighteenth and Early Nineteenth Centuries', unpublished PhD thesis, University of Wolverhampton, 2010

Dean, D. and M. Overton, 'Wealth, Indebtedness, Consumption and the Lifecycle in Early Modern England', paper presented to the 14th International Economic History Congress (http://www.helsinki.fi/iehc2006/papers3/Overton122.pdf)

Goose, N., 'Variations in the Demographic Profile of Almshouse Residents over Time and Space', The Local Population Studies Society Autumn Conference, Cambridge, 21 November 2009

Goose, N., 'The English Almshouse and the Mixed Economy of Welfare, c. 1500–1900', Social Science History Conference, Ghent, 13–16 April 2010

Ponsonby, M., 'The Consumption of Furniture and Furnishings for the Home in the West Midlands using Local Suppliers, 1760–1860', unpublished PhD thesis, University of Wolverhampton, 2001

Index

The singletons referred to in the text are listed by name and marital status at the time when the source(s) were produced. Thus,

B Bachelor
S Spinster
W Widowed
B/W or S/W Single but unknown status
B+S Two singletons sharing a home

Abingdon, Wiltshire 14
Accounts 4, 5, 31, 65, 66, 90, 143,
    185n124
Acton, Eliza, *Modern Cookery for Private
    Families* (1845) 115
Addis, Susanna (W) 170
Advice literature, *see* conduct literature
Alfreton, Derbyshire 88
Aliston, Thomas (B/W) 183
Almshouse 5, 61, 181–200, 204
Anderson, John (B/W) 160
Anderson, M. 152
Annuities, *see also* bond 43, 55n7, 61,
    63n33, 150, 160, 162
Anon, *Practical Economy* (1822) 131
Anon, *The Accomplish'd Housewife: or
    the Gentlewoman's Companion*
    (1745) 91
Anon, *The Family Economist: a Penny
    Monthly for the Industrious
    Classes* (1853) 91
Anon, *The Footman's Directory and
    Butler's Remembrancer* (1823)
    93–4, 125n53
Anon, *The Home Book* 1829 58–60
Anon, *The Servants' Guide and Family
    Manual* (1830) 136
Antiquarian 26, 55, 110n6, 131, 134, 136,
    138, 140–1, 142–3, 144, 181
Antique 57, 131, 134, 138, 141

Apprentice/ship 12, 15, 16, 31, 45, 55, 63,
    79, 149, 150, 152, 153, 179
Arnsworth, Miss E. (S) 86–7
Artisans 2, 90, 123
Artist 62, 121, 123, 145, 155–6, 158–9
Astronomer 66–7, 17
Athenaeum 8
Attorney 4, 8, 127, 154
Auctions/Auctioneers 4, 43, 72, 84, 144
Austen, Jane, *Mansfield Park* (1814) 178

Bachelor 1, 4, 6, 24–5, 35–6, 55, 60–2, 66,
    81–2, 92, 100–1, 104–5, 117–23,
    132, 139, 152, 158–9, 163–4, 181,
    186, 188–9, 201, 203
Backworth, Tyne and Wear 149
Bakehouse 77
Baker, John (W) 26
Baking 75, 116
Baldwyn, Edward (B/W) 76, 119
Barber-surgeon 164
Barrister 1, 26n73
Barry, Jonathan 2
Bateman, Richard (B) 139–40
Bath, Somerset 66, 82, 142
Bayley, Sarah (S) 60
Bayley, Thomas (B) 62
Beaconsfield, Buckinghamshire 1
Beauchamp, Anne (and Simon) (W) 44–5,
    47
Bed (shared) 80, 143
Bed/stead 40, 42, 48, 49, 54, 66, 69, 72, 85,
    87, 95, 98, 100, 105–6, 153, 160,
    161, 164, 194, 195
Bedchamber/bedroom, *see also* chamber
    54, 63, 67, 73, 76, 82, 85, 86,
    89–90, 91, 95, 96, 97, 99, 138, 140,
    143, 155, 172, 173, 175, 176, 178,
    179, 180, 185, 197
Beddard, Ann (S/W) 82

QM LIBRARY
(MILE END)